W9-BJI-863

Bicycling the
PACIFIC COAST

SECOND EDITION

by Tom Kirkendall and Vicky Spring

THE MOUNTAINEERS

The Mountaineers: Organized 1906 "... *to explore, study, preserve, and enjoy the natural beauty of the Northwest.*"

© 1990 by Tom Kirkendall and Vicky Spring
All rights reserved

4 3 2 1
5 4 3 2

No part of this book may be reproduced in any form, or by any electronic, mechanical, or other means, without permission in writing from the publisher.

Published by The Mountaineers
1011 S.W. Klickitat Way, Suite 107, Seattle, WA 98134
Published simultaneously in Canada
by Douglas & McIntyre, Ltd.,
1615 Venables Street, Vancouver, B.C. V5L 2H1
Published simultaneously in Great Britain
by Cordee
3a DeMontfort St., Leicester, England LE1 7HD

Manufactured in the United States of America
Edited by Julia Coffey
Cover design by Brian Metz
Layout by Bridget Culligan
Cover photographs: Pigeon Point Lighthouse on the California coast Inset: Santa Barbara
Frontispiece: Point Arena Lighthouse on the California coast

Library of Congress Cataloging in Publication Data
Kirkendall, Tom.
  Bicycling the Pacific Coast / by Tom Kirkendall and Vicky Spring.
    p.   cm.
  Includes bibliographical references.
  ISBN 0-89886-232-9
  1. Bicycle touring--Pacific coast (North America)--Guide-books.
  2. Pacific coast (North America)--Description and travel--Guide
  -books.   I. Spring, Vicky, 1953-   II. Title.
  GV1046.P17K57   1989
  796.6'4'097--dc20   89-13791
                                                              CIP

CONTENTS

♡	CANADIAN HIGHWAY	Å	HIKER-BIKER CAMPGROUND
▭	US HIGHWAY	▲	CAMPGROUND
○	STATE HIGHWAY	⌂	HOSTEL
♡	INTERSTATE HIGHWAY	o	CITY OR TOWN
────	MAIN ROUTE	△	POINT OF INTEREST
────	ALTERNATE OR SIDE ROAD	✈	AIRPORT
════	FREEWAY	─▣─	TUNNEL
──►	ONE WAY STREET	─ ─ ─ ─	FERRY
▬▬▬	GRAVEL ROAD	~·~··~·~	RIVER
··········	BIKE PATH	──·· ──	STATE OR COUNTRY BORDER
┼	UNDERPASS	──· ──	COUNTY BORDER
┼	OVERPASS OR CROSS STREET		

PREFACE

Why North to South?

If Tom had decided to ride the Pacific coast from Canada to Mexico in 1981, he would have had a great time, and this book would never have been written. However, in 1981 Tom decided to ride from Mexico to Canada, and the results are as follows.

I rode with him for the first four days, ending the short trip with a sunburn and a great enthusiasm for bicycle touring. As he continued to pedal on, I drove north, heading to a summer job knowing that I was missing a great ride.

As a West Coast native, I am proud of our beautiful coast, and expected Tom to be thrilled by the scenery as well as by the challenge of the ride. I was terribly envious.

But something happened as Tom headed on by himself. North of Santa Barbara, he encountered stiff headwinds that blew the

Hiker-biker site at Manchester State Beach in California

3

Sliding in the sand dunes at Pismo Beach

fun right out of his adventure. Scenery and the thrill of exploring became secondary to his daily battle with the wind. The wind created an invisible barrier that had to be constantly fought. It beat dirt into his face, produced an annoying whistling sound through his helmet, and attempted to push him back to Mexico. By San Francisco, riding had become a chore. In Oregon 80-mile-per-hour winds blew him to a stop while going down a steep hill. In Washington, he had three hours of peace when a very wet storm blew through from the south. It was at the Canadian border when he started enjoying the trip again, after he turned south and let the wind push him back to the nearest bus station.

When describing that trip, Tom will pull out his trip journal in which he wrote all his thoughts and impressions: the winds consistently blew from the north; the only time the wind blew from the south was during a rainstorm. His journal describes how he got up early in the morning to avoid the winds that blew up to 50 miles per hour by the afternoon. The journal describes the miles covered each day, the food he ate, and the interesting people he met along the way, but nowhere is there any mention of beautiful vista points, magnificent redwood forests, sea otters, sea lions, lighthouses, sand dunes, and fascinating old forts. Nowhere is there any mention of the word *fun*.

The following summer, Tom and I took a tour back down the coast to prove it *can* be fun. It was an incredible trip. Oh yes, the wind was still blowing, but this time, it was pushing us down the coast. Near the Sea Lion Caves in Oregon, I had to apply my brakes to stop on a steep uphill grade. The miles flew by, and we had plenty of extra time and energy to stop and explore the forest and beaches. We were surprised to note that the Highway Department expects cyclists to travel from north to south. We frequently had a good shoulder on the southbound side of the road but cyclists dodged trucks and cars on the shoulderless northbound lanes.

To help other cyclists avoid the disappointment of northbound travel, we spent the following year organizing this guide from Canada to Mexico.

We may be biased but we believe that magnificent and varied scenery, a temperate climate, and the numerous public facilities designed especially for cyclists make the Pacific coast the best long-distance tour in the country. When you plan your first tour down the coast, take advantage of the tail winds, head south, and leave yourself plenty of time and energy to explore and enjoy the coast.

Vicky Spring
Seattle, 1989

Highway 101 hugs the coastline heading south around Cape Perpetua

INTRODUCTION

This book is a guide to the Pacific coast bicycle route from the forests of British Columbia south along some of the world's most scenic coastline to palm-lined beaches and the Mexican border. More than a route, this is an adventure that passes through portions of two national parks, a national recreation area, several national historical monuments, innumerable state parks, museums, forts, and lighthouses. Along the route are small friendly towns with bakeries and art galleries, huge bustling metropolises with fascinating museums and excellent restaurants, beautiful forests laced with trails, lonely seacoasts, and wind-sculptured sand dunes. Included in the adventure are sea otters, sea lions, sea gulls, pelicans, elk, raccoons, chipmunks, deer, and an amazing cross section of people.

It is difficult to draw a generalized description of the Pacific coast. Nearly all types of road conditions, terrain, and weather may be encountered. A few broad generalities, open to exception, may be drawn as follows: wind blows from the north in good weather and from the south in bad; the chance of bad weather decreases as you travel south; and the number of facilities for cyclists (and the number of cyclists) increases to the south.

The Pacific Coast Bicycle Route is 1,987.3 miles long, excluding side trips. Following the day-by-day descriptions, the entire route may be cycled in 38 days. Some cyclists will ride it in less time. Others will want more time to explore areas of special interest, take side trips, and enjoy leisurely rest days.

For the purpose of simplicity, the book is divided into four chapters: British Columbia, Washington, Oregon, and California. However, the text and maps are arranged so that users may pick out the portions that interest them.

No formalized bicycle route exists for the coast of British Columbia or Washington. However, Oregon and California both established coastal bike routes for the American Bicentennial in 1976, and unless safer or more scenic routes were found, the Pacific Coast Bicycle Route follows established routes.

This book was designed for the cyclists on a budget, for those who stay in a campground and cook their own food. However, credit card cyclists will find it easy to adapt the information to suit their own needs, as restaurants and motels are plentiful on the coast.

Pedaling Through the Pages

At the start of each of the four chapters is a discussion of the weather, camping, road conditions, and any problems or conditions unique to that state or province. The chapters are then divided into day rides, starting and ending at campgrounds. The day rides average 52 miles but vary from 28.9 miles to 77.3 miles, depending on the availability of campsites and number of points of interest along the ride. If the days suggested are too short, cycle further. If they are too long, shorten them. Most important, have fun in your own special way.

Each day's ride includes a discussion of highlights, road conditions, possible problems, and suggested alternative camping areas (if any); a map; and a mileage log listing road directions, side trips, and points of interest.

When the route is on a major highway, mileages are accompanied by a milepost number (mp), except in British Columbia. Mileposts are small signs along the road with a number that indicates the miles from a county or state line. (Mileposts are used by the highway maintenance crews to accurately locate problems. They are not always spaced correctly and some are missing.) For the scope of this book, mileposts serve as another tool to aid in route-finding, eliminating the necessity of watching your cycle computer. In Washington and Oregon, mileposts do not list tenths or hundredths. We have added tenths to the mileage logs to help riders determine whether the point listed is before or after the milepost. In California, mileposts list mileages to the hundredth place. No mileposts were noted in British Columbia. Canada is on the metric system, and kilometer posts, when present, occur once every 5 kilometers and are situated for easy reading by the northbound traveler only.

Maps

Additional up-to-date maps and information are always handy. We suggest you obtain city maps of all the major cities you will be visiting (if following the entire route, that means Vancouver, Victoria, San Francisco, Los Angeles, and San Diego). Trace the bike route on these maps to give you a better idea of where you are going before you head into the city. Automobile clubs such as AAA are good sources for city street maps.

Bicycle maps are also available from the individual states and provinces along the coast; these maps note routes, bicycle laws, restrictions, and some facilities.

For British Columbia, write to:

    Ministry of Tourism
    Tourism British Columbia
    1117 Wharf Street
    Victoria, British Columbia
    V8W 1T7

The Washington State publication (not recommended), "Wash-

Left, *example of the milepost signs found in Washington and Oregon*
Right, *a California milepost sign indicating highway number at the top with the county name (abbreviated) in the center and the miles below*

ington Bike Map and Freeway Guide," is available for a small fee by writing:

> Public Affairs Office
> Washington State Department of Transportation
> Transportation Building, KF-01
> Olympia, Washington 98504

Oregon offers two useful publications; obtain the "Oregon Coast Bike Route" and the "Oregon Bicycling Guide," by writing:

> Bicycle Program Manager
> Oregon Department of Transportation
> Room 200, Transportation Building
> Salem, Oregon 97310

In California, each district along the coast produces its own "Bicycle Touring Guide." The coast districts are 1, 4, 5, 7, and 11. These guides are detailed but difficult to use. No guide is available for District 7, which covers Ventura, Los Angeles, and Orange counties. The rest may be obtained by writing the individual districts as follows:

District 1	District 4
P.O. Box 3700	P.O. Box 7310
Eureka, CA 95501	San Francisco, CA 94120
District 5	District 11
P.O. Box "L"	P.O. Box 81406
San Luis Obispo, CA 93403	San Diego, CA 92138

9

Hiker-Biker Camps

A hiker-biker camp is a special area in a campground set aside for people traveling alone or in small groups using nonmotorized forms of transportation. Maximum stay is two nights unless otherwise noted. These camps vary in size and fee charged. Some may lack certain conveniences, such as nearby water or restrooms. Space is available on a first-come basis.

The hiker-biker system of campsites is well organized in Washington, Oregon, and California. In these three states, there is virtually no need to worry about full campgrounds or finding a place to stay on busy summer weekends. The fee is moderate, and space is available for a large number of cyclists. Hiker-biker sites may be found in state parks, some Forest Service campgrounds, and a few county parks. As of 1989, only one park on the coast route had a hiker-biker camp (called a campers' field). More are planned for the future.

Hiker-biker sites are a great help to cyclists. When using these sites PLEASE remember they are a privilege and not a right. The fee is modest, so pay it. The campground officials are not raking in a profit from hiker-biker sites, so help them out by keeping

Co-author Tom Kirkendall replacing a broken spoke, a common roadside repair

them clean. Hiker-biker areas may be eliminated if there is too much upkeep involved. Most important, let the campground officials know how much you appreciate having sites like these available to cyclists.

If you are traveling in a group of four or more, a regular campsite will always be less expensive than a hiker-biker site. If you are traveling with a support vehicle, you are required to use a regular campsite. Write ahead to the individual campgrounds to make a reservation.

In southern California, the hiker-biker sites have become favored hangouts for transients. In response to this serious problem, the official hiker-biker sites have been closed in some campgrounds. No cyclists will be turned away from these campgrounds; however, you may be moved from one site to another until the official site for the day is chosen.

Hostels

Twenty-five hostels are located on or near the coast route. Hostels are considerably more expensive than a campsite, but a lot cheaper (for one person) than a motel. If you run into a streak of wet weather, you may be glad to spend a night indoors. For more current information about hostel locations and charges, write:

American Youth Hostels
P.O. Box 37613
Washington, D.C. 20013-7613

Getting Ready to Tour

Before starting a long bicycle tour, it is important to get your body and bicycle into the best shape possible. Numerous excellent books thoroughly cover the subject of how to tour, so we will not pursue it here. (See Recommended Reading.) These books are available at book stores and most bicycle shops. A fairly complete catalog of all books pertaining to bicycle touring is available from Bikecentennial, P.O. Box 8308; Missoula, Montana 59807.

Riding Safely

The first time you ride your fully loaded touring bike is a shock, even to the most seasoned rider. When loaded with an extra 20 to 30 pounds of gear, a lightweight bike behaves like a lopsided tortoise on level ground, and what it does on the uphills defies description. Of course, on the downhill, it takes off like a locomotive. Start off slowly, and take an hour or so to readjust your balance to the extra weight.

On the road, a cyclist's first line of defense is to be as visible as possible to motorists. A bright-colored helmet, brilliantly colored clothing and/or bright fluorescent vests or fanny triangles, and eye-catching touring bags will greatly increase the chances of being seen from a distance, giving motorists a chance to slow down or move to another lane.

Along the Pacific coast, a cyclist has the same rights and obligations as the driver of a motor vehicle, which means riding single file except to pass, having one hand on the handlebars at all times, obeying stop signs and traffic signals before turning or stopping, and moving as far off the road as possible for rest or repairs.

Large trucks are intimidating to many cyclists, with good reason. An 80,000-pound truck cannot stop quickly or swerve as sharply as a small car if it comes unexpectedly upon a cyclist in the middle of the road. As a large truck passes, its slipstream pulls the relatively lightweight bicycle in towards the center of the road.

The following suggestions were made by a logging truck driver: Do not ride in the center of the lane; ride as far to the right as possible, preferably on or to the right of the white line. When traveling in a group, do not string out in a long line down the road; break into groups of two or three, and keep at least one-quarter mile between groups to allow trucks time to swing out to pass riders then get back into their lane. When the driver tries to pass a long group, he may be forced to swing in close if he meets oncoming traffic.

Cyclists should be especially cautious in popular tourist areas. Many people are unfamiliar and uncomfortable with the large mobile home they are driving. They are less likely to move over when passing, and much more likely than a commercial truck driver to panic in an emergency.

The Necessities

Three necessities are universal to all touring cyclists: food, restrooms, and water. Travel tends to degenerate into a constant search for one or all of these three basics. Public restrooms and water are easily found at numerous parks along the coast. However, in some areas, you are faced with long stretches without any kind of facility at all. Do not plague the small stores and gas stations looking for water or looking to leave some. When necessity forces the use of private facilities, try to incorporate this stop with acquisition of the first necessity—food. Do your best to leave a good impression or the next group may be faced with a NO CYCLISTS sign.

Leaving Valuables Behind

The Pacific coast is a popular area for vacations and a prime location for thieves. It takes only a second for a thief to grab a touring bag—or your entire bike—and throw it into the back of a truck. There is no perfect answer to this problem. Some cyclists never leave gear unattended, making sure one person stays with the bicycles at all times. For small groups this solution is impractical. Other groups leave their bikes then worry about them the entire time they are away.

Groups having the most fun are those that take reasonable precautions, then concentrate on having a good time. If leaving a loaded bike take valuables—money, credit cards, and camera—along. Carry a good bicycle lock and always use it. In camp, get to know your neighbors and watch gear for each other.

Stashing gear when heading off the main route on a side trip is common, though potentially hazardous. When stashing gear, make sure no one sees the hiding place, and check to be sure it's not visible from the road.

The First Principle of Bicycle Touring

The first and foremost principle in bicycle touring is to have fun. If the days suggested in this book are too short, cycle farther. If they are too long, shorten them. Take additional side trips or add rest days. Just be sure to have FUN.

A Note About Safety

Safety is an important concern in all outdoor activities. No guidebook can alert you to every hazard or anticipate the limitations of every reader. Therefore, the descriptions of roads, trails, routes, and natural features in this book are not representations that a particular place or excursion will be safe for your party. When you follow any of the routes described in this book, you assume responsibility for your own safety. Under normal conditions, such excursions require the usual attention to traffic, road and trail conditions, weather, terrain, the capabilities of your party, and other factors. Keeping informed on current conditions and exercising common sense are the keys to a safe, enjoyable outing.

The Publisher

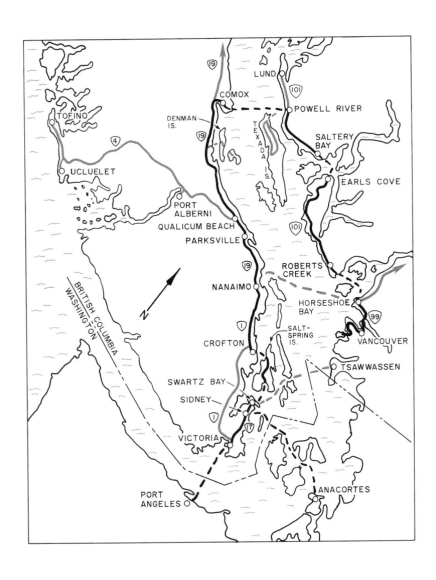

Right, *Horseshoe Bay, gateway to the Sunshine Coast*

14

BRITISH COLUMBIA

The 246.9 miles of cycling that make up the British Columbia portion of the Pacific Coast Bicycle Route are unique: the Pacific Ocean is never seen, a minimum of 4 hours and 20 minutes will be spent on the six different ferries that are necessary to the basic route, and for 115.1 miles you will cycle north rather than south.

The British Columbia ride starts in Vancouver and heads north up the beautiful Sunshine Coast to Powell River, a small town near the northern end of Highway 101, which is the true beginning of the Pacific Coast Bicycle Route. From Powell River, the route heads west across the Strait of Georgia to Vancouver Island, where it turns south through miles of scenic country and several lovely cities rich with Canadian history. The route ends in Victoria, where you can celebrate with an authentic English tea at the Empress Hotel.

Hopping from peninsula to islands, the route is connected by the British Columbia ferry system. The ferries are reliable, comfortable, and some are downright luxurious. On clear days, the ferry rides seem like expensive cruises to exotic places, where ice-covered peaks form a beautiful backdrop as the boat winds its way through narrow passages between forested islands. Cyclists who become hooked on the British Columbia ferries may find several extra excuses to ride them on side trips to islands off the main route.

Despite being the northernmost section of the Pacific coast ride, temperatures are mild, averaging 64 degrees in the summer, and rainfall is just less than 40 inches a year. Riding is best from May through September, when rainfall is at a minimum and daylight hours at a maximum. Wind is generally not a problem as most of the route is protected by dense forest.

When packing for a ride in British Columbia, plan for wet, cool, weather, and then be pleasantly surprised if it's sunny. Fenders and rain gear are recommended equipment. Carry a tent or a very good tarp as well as a small stove for hot food and drinks at the end of the day.

Road conditions for bicycling in British Columbia are poor. The roads on the mainland side are narrow, two-laned, and without shoulders. Traffic is moderate except on weekends or during vacations. On Vancouver Island, some sections of the highway have been upgraded to include an adequate shoulder; however, travel on unimproved sections is hazardous due to the steady flow of oversized tourist vehicles and trucks. Because of the poor roads, British Columbia is recommended for cyclists who have had previous touring experience and who are in good condition.

Distances in the trip logs are given first in miles and then in kilometers. No kilometer posts are noted. North of Vancouver, these posts are few and far between. On Vancouver Island, they are located every 5 kilometers, all facing north and nearly invisible to southbound travelers.

The main difficulty for cyclists in British Columbia is finding a campsite. While provincial parks are numerous, only one has a hiker-biker site, called a camper's field. At the remainder of the campgrounds, sites are available on a first-come basis only. Start your days early in order to get into camp in time to claim a site for the night. Try to schedule trips to avoid weekends during the busy vacation months of July and August.

The city of Vancouver is the center of West Coast Canadian commerce, and is readily accessible by air, train, or bus.

United States residents entering Canada should carry some identification establishing their citizenship. Technically, this means a birth certificate, passport, or voters registration; however, a driver's license is usually all that is needed. Carry sufficient money—$20 per person per day, or a major credit card, is required.

At the end of the British Columbia portion of the route are numerous options. To continue south, cyclists may take a Washington State ferry from Sydney, British Columbia, through the San Juan Islands to Anacortes following Washington's Inland Route, or a ferry from Victoria to Port Angeles, Washington, if the Peninsula Route is preferred. Other options are a bus, or, in the summer, a ferry to Seattle.

Cyclists wishing to cycle only British Columbia may return to Vancouver by ferry from Nanaimo to Horseshoe Bay, or from Swartz Bay to Tsawwassen. (If returning by Tsawwassen, check with the Tunnel Office, 604-277-2115, to be sure the shuttle bus is running at the George Massey Tunnel on Highway 99. Shuttle service is provided daily from June through August, and on weekends in September and the last two weeks of May. The bus starts from the Highway Patrol building at one end, and the Town and Country Motel at the other. If the shuttle is not running, be prepared for a 7.5-mile (12-km) detour across the Fraser River via the Alex Fraser Bridge.)

Vancouver to Roberts Creek Provincial Park (46.4 Miles/74.2 Kilometers)

Vancouver is a beautiful city, and one of the most difficult on the entire Pacific coast to bicycle through. With no major freeway to take the brunt of traffic through the downtown area, the narrow city streets are exceptionally busy. Cyclists in Vancouver—and there are a lot of them—ride well out in the center of the lane and seem oblivious to traffic. As a one-time visitor, you probably will not have time to achieve that kind of confidence in the drivers. You will also be faced with route-finding on streets that wind over and around rolling hills, requiring careful attention to book and map. If you get off-route, ask a local cyclist.

Several city parks provide opportunities along the way to stop, rest frazzled nerves, and take in the outstanding views. The largest is Stanley Park, located on a point at the edge of English Bay. It has a children's zoo, aquarium, totem poles, hiking trails, and a bike route on the water's edge. With a perfect view over sparkling water to the city's skyline and towering, snow-capped mountains beyond, the park is popular with local residents and visitors alike.

The route described through Vancouver is neither the shortest nor straightest. In order to avoid the more congested streets, the route follows the coastline, passing through miles of parkland

around the University of British Columbia and the popular
beaches of English Bay. A short section of city streets must be
traversed through the heart of downtown before ducking into the
protection of Stanley Park.

From Stanley Park, the route crosses the Lions Gate Bridge to

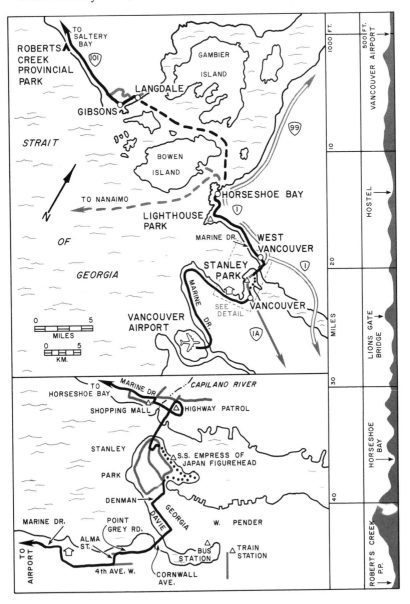

West Vancouver, the last major city before Victoria, at the end of the British Columbia ride.

North from West Vancouver, a narrow two-lane road leads to Horseshoe Bay, where a luxurious ferry is taken to Langdale and the start of the Sunshine Coast. Roads are narrow with little shoulder, and the terrain is rolling. This is a popular resort area and heavy traffic can be expected on weekends and holidays. After a ferry docks, there is a rush of traffic. If you pull over to the side for a few minutes, the roads will rapidly clear out.

As Vancouver is the starting point of the Pacific coast bicycle route, most cyclists will arrive by bus, train, or air. Since the airport is the farthest point south, the trip description and mileage start from there. For those arriving by ground transportation, the trip is 17 miles (27.4 kilometers) shorter. If you arrive late, the youth hostel at Jericho Beach Park, (phone 604-224-3208), is a convenient place to spend the night. The hostel is located on the route from the airport. Those arriving by bus or train may find it by following the route in reverse from downtown Vancouver.

Directions to the bicycle route from the train and bus station are as follows: Arriving by bus, head west on Dunsmuir St. for a half block to Cambie St., turn left (south) for one block, and then turn right on Georgia St. and follow it into Stanley Park. If arriving by rail, follow Main St. north 0.5 mile (0.8 kilometer), turn left on W. Pender and follow it into Stanley Park.

MILEAGE LOG

0.0 mi/0.0 km From Vancouver International Airport, cycle the shoulderless main road (Grant MacConache Way) out of the terminal area. Go straight, following signs to Vancouver and the Arthur Lang Bridge.

1.9 mi/3.0 km Cross Arthur Lang Bridge in the comfortable security of a 3-foot (1-meter) shoulder.

2.2 mi/3.5 km At the north end of the bridge, take the Granville St. exit.

2.7 mi/4.3 km Take the first left off Granville St. and follow the Bypass to S.W. Marine Dr., then make an immediate right on S.W. Marine Dr.

3.0 mi/4.8 km Junction; turn left on W. 70th St., which becomes S.W. Marine Dr. again. Pass a couple of small city parks as S.W. Marine Dr. winds its way through expensive residential neighborhoods on a narrow, bumpy road with moderate traffic.

5.0 mi/8.0 km Junction with W. 49th St. Continue straight ahead.

6.1 mi/9.7 km Major junction with 41st St. As you enter the University Endowment Lands, the road broadens to a four-lane highway with wide shoulders.

7.6 mi/12.2 km Pass a historical site on left (west) wide of Marine Dr., where an information board explains the exploration of the Fraser River, once mistaken for the Columbia River.

8.8 mi/14.0 km The road divides. Keep left, staying on Marine Dr., which soon narrows. The road on the right goes to the University of British Columbia.

9.0 mi/14.4 km Junction; stay on the left side of the university buildings.

9.8 mi/15.6 km Beach access trail, popular with students.

10.5 mi/16.8 km Junction; go left on N.W. Marine Dr. and descend a steep hill with excellent views over English Bay to the Coast Range.

12.9 mi/20.6 km N.W. Marine Dr. makes a sharp right, then a left while descending to English Bay at a section known as the Spanish Banks. The road then follows the edge of the bay.

13.3 mi/21.2 km Jericho Beach Park and hostel. The hostel is located in a three-story white building on the left side of the road. The park is a popular sailboarding area; rentals are available. Follow N.W. Marine Dr. up a short hill.

13.6 mi/21.7 km Turn left on W. 4th Ave., a four-lane road. Traffic volume increases.

14.2 mi/22.7 km At the traffic light, turn left (north) on Alma St. and follow it to Point Grey Rd.

14.5 mi/23.2 km Head right (east) on Point Grey Rd., a two-lane city street following the water's edge.

15.8 mi/25.2 km Point Grey Rd. bends right and turns into Cornwall St., which is narrow and busy. Pass the entrance to Vanier Park; beaches, maritime museum, planetarium, and central museum.

16.5 mi/26.4 km Cross the Burrard Bridge on a wide shoulder. Ignore the bike route signs at the north end and be prepared for a left turn at the second stoplight after the bridge.

17.2 mi/27.5 km Turn left (west) on Davie St.

20.0 mi/32.0 km Turn right (northeast) on Denman St.

20.5 mi/32.8 km Cycle left (west) on Georgia St. and follow it to Stanley Park.

20.9 mi/33.4 km Head right (north) on Scenic Dr. at the park entrance. Leave the road to the cars and drop down to the bike path on the seawall to enjoy views of water, city, and mountains. Follow the seawall around the park past the yacht club, Brockton Point Lighthouse, a metal sculpture of a girl in a wet suit sitting on a rock; restrooms, and water.

22.7 mi/36.3 km At 0.6 mile (0.9 kilometer), beyond the S.S. *Empress of Japan* figurehead, go back up to Scenic Dr. and fol-

Cyclists in Stanley Park

low signs uphill to Lions Gate Bridge.

23.4 mi/37.4 km Turn right (north) on combined Highways 99 and 1A, staying on the elevated shoulder to cross the Lions Gate Bridge.

24.6 mi/39.4 km At the north end of the bridge, just after the Highway Patrol building, go right on a service road.

24.8 mi/39.6 km Loop under Lions Gate Bridge and head to the right (north) following a narrow, shoulderless road past a trailer court and over the Capilano River to a large shopping mall.

25.0 mi/40.0 km Turn right (east) at the stop sign.

25.1 mi/40.1 km Go left (north) on Marine Dr., a busy six-lane city street with no shoulders.

25.8 mi/41.2 km Turn left (south) on 13th St. (the first street beyond a municipal park), leaving the rush behind.

25.9 mi/41.4 km Take the first right on Bellevue Ave.

27.4 mi/43.8 km Turn left (south) on 25th St., cross the railroad tracks, and take an immediate right, following a marked bike route.

28.0 mi/44.8 km Bike route ends; turn right (east) on 29th St.

28.1 mi/44.9 km Turn left (west) on Marine Dr., which is narrow, winding, and shoulderless. There are blind corners, so use caution as you climb over a series of steep rolling hills.

31.5 mi/50.4 km Pass the entrance to Lighthouse Park, located on the left side of Marine Dr. The access road descends 0.3 mile (0.5 kilometer) to a trailhead. If time allows, hike 0.5 mile (0.75 kilometer) through forest to a scenic lighthouse. Other park trails lead to viewpoints and fields. Water and restrooms are available near the lighthouse.

33.3 mi./53.2 km Pass Thunderbird Marina on the left and small convenience store on the right.

34.8 mi/55.6 km At the Highway 1 overpass, turn left (west), following the signs to Horseshoe Bay.

35.1 mi/56.1 km Turn right (north) on Nelson Rd. and descend.

35.2 mi/56.3 km Turn right on Chatham Rd.

35.3 mi/56.5 km Turn left on Royal and descend to the ferry dock. Tickets to Langdale may be purchased at the foot passenger window or up the road at the automobile ticket booth. Groceries and fast foods may be purchased in Horseshoe Bay. The ferry crossing is an enjoyable 40-minute cruise through island-studded Howe Sound. When the ferry docks at Langdale (no stores), it is best to let all the traffic zip by before starting.

35.5 mi/56.8 km Leaving the ferry dock, climb a short hill.

35.7 mi/57.1 km Turn left (south) at the light, heading towards Gibsons.

36.1 mi/57.7 km Road forks; stay left on Highway 101.

38.2 mi/61.1 km Gibsons; tourist facilities and last grocery stores before Roberts Creek Provincial Park. Follow Highway 101 up a very steep hill, then head north out of town. Shoulders are narrow, and traffic volume is generally light.

44.0 mi/70.4 km Cliff Gilkner Park; outhouses, picnic tables, and a short hiking trail to waterfall.

46.0 mi/73.6 km Roberts Creek Provincial Park picnic area; restrooms, water, beach access 0.5 mile (0.8 kilometer) off the highway on the left.

46.4 mi/74.2 km Roberts Creek Provincial Park (Sechelt Campground) on left (west) side of Highway 101. This campground has graveled campsites, running water, but no showers or hiker-biker site. If campground is full, continue on to one of several private campgrounds or Porpoise Bay Provincial Park.

Roberts Creek Provincial Park to Saltery Bay Provincial Park (41.7 Miles/66.7 Kilometers)

Narrow, winding roads and a series of long, steep hills provide challenging riding north of Roberts Creek Provincial Park. The scenery varies from enjoyable on the forest-lined road to good at the very occasional viewpoints over Malaspina Strait, where you may catch tantalizing glimpses of little rocky islands and harbors accessible only by boat.

The route heads up the Sechelt Peninsula on Highway 101 through lush forest to Earls Cove and the ferry to Saltery Bay. Check your schedule before starting off in the morning, and plan

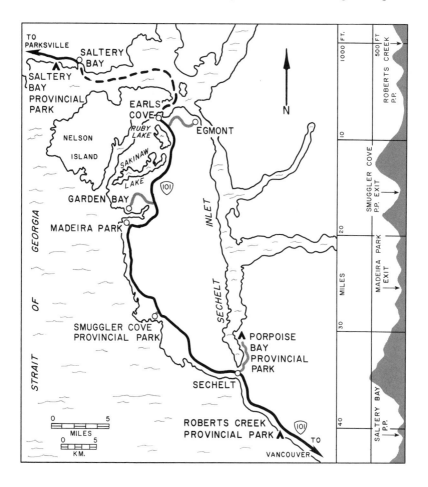

Tidal surge at Skookumchuck Narrows

your day's activities around the ferry departure time. The ferry ride is a relaxing 50-minute cruise with views of the Coast Range and forested islands. Once off the ferry, it's only a short, 0.9-mile (1.4-kilometer) ride to the campground. End your day by watching the sunset from the benches on the rocky shore of Saltery Bay.

One of the highlights of the Sechelt Peninsula is the Skookumchuck Narrows, where the tidal force of three inlets reaches phenomenal proportions. While it is best to visit at high or low tide, boats working their way through the narrows offer an exciting spectacle at any time of the day. The narrows are reached by a 3.4-mile (5.6-kilometer) side trip towards Egmont, followed by a 2.5-mile (4-kilometer) walk through inviting forest, to viewpoints overlooking the narrows. Plan to spend some time watching boats pass in and out of the inlet.

In spring and fall, traffic on this section of the route is light and drivers generally very courteous, except when they're rushing to catch a ferry. In the summer, however, oversized RVs crowd the highway, and cyclists must ride defensively.

There are only two places to stock up on supplies—Sechelt and Madiera Park. Grocery supplies are not available near Saltery Bay Provincial Park.

MILEAGE LOG

0.0 mi/0.0 km From Roberts Creek Provincial Park, follow Highway 101 north through heavy timber.

1.7 mi/2.7 km Wilson Creek, a private campground.

2.4 mi/3.8 km Brookman Park, a small park with picnic tables.

2.5 mi/4.0 km A short section of highway right along the water's edge at Davis Bay, with unobstructed views over the Strait of Georgia.

5.3 mi/8.5 km Sechelt, a tourist-oriented town with grocery stores, tourist facilities, and a small city park. The town sits on a narrow sand bar, which is all that connects the mainland with the Sechelt Peninsula to the north. A short *SIDE TRIP* up Wharf St. from the center of town leads to Porpoise Bay on the beautiful southern end of Sechelt Inlet. To further explore the bay, follow Porpoise Rd. northeast 5 miles (8 kilometers) to the provincial park: camping, water, showers, and short hikes. Continuing north, Highway 101 spends more time climbing than descending as it rolls on through heavy forest.

13.0 mi/20.8 km Pass a small lake on the east side of Highway 101, a good spot for a breather. The road begins a long descent.

16.7 mi/26.9 km Smuggler Cove Provincial Park turnoff. This park is designed for approach by water, with only a few rough trails from the road. Picnicking is allowed on the beaches but no camping.

19.5 mi/31.2 km Intriguing views of rocky coves, islands, and summer homes, accessible only by boat.

25.2 mi/40.3 km A handy information sign notes location of the grocery store in the town ahead.

27.4 mi/43.8 km A large supermarket lies 0.1 mile (0.2 kilometer) west (left) of Highway 101 in Madiera Park at the Pender

Cove Shopping Center. This is the last chance to shop before Saltery Bay Provincial Park.

31.0 mi/49.6 km Garden Bay turnoff, a small tourist town on the north side of scenic Pender Harbor 6 miles (10 kilometers) west of Highway 101. Beyond the turnoff are more rolling hills and views of two large lakes. The first is Sakinaw Lake, which lies to the west, below the highway.

37.5 mi/60.0 km Highway 101 passes island-dotted Ruby Lake. The road climbs above the east side of the lake, and then begins its final descent towards Earls Cove.

40.3 mi/64.5 km *SIDE TRIP* to Skookumchuck Narrows Provincial Park. Follow the Egmont Rd. for 3.5 miles (5.6 kilometers) east over several short, steep hills. The trail starts from a small parking area on the right side of the road. Push or ride your bikes down the first section of the trail on a dirt road. Mountain bikes can be ridden to the end of the road; touring bikes should be securely locked to a tree. At the Narrows, park facilities are limited to picnic tables and an outhouse.

40.8 mi/65.3 km Earls Cove ferry terminal. A waiting room and small restaurant help pass the time. There is no toll booth; fees were included in the price of the previous ferry ride. The scenery is beautiful, making the 50-minute ride pass quickly. The ferry heads east to avoid the large mass of Nelson Island, providing a glimpse of the northern end of Sechelt Inlet and the southern ends of Prince of Wales Reach and Hotham Sound. Miles of green forest connecting the rocky bays to the snow- and ice-covered Coast Range mountains confirm the feeling of being on the edge of the untamed north. Once across, cycle up a short hill away from the dock, then go left, following Highway 101 as it heads northwest.

41.7 mi/66.7 km Saltery Bay Provincial Park, a forested campground with running water, pit toilets, and easy beach access.

Saltery Bay Provincial Park to Rathtrevor Beach Provincial Park (74.6 Miles/119.4 Kilometers)

Saltery Bay Provincial Park to Rathtrevor Beach Provincial Park is not only the longest section of the British Columbia ride; it also includes a 75-minute ferry ride from the mainland to Vancouver Island. Start your day early and pedal hard to be in time for the

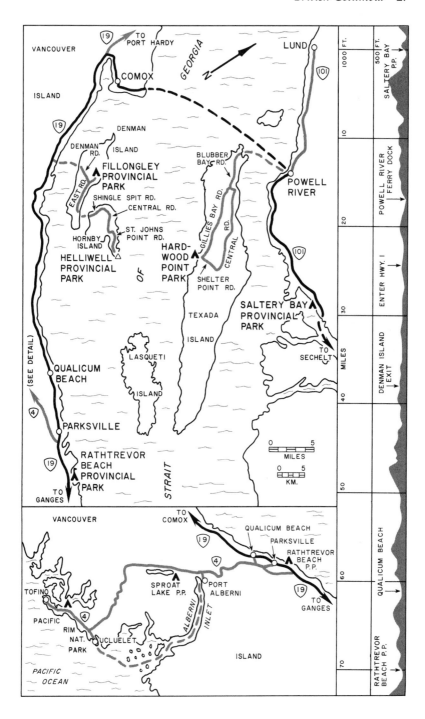

first ferry departure of the day. The Powell River to Vancouver Island ferry is more like a cruise ship than an auto transport. Enjoy the large sitting and dining rooms, decks for lounging or strolling, and tremendous views. On cold, wet days, it is tempting to pay passage back and forth a few times.

On the northern end of Vancouver Island, campgrounds, stores, and views are spread far apart, so the ferry dock at Little River marks the true starting point for the journey south to Mexico. Roads are good and shoulders adequate in most areas; however, Highway 19 is the only route north and south on the island. Expect a heavy volume of commercial traffic at all times and considerable tourist traffic during the summer and on weekends. The

Road sign in Lund

terrain consists of low, rolling hills with an occasional spectacular view across the Strait of Georgia to the mainland.

If you would like to spend some extra time in this area, consider one or more of four possible side trips off the suggested route which could extend this section from one day to a week. The first is a 35.6-mile (57-kilometer) round trip to Lund, at the northern end of Highway 101. It's 1,856.8 miles from Lund to the south end of the Pacific Coast Bicycle Route at San Ysidro, California. The road to Lund is narrow, with few views.

The second side trip is to the islands of Texada, just a short ferry ride from Powell River. Several industries are located on Texada Island: limestone quarries, an iron ore mine, and timber. However, intermixed with all this enterprise is some spectacular scenery and very little tourist traffic. Camping is available on the island at Harwood Park.

Once on Vancouver Island, an extra day may be spent hopping between Denman and Hornby islands. Denman Island is first, then Hornby Island, which has an extinct volcano rising out of its center. Camping is available at Fillongley Provincial Park on Denman Island. Hornby Island has two provincial park day-use areas.

The fourth potential side trip starts from Parksville, near the end of the day's ride and heads west across Vancouver Island 29 miles (47 kilometers) to Port Alberni. Here, you may put your bicycle on a boat and cruise down Barkley Sound, past the Broken Island Group, to Ucluelet and the Pacific Rim National Park. Once at the park, there are long, sandy beaches, trails, a rain forest, fishing villages, and tourist attractions such as rental canoes, boat trips, campgrounds, and grocery stores.

MILEAGE LOG

0.0 mi/0.0 km From Saltery Bay Provincial Park, follow Highway 101, climbing and descending over rolling countryside past several small grocery stores. Views are few.

1.2 mi/1.9 km Saltery Bay picnic area; water, restrooms, and limited beach access.

2.9 mi/4.6 km Viewpoint overlooking Texada Island.

7.3 mi/11.7 km Small gas station/grocery store.

7.6 mi/12.2 km Commercial campsite located on the beach.

8.5 mi/13.6 km Long Beach Spawning Channel; picnic tables. Peak spawning time from late August to October in odd years.

10.0 mi/16.0 km Black Point grocery store.

13.6 mi/21.8 km Myrtle Point; small grocery store and commercial campground.

18.3 mi/29.3 km Enter Powell River, a surprisingly large community nestled along the water's edge; commercial campground, grocery stores, and small cycle shop. To the north is the Powell River newspaper plant, the world's largest. A roadside information board relates some of the history of the plant, which may be toured on weekdays.

19.0 mi/30.4 km Turn left and follow the signs to the Vancouver Island ferry. This turn marks the start of the side trips to Lund and Texada Island. For details, see end of this mileage log.

19.1 mi/30.6 km After the 75-minute crossing, depart from the pleasant luxury of the ferry at Little River, then wait for the traffic to go by before heading south on a narrow and shoulderless road.

19.4 mi/31.3 km Pass a private campground.

21.2 mi/33.9 km A large four-way junction. Continue straight ahead (south) on Anderton Rd., which widens to include a shoulder as it passes over nearly level terrain.

23.2 mi/37.1 km Comox; bicycle shop and grocery stores.

24.0 mi/38.4 km Turn right at T-intersection, toward the business section of town. The route passes over low-lying marshlands with views of the snow-capped peaks of Vancouver Island and a special area for bird watching.

26.7 mi/42.7 km Following the signs to Highway 19, turn left at the traffic light, and cross a short drawbridge.

26.9 mi/43.0 km Turn left (south) on Highway 19. The shoulder, though generally good, disappears in spots; the terrain is nearly level. Several large grocery stores in the next mile (1.6 kilometer).

32.3 mi/51.7 km Shoulder disappears for a hectic 0.5 mile (0.8 kilometer), then returns. It will do this several times during the remainder of the day's ride.

35.8 mi/57.7 km Union Bay; small market and beach access.

38.2 mi/61.1 km Buckley Bay rest area, located on the left-hand side of the road, has an excellent view, beach access, and outhouse, but no water.

40.2 mi/64.3 km Start of Denman and Hornby islands *SIDE TRIP.* For details, see end of this mileage log.

41.3 mi/66.1 km Fanny Bay; restaurant and small grocery store.

52.4 mi/83.8 km Georgia Park; small grocery store.

63.0 mi/100.8 km Cedar Grove; a private campground with a water slide and nearby store.

63.6 mi/101.8 km Qualicum Beach; Grocery stores and nice grassy park along the edge of the bay, which has restrooms. Highway 19 narrows through town. Pass the first of three turnoffs to Port Alberni.

69.1 mi/110.6 km Lasqueti Island ferry turnoff. The island has gravel roads and no campgrounds. Several privately operated campgrounds are located near the turnoff.

70.5 mi/112.8 km Parksville. Stock up on food supplies for the night.

72.0 mi/115.2 km Second turnoff to Port Alberni and Pacific Rim National Park. See end of this mileage log for details.

73.4 mi/117.4 km Cross Englishman River, then climb a short hill.

73.8 mi/118.0 km Near the top of the hill, turn left to Rathtrevor Beach Provincial Park.

74.6 mi/119.4 km Rathtrevor Beach Provincial Park; camping, hiker-biker site (called the hikers' field), restrooms, water, showers, and beach access.

Lund Side Trip

Cyclists continuing north to Lund, at the end of Highway 101, should stay on the main road through Powell River. There are few views along the 14-mile (23-kilometer) ride. Several private campgrounds are passed en route, and groceries may be purchased at Powell River and Lund.

Texada Island Side Trip

From the same dock as the Vancouver Island ferry, catch the small ferry from Powell River to Blubber Bay, an old whaling port on Texada Island. There is a long, steep climb on Blubber Bay Rd. to a junction at 4.5 miles (7.2 kilometers). Head right on Gillies Bay Rd. for 8 miles (11.2 kilometers) to the small community of Gillies Bay, then on for 2 more miles (3.2 kilometers) to Hardwood Point Campground, located in one of the most scenic areas on the island.

A loop may be made on the way back to the ferry by heading east from the park on Shelter Point Rd., then north on Central Rd. to Blubber Bay Rd. These roads pass through the heartland of the island and are very steep in some sections. At Blubber Bay, purchase a ferry ticket to Comox on Vancouver Island with a stopover at Powell River—this is cheaper than two separate tickets.

Denman and Hornby Islands Side Trip

Take the ferry across Buckley Bay to Denman Island. Since many of the island's roads are not paved, head directly across the island from the ferry landing. Follow Denman Rd. 3 miles (5 kilometers) to Swan Rd., turn left for 1 mile (1.6 kilometers) to Fillongley Provincial Park; camping, water, restrooms, nature walks, and beach access. Set up camp here before continuing on.

From the provincial park turnoff, continue on Denman Rd., then on East Rd., riding along the shores of Lambert Channel for 3.4 miles (5.5 kilometers) to the Hornby Island ferry. This island has several resorts but no camping. Ride to Helliwell Park on the east end of the island. It can be reached by following Shingle Spit

Rd., for 2.2 miles (3.5 kilometers). Turn left on Central Rd. for 4.1 miles (6.5 kilometers), then go right on St. Johns Rd. (gravel) for the final 2.2 miles (3.5 kilometers) to the park.

Pacific Rim National Park Side Trip

From Parksville, take Highway 4 west 29 miles (47 kilometers) to Port Alberni. The road is hilly and twisting, passing lakes, Little Qualicum Falls Provincial Park, the Cathedral Grove Provincial Park, where trees are 300 to 800 years old. The road crosses 1,230-foot (375-meter) Port Alberni Summit at 25 miles (40 kilometers), then descends to town. Stop at the visitor information center at the east end of town to pick up maps and information on campgrounds, roads, and the sailing schedule for the Lady Rose. Facilities in Port Alberni include several commercial campgrounds, supermarkets, motels, and restaurants.

From Port Alberni, take the beautiful and scenic boat ride on the Lady Rose to Ucluelet. The alternative is to ride 60 miles (90 kilometers) to the coast on Highway 4, which is steep, narrow, and busy, but very scenic. Evenings are the best time to ride, when the logging trucks are off the road. The Lady Rose leaves Port Alberni at 8:00 A.M. on alternating days and carries only 100 people. Be sure to sign up early and specify that you will be taking your bicycle with you. If riding, stock up on supplies at Port Alberni.

Once you reach Ucluelet, ride north to find camping, hiking, long, sandy beaches, trails, and the rain forest.

Rathtrevor Beach Provincial Park to Mouat Provincial Park (55.3 Miles/88.5 Kilometers)

Spanning great changes in scenery and climate, the ride from Rathtrevor Beach Provincial Park to Mouat Provincial Park brings you out of the raw north to the warmth of the Gulf Islands. From the summits of the Coast Range gleaming across the island-studded Strait of Georgia, to ships and boats cruising this inland passage to and from Alaska, the scenery is outstanding.

In this section, the route follows Highway 19 along the east coast of Vancouver Island. Just north of Nanaimo, the Trans-Canada Highway 1 joins with Highway 19. From this point south, the road is extremely busy, and occasionally without a shoulder. To end the day, the route leaves the hustle and bustle of the main highway and jogs east on rural roads to catch the ferry to Salt-

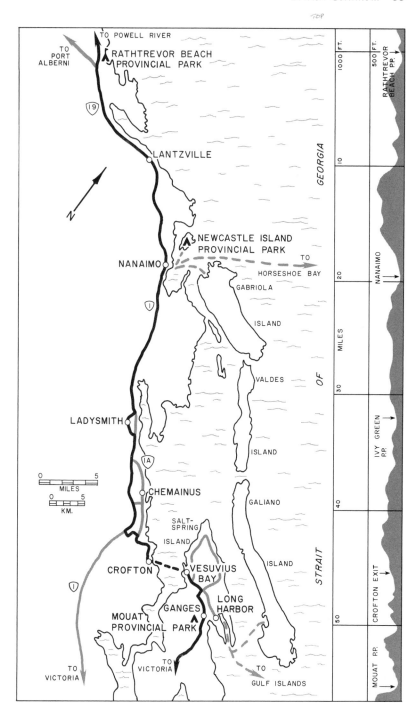

spring Island, one of the Gulf Islands (which are the northern extension of the San Juan Islands).

The main points of interest in this section center around the town of Nanaimo. At the hub of this thoroughly modern area, is the old town, with beautiful rock buildings and immaculate parks. Stop at the tourist center and pick up a tour map outlining various points of interest, from rose gardens to totem poles and petroglyphs. Spend time at the small but well-designed museum, and explore a coal mine and coal miner's cottage, an important part of Nanaimo's (and my) heritage.

In the center of Nanaimo's harbor lies Newcastle Island, a provincial park. The island is a perfect picnic spot, and the ferries run frequently throughout the day during the summer months. Enjoy an hour on the island, hike its many trails, or spend the night at the campground.

MILEAGE LOG

0.0 mi/0.0 km From Rathtrevor Beach Provincial Park, enjoy a final view of the Sunshine Coast across the Strait of Georgia, then cycle west on the park access road back to Highway 19.

0.8 mi/1.3 km Head south on Highway 19. The road is busy, the shoulders good, and the scenery excellent.

2.3 mi/3.7 km Final turnoff to Port Alberni and Pacific Rim National Park. Beyond this junction, the road is forested until it rounds the end of Nanoose Bay.

7.3 mi/11.7 km Rest area, on the edge of Nanoose Bay; outhouses, picnic tables, but no water. This inlet is beautiful when the tide is in, and an enticing clam-digging area when the tide is out. Across the inlet from the highway is a naval station, where large ships of war are frequently moored. Beyond the bay, the road turns inland, past several privately operated campgrounds.

8.7 mi/13.9 km Lantzville, a small commercial area with most of its facilities located off the main highway. Soon after Lantzville, forests are replaced by farms, which in turn are replaced by shopping centers, gas stations, and warehouses as Highway 19 enters Nanaimo.

13.1 mi/21.0 km Nanaimo; all facilities, including bike shops and grocery stores. Traffic becomes heavy as the road gets closer to the center of town.

18.2 mi/29.1 km City bike route goes left and crosses under the highway. This route offers no discernible advantage and will return to the main highway in 0.3 mile (0.5 kilometer).

18.3 mi/29.3 km Nanaimo–Horseshoe Bay ferry traffic turns left on Departure Bay Rd. Cyclists who run out of time may

Waiting at Crofton for the ferry to Saltspring Island

shorten their trip by taking this ferry back to Vancouver. The ferry turnoff marks the joining of Highway 19 with the Trans-Canada Highway 1. From this point south, the road is extremely busy. To mark this event the road narrows and the shoulder ends. Use caution as you descend into town.

20.0 mi/32.0 km Pass the visitor information center on the left side of the highway. Use caution when crossing over to the center to pick up your city map.

20.2 mi/32.3 km Turn left (east) off the main highway onto Comox Rd. at the heart of Nanaimo. Descend into the heart of the old town. *SIDE TRIP* to Newcastle Island Provincial Park. Ride approximately 500 feet (150 meters) on Comox Rd., take a left, and descend to the ferry terminal at Maffeo Sutton Park, located directly behind the arena. The island park has campsites, fast food, swimming, playfields, and enough artifacts to keep a history buff happy for several days.

20.4 mi/32.6 km Comox Rd. bends to the right and turns into Front St. Pass to the right of the Bastion, an old Hudson Bay Company fort turned museum, open in the summer .

21.7 mi/34.7 km *SIDE TRIP* to the Nanaimo Museum. The building sits atop a small knoll with access up a short, steep road. View from the top is excellent.

21.8 mi/34.9 km Pass Gabriola Island ferry dock. There are 20 miles (32 kilometers) of pleasant touring on the island. No camping.

21.9 mi/35.0 km The road divides; stay to the left, following the waterfront as Front St. turns into Esplanade.

22.0 mi/35.2 km Turn right on Crace St. and follow the city bike route signs.

22.1 mi/35.4 km Take the first left on Haliburton and ride south on a residential street.

24.1 mi/38.6 km Just before reaching Trans-Canada Highway 1, turn left on Chase River Rd.

24.3 mi/38.9 km The road ends at Trans-Canada Highway 1 exit. Carefully cross the road just before the exit and ride the sidewalk south to the next intersection.

24.6 mi/39.4 km Return to Trans-Canada Highway 1 at the traffic signal and continue south. It is a wide 4-laner here, with an excellent shoulder.

29.5 mi/47.2 km Pass a rest area on the left side of the highway; no water.

32.3 mi/51.7 km The highway narrows to two lanes and the shoulder ends temporarily. Traffic is very heavy, so ride with caution.

33.4 mi/53.4 km Small rest area; no facilities. The shoulder returns here but will continue to come and go for the next 5 miles.

35.3 mi/56.5 km Ladysmith; commercial district and grocery stores are located off Trans-Canada Highway 1.

35.5 mi/56.8 km *ALTERNATE ROUTE* through Ladysmith. Exit the Trans-Canada Highway 1 here for the comparative quiet of the city streets. Follow the main road through town and back to the highway.

37.4 mi/59.8 km Alternate Route returns to Trans-Canada Highway 1. For the next 2.5 miles (4.0 kilometers), the highway is shoulderless.

37.6 mi/60.2 km The Chemainus turnoff is the start of an *ALTERNATE ROUTE* to Crofton. Highway 1A through Chemainus offers a scenic escape from the Trans-Canada Highway 1. The road is narrow and recommended only on weekends, when the lumber mills are closed.

39.9 mi/63.8 km The highway widens to four lanes with a delightful shoulder.

46.3 mi/74.1 km Cross a large bridge, then prepare for a left turn.

46.5 mi/74.4 km Take a left turn off Tans-Canada Highway 1 and head east, following signs to Crofton and Saltspring Island ferry.

46.9 mi/75.0 km Intersection. Go left on narrow road through a residential area.

47.9 mi/76.6 km Road ends. Turn right, joining Highway 1A from Chemainus, and follow the narrow road over several very short, steep hills to Crofton.

50.2 mi/80.3 km A large lumber mill marks the entrance to Crofton. In town, you will find a supermarket and a view of Mount Baker over Saltspring Island on a clear day.

50.7 mi/81.1 km Ferry terminal. After a 20-minute ride, the ferry docks on Saltspring Island at Vesuvius Bay. Head up the steep hill following Vesuvius Rd. Riding on the island is fun, and many cyclists relax their strict road disciplines on the quiet country roads. Unfortunately, though traffic on the island is sparse, cars travel at high speeds. Remember to ride defensively while enjoying the scenery.

51.9 mi/83.6 km Intersection. Turn right (south) and follow the roller-coaster road through island farmlands.

54.4 mi/87.6 km Ganges; a small tourist town with grocery store, bakery, picturesque harbor, and small picnic area. Ride through town to a T-intersection facing the picnic area. Turn right and cycle 300 feet (0.1 kilometer) to the base of a steep hill, then turn right on an unmarked road full of potholes.

55.3 mi/88.5 km Mouat Provincial Park campground; running water and pit toilets. Saltspring Island may be used as a stepping stone south, or as the start of an island-hopping tour of the Gulf Islands. From the east side of the island, the Long Harbor ferry goes to Mayne, Galiano, and Pender islands. There are campsites on Pender and Galiano islands, and excellent riding on all three.

Mouat Provincial Park to Victoria (28.9 Miles/46.6 Kilometers)

The final leg of the British Columbia section of the Pacific coast bicycle route has three possible endings. Cyclists heading back to Vancouver take the ferry from Swartz Bay to Tsawwassen. If planning to head south on the Inland route through Washington, ride to Sidney and take the San Juan Islands ferry east to Anacortes. The Coho ferry to Port Angeles is the proper choice if the objective is the Peninsula route through Washington. It departs from the heart of downtown Victoria. (The San Juan Island and Coho ferries have limited daily departures; check with a tourist information center for an up-to-date schedule.)

No matter what route off Vancouver Island is chosen, plan to spend at least half a day touring Victoria. The city, often accused

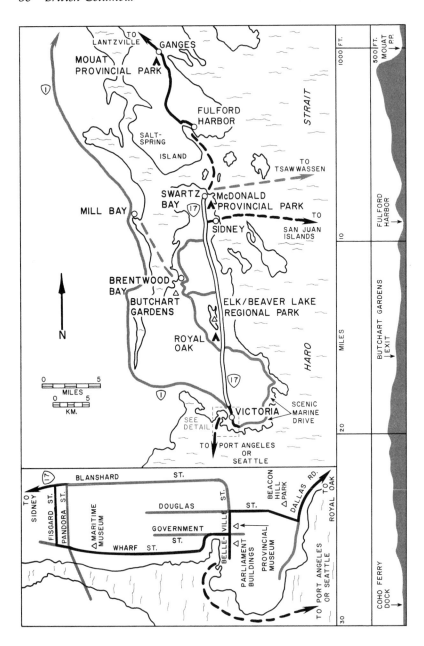

of being more English than England, is easy to explore by bicycle. Major attractions are within a few blocks of each other, and there are several scenic rides through beautifully maintained parks. Popular attractions include the Maritime Museum and Provincial Museum (hours can be spent here), Thunderbird Park, Empress Hotel, the Parliament buildings, and Beacon Hill Park, with beautiful gardens and an excellent view south. Stop at any tourist information office for a city map.

Just north of Victoria is the spectacular Butchart Gardens, open year around. The thirty-five-acre gardens display almost every variety and color of flower known to man in such exotic settings as the Sunken Garden, English Rose Garden, Japanese Garden, and Italian Garden.

The only provincial campground between Mouat Provincial Park and Victoria is located near Swartz Bay, 19 miles (30.6 kilometers) north of the city. There is one excellent private campground on the route, located 6.4 miles (10.3 kilometers) north of Victoria, which has walk-in tent sites out of sight and sound of the main highway. In downtown Victoria, you may stay at a hostel located on 516 Yates St. Call ahead for reservations, (604) 385-4511.

MILEAGE LOG

0.0 mi/0.0 km From Mouat Provincial Park, turn right on the main island road heading south. It's a warm 1-mile (1.6-kilometer) climb before the road levels off, followed by a long, sweeping downhill whisking you past pastoral island scenery.

7.6 mi/12.2 km Stop sign; turn left towards Fulford Harbor, past a small park on the right.

8.6 mi/13.8 km Fulford Harbor. Descend to the ferry dock and the main part of town; grocery store and small restaurant. The crossing from Saltspring Island to Swartz Bay on the Saanich Peninsula of Vancouver Island takes 20 minutes, much too brief to fully appreciate the view that stretches across the Gulf Islands to Mount Baker in Washington State.

8.7 mi/14.0 km After docking at Swartz Bay on Vancouver Island, follow Highway 17 south to Victoria. Shoulders are good to within 1 mile (1.6 kilometer) of the downtown area.

9.8 mi/15.8 km McDonald Provincial Park is located on the left-hand side of Highway 17; camping, picnicking, water, restrooms, and beach access.

10.9 mi/17.5 km Tourist information. Stop here to pick up a map of downtown Victoria and the entire Saanich Peninsula.

12.1 mi/19.5 km Sydney exit. Turn left for ferry service to the San Juan Islands and Anacortes.

13.1 mi/21.2 km Mill Bay ferry exit. This ferry connects Mill Bay with Brentwood (on the Saanich Peninsula).

16.0 mi/25.7 km Butchart Gardens exit; admission charged. Follow the road signs to the gardens. The gardens may also be reached from Royal Oak Campground, a few miles ahead.

20.5 mi/33.1 km Elk/Beaver Lake Regional Park, a large day-use area; picnicking, swimming, restrooms, and water.

21.1 mi/33.8 km Beaver Lake Park and Royal Oak exit. Use this exit if you are planning to camp. Parallel Highway 17 for 0.3 mile (0.5 kilometer) to Royal Oak Campground and hot showers.

22.5 mi/36.3 km Royal Oak Dr.; second and last access to Royal Oak Campground. From this point on, the traffic volume increases and the shoulder narrows and eventually disappears. To reach the center of town, follow Highway 17 until it becomes Blanshard St., then turn right on Fisgard St.

27.9 mi/45.0 km Turn right on Fisgard St. and cycle through Victoria's Chinatown.

28.1 mi/45.2 km Fisgard St. ends; go left on Store St. and follow it until Wharf St. joins on the right. The Victoria Hostel is here on the corner of Wharf and Yates streets.

28.3 mi/45.5 km Continues straight on Wharf St. paralleling the Inner Harbor. At the end of the next block is Bastion Square, where the Maritime Museum of British Columbia is located.

28.7 mi/46.2 km Wharf St. ends; go right on Government St.

28.8 mi/46.4 Intersection of Government St. and Belleville St. The Provincial Museum is the large building across Belleville St. on the left; the Parliament buildings are on the right. To reach the Coho Ferry to Port Angeles, Washington, go right on Belleville St. for one block.

28.9 mi/46.6 km Coho Ferry terminal. The dock is nearly overshadowed by its large neighbor, the twice-a-day ferry to Seattle, which runs during summer months only.

Victoria Scenic Tour

After visiting the center of town, take a scenic ride along the shores of the Strait of Juan de Fuca. Starting at the Parliament buildings, head east on Belleville St. for one block to Douglas St. and the Trans-Canada Highway 1. Go right (south) and parallel the park until you near the waterfront. Turn left (east) on Dallas Rd. and cycle through Beacon Hill Park to reach a spectacular viewpoint south over Juan de Fuca Strait to the ice-clad Olympic Mountains. Lock up the bikes and walk the park trails through immaculate gardens to the world's largest totem pole.

For cyclists with energy for a few extra hills and a good city map in hand, try this alternate route from Beacon Hill Park back to

Royal Oak campground. Follow Dallas Rd. east along the shores of the strait for 3.4 miles (5.5 kilometers) past scenic Clover Point and Gonzales Bay to reach Crescent Street. Turn right, following the SCENIC MARINE DRIVE signs back to Royal Oak Dr. and then head west to Highway 17 and Royal Oak Campground.

Totem Pole Park, downtown Victoria

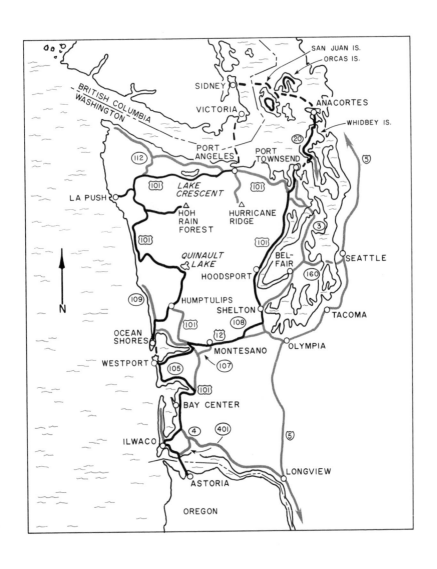

LA PUSH

Right, *sunset at San Juan County Park on San Juan Island*

WASHINGTON

The state of Washington prides itself on its rich, green forests, lush vegetation, lakes, rivers, rugged coastline, and glacier-capped mountains. If you think that all the verdant growth and abundant water are indicators of a very moist climate, you are correct. The generous and frequent rainfall discourages some cyclists but the hardy don raincoats and find much to enjoy. Of course, everyone hopes to catch one or more of the 60 days a year when it is perfectly clear, the sky a sparkly blue, and the great snow- and ice-covered peaks of the Cascade and Olympic ranges gleam brightly over the open waterways and forested foothills.

Two different routes through the northern portion of the state are catalogued in this section. We have named them the Peninsula route and the Inland route. The Peninsula Route heads south from Victoria, British Columbia, to Port Angeles by ferry, and then around the west side of the Olympic Peninsula on U.S. 101, totaling 344.5 miles to the Oregon border. The Inland Route travels down the Puget Sound, island-hopping from the San Juan Islands to Fidalgo and Whidbey islands. The route then crosses to the west side of the Sound and follows the Hood Canal to Shelton before turning west to join the Peninsula Route at Aberdeen, a total of 329.9 miles to the Oregon border.

The two routes are designed for riders with different goals. Riders taking the Peninsula Route should not be planning a quick dash through the state. To fully enjoy the Olympic Peninsula, it's necessary to take long side trips off U.S. 101 and pedal up steep roads to alpine meadows to watch mountain goats ambling across cliffs; descend long, narrow roads to beachcomb the rugged coast; and follow forest roads inland to wander through the moss-hung rain forests. Weather plays an important role on the Olympic Peninsula, and riders should be prepared for heavy fogs and rain (over 140 inches of rain fall each year in the Hoh River valley). The roads around the Olympic Peninsula are narrow, and see considerable logging truck traffic. Grocery stores, restaurants, and mo-

North Head Lighthouse

tels are few and far between, making this route best for more experienced cyclists who are prepared to camp and carry their food supplies for long distances.

If you are not interested in long side trips and miles of forest or prefer your route to be dotted with bakeries and ice cream shops, then the Inland Route is the way to go. Points of interest are easily accessible from the main route. Riding conditions are generally good, and the climate, protected by a coastal range of mountains, is much drier. In addition to numerous state parks, old forts, and Victorian towns, riders can expect to enjoy beautiful scenery and classic Northwest views. The route starts with a ferry ride to one of the best-known cycling areas in the country, the San Juan Islands, then heads south along the edge of the scenic Hood Canal. Moderately rolling terrain and good roads make this route enjoyable for all cyclists.

All state parks in Washington have primitive campsites for cyclists. These sites are small, with trail access to the water and restrooms. Cyclists are charged per tent (or tarp), rather than per person. These sites do not require reservations and are never "full." National Forest and National Park campgrounds are filled on a first-come basis, and finding a campsite may be difficult on weekends and holidays. To ensure a site in these campgrounds, it's best to make camp by early afternoon.

National Park campgrounds are open year-round. Most Forest Service camps close from October through April. State parks open for winter camping are Moran, Fort Casey, Belfair, and Fort Canby.

Due to the moist climate, fenders and rain gear are recommended for cycling in Washington. Take a tent or heavy-duty tarp and a stove, so you can cook at least one hot meal each day when it's raining, However, it's a documented fact that if you load up on rain gear and warm clothing, and forget your sunglasses, you will have excellent weather the entire time you are in the state.

The climate is mild. Temperatures average in the low 60s during June, July, and August. Winds blow from the south when the weather is bad and from the north when it's good. Rainfall averages 33 inches a year on the Inland Route, and up to 144 inches a year on portions of the Peninsula Route.

Mileposts in Washington decrease from north to south, and only whole numbers are indicated. Tenths have been added to the mileage logs to increase accuracy. For cyclists heading north to south, if the milepost number reads 25.7 in the mileage log, the point indicated will be passed 0.7 mile before milepost 25 (or 0.3 mile after milepost 26).

Finding an easily accessible point to start the Washington tour is difficult. Ideally, the tour should start from the Canadian border at Victoria; however, it's less expensive to fly to either Vancouver or Seattle and ride (very easy), or take ground transport to Victoria. Air, train, and bus service to Vancouver is excellent. From the Vancouver Airport, it is a relatively straightforward ride to Tsawwassen, where you pick up the ferry to Swartz Bay. (See introduction to British Columbia for details.) Air, train, and bus service to Seattle is also excellent. Seattle has the added advantage of direct ferry service to Victoria on the Princess Marguerite (leaving in the early morning from mid-May through September only). Port Angeles, the starting point for the Peninsula Route, is an easy two-day ride from Seattle. It also can be reached by Greyhound bus from Seattle or by ferry from Victoria.

Cyclists choosing to start from the Seattle–Tacoma International Airport (located at the south end of Seattle), are faced with a maze of freeways closed to nonmotorized traffic. If heading west to intercept the Pacific Coast Bicycle Route, pack your gear onto your bike and descend to the base of the parking garage. Head west into the darkest regions of the garage to Air Cargo Rd. (also called Airport Service Rd.), and follow it north. The road parallels the airport for 1.3 miles, to its end. Cross S. 154th St. and continue straight on 24th Ave. for another 1.1 miles before turning left (west) on S. 136th St. for 0.5 mile. At 4th Ave. S.W., take a right and head north, following city bike-route signs for the next 2.1 miles. At S.W. 108th St., turn left (west) through residential streets; S.W. 108th St. becomes 107th, then S.W. 106th St. After heading west for 2.9 miles 106th ends. Turn right (north) on Marine View Dr. for 0.8 mile. At S.W. Wildwood, turn left (west) and descend to the Fauntleroy ferry dock. Be sure to catch a ferry going all the way across the Puget Sound to Southworth. Once on the west side of the Puget Sound, follow Highway 160 west 11.7 miles to meet Highway 3 just south of Bremerton. Head west on Highway 3 for 7.4 miles to Belfair, then continue east on Highway 106 for 19 more miles to join the Inland Route just south of the town of Potlatch. If cycling up to Port Angeles, head north on Highway 3 to the Hood Canal Bridge, then west on Highway 104 to U.S. 101; shoulder is excellent the entire way.

For cyclists heading to the center of Seattle to catch a bus, the Princess Marguerite to Victoria, the ferry to Bremerton or Winslow, or simply to spend some time in the downtown area, continue straight on 24th Ave. S. to its end, then go right (east) on S. 116th Way and descend 0.5 mile to Pacific Highway S. After 0.6 mile, take a sharp right on Airport Way and follow it north for 6.9 miles to Royal Brougham. Head left (west) to Alaskan Way S., then turn right (north), past the Alaska Ferry and Washington State ferries to Winslow and Bremerton, to the Victoria ferry at Pier 69. If heading to the Greyhound bus station, head up Broad

Olympic Mountains viewed from Highway 101 near Shelton on the Inland Route

St. to 2nd Ave. and turn right (south). Go left on Stewart to 8th and the bus station. (Note: it is difficult to get bike boxes here.)

If ending your trip at the southern end of the state, it is best to cross the Columbia River to Astoria, Oregon, then ride inland on Highway 30 to Portland, or box the bikes and take a Greyhound bus to Seattle or Portland. A bicycle shop is a possible source of bike boxes for bus travel. See the introduction to Oregon for bike routes to the bus, train station, and airport in Portland.

For Washington State road and bicycle maps write: Washington State Department of Transportation, Public Affairs Office, Transportation Building, KF-01, Olympia, WA 98504; phone 206-753-2150. (The road maps are very good, but the bicycle map is not.) For a Seattle bicycle map write: Seattle Engineering Department, Bicycle Program, Room 612, Municipal Building, Seattle, WA 98104; phone 206-625-5177.

Inland Route: The San Juan Islands (57.9 Miles)

The Inland Route through Washington heads east from Sidney, British Columbia by ferry through the San Juan Islands to Anacortes. While touring the islands is not essential to the southward journey, it is an opportunity you should not pass up.

The San Juan Islands are a cyclist's paradise. Even their size is perfect—too small to be toured enjoyably by car, and too large to be easily explored on foot. The islands which have ferry service are the ideal size for a day-long tour including plenty of time to explore the numerous viewpoints and historic monuments.

Of the many islands that make up the San Juans, only four have state ferry service—San Juan, Orcas, Shaw, and Lopez. These four islands offer good riding and camping (limited on Shaw). Shaw and Lopez offer pleasant roads with low traffic volume, but are very limited in the way of scenic or historical highlights, and will not be mentioned further here. San Juan and Orcas offer numerous points of interest, and should not be missed by southbound cyclists, even those with tight schedules.

San Juan Island is the first ferry stop from Sydney, British Columbia, and is the site of the farcical Pig War between the Americans and the English. The war, allegedly, over a pig, actually disputed the boundary between Canada and the United States. It lasted from 1859 to 1871, with only one shot fired, and only one casualty: the pig. The sites of the two camps are on opposite sides of the island—and are a "musts" on the tour itinerary.

Roche Harbor is of scenic and historical interest. Hotel de Haro has housed two American presidents and is now the center of a yachtsmen's paradise. Near the harbor is the Afterglow Vista Mausoleum, the bizarre and strangely beautiful tomb of the McMillin family, who made a fortune mining lime in the area. In the center of the mausoleum is a marble dining table with chairs arranged as they had been during the family's life.

San Juan Island has several private campsites and a county park with a hiker-biker site. (This is a very popular park; call ahead for reservations at 206-378-2992.) The Elite Hotel Hostel in Friday Harbor allows you to enjoy a soak in a hot tub. (During the summer, call ahead for reservations at 206-378-5555.)

Orcas Island's chief attraction is Moran State Park, which covers over 4,900 acres. The park has two large lakes, numerous hiking trails, campgrounds, and outstanding viewpoints over Puget Sound from the summit of Mount Constitution. If time allows, explore the miles of back roads off the main island tour,

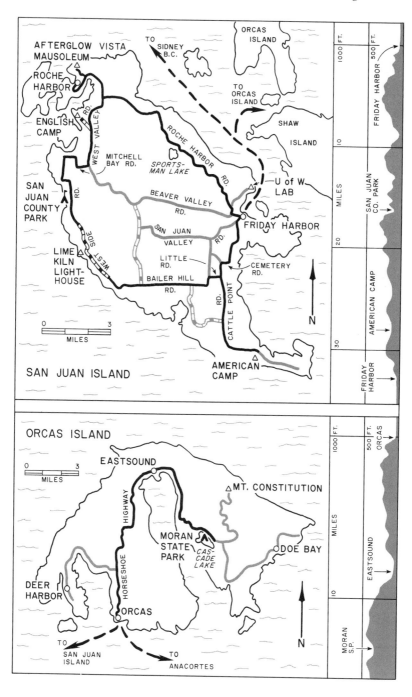

SAN JUAN ISLAND

AFTERGLOW VISTA
MAUSOLEUM
ROCHE HARBOR
ENGLISH CAMP
SAN JUAN COUNTY PARK
LIME KILN LIGHTHOUSE

TO SIDNEY B.C.
ORCAS ISLAND
TO ORCAS ISLAND
SHAW ISLAND
U of W LAB
FRIDAY HARBOR

RD.
WEST VALLEY
MITCHELL BAY RD.
SPORTSMAN LAKE
ROCHE HARBOR RD.
BEAVER VALLEY RD.
SAN JUAN VALLEY
WEST SIDE
LITTLE RD.
BAILER HILL RD.
CEMETERY RD.
CATTLE POINT
RD.

AMERICAN CAMP

0 3
MILES

N

1000 FT. 500 FT. FRIDAY HARBOR
10
MILES SAN JUAN CO. PARK
20
AMERICAN CAMP
30
FRIDAY HARBOR

ORCAS ISLAND

EASTSOUND
MT. CONSTITUTION
MORAN STATE PARK
CASCADE LAKE
DOE BAY
DEER HARBOR
ORCAS
HIGHWAY
HORSESHOE

TO SAN JUAN ISLAND
TO ANACORTES

0 3
MILES

N

1000 FT. 500 FT. ORCAS
MILES EASTSOUND
10
MORAN S.P.

Country road on San Juan Island

which lead to beautiful secluded coves and small resorts, including the Doe Bay Village Hostel (call 206-376-2291 for reservations). Sea kayaks may be rented if you wish to continue your explorations on the water.

The San Juan and Orcas island tours are best spread out over two days. Spend the first night at San Juan County Park and the second at Moran State Park. The ride back across Orcas Island fits nicely into the next section heading south from Anacortes to Fort Worden.

Island travel is popular, and spring and fall are the recommended times to avoid crowds.

MILEAGE LOG

San Juan Island

0.0 Leave the ferry at Friday Harbor and head uphill; tourist shops, whale museum, grocery stores, hostel, bakery, and bike shop.

0.2 At Second St., turn right, heading up and out of town.

0.4 Turn right on Tucker St., which dips down past small resorts and a delightful view over Friday Harbor to Mount Baker.

0.7 Intersection. The right fork leads to the University of Washington's marine research laboratories, open to the public Wednesdays and Saturdays from 2:00 P.M. to 4:00 P.M. during the summer. Take the left fork and continue around the island on Roche Harbor Rd.

4.5 Pass Sportsman Lake, popular with bird watchers and fishermen.

7.0 Roche Harbor–English Camp junction. Bear right to Roche Harbor if making the full island tour.

8.2 Roche Harbor. Pass the entrance gate and take a left. Coast down the steep road to the harbor and hotel.

8.6 After checking out the area, return to the entrance gate and turn north for 0.2 mile to the mausoleum trail.

8.8 Afterglow Mausoleum Trail, a short 0.25-mile walk. Imagine the area as it was when the mausoleum was built, with a sweeping view west over Haro Strait.

9.8 Return to Roche Harbor–English Camp junction and head south to English Camp on the West Valley Rd. The terrain is rolling (hills moderate to steep), the road is narrow and shaded.

11.5 English Camp National Historic Park. Walk or ride the short dirt access road then walk the trail down to the camp area. Tour the restored buildings on the pretty little harbor, then hike one of the park trails. A visitor center offers a movie, information, a small museum, and restrooms, but no running water.

13.3 Intersection. Turn right on Mitchell Bay Rd. towards Snug Harbor. (West Valley Rd. continues back across the island to Friday Harbor.)

14.6 Curve left on the West Side Rd.

16.4 San Juan County Park; hiker-biker site, restrooms, but no showers. The closest grocery stores are located in Friday Harbor. The park has a lovely western exposure for watching the sun set over Vancouver Island and the Olympic Mountains. This is a popular whale-watch area.

17.7 Paved road ends. The next 2.5 miles are gravel.

19.7 Turnoff to Lime Kiln Lighthouse and the remains of a lime mine.

20.2 Pavement. The road parallels the coastline. Views are excellent south to the Olympic Peninsula and west to Victoria.

21.7 West Side Rd. bends east, becomes Bailer Hill Rd. and heads inland across green farmland.

24.8 Turn right on Little Rd.

Cyclist ascending Mount Constitution on Orcas Island

25.2 Intersection. Go right again on Cattle Point Rd. and follow it to windswept American Camp.

28.0 American Camp National Historic Park; information center, restrooms, and drinking water. A nature trail winds around the camp site to an excellent viewpoint over Cattle Point. From American Camp, cycle north back along Cattle Point Rd. for 3.2 miles, passing the Little Rd. turnoff.

31.2 Turn right at Cemetery Rd. and head downhill.

31.8 Bear left as Cemetery Rd. joins Argyle Rd.

31.9 Return to Friday Harbor, completing the San Juan Island tour.

Orcas Island

0.0 The ferry docks at the little town of Orcas; small grocery store and several restaurants. Following the Horseshoe Highway, the tour starts by climbing the first of numerous steep hills while heading across the center of the island. The road is narrow: watch for cars.

4.5 Bicyclist rest stop; no facilities.

8.3 Eastsound, largest town on Orcas Island; large grocery store, small pioneer museum, and a combination bicycle–chain saw shop. The town is scenically situated on the edge of East Sound, a long, narrow passage which nearly cuts the island in two.

8.8 Start of steep climb to Moran State Park.

12.5 Moran State Park entrance. Road descends to Cascade Lake.

13.0 First of three campgrounds along Cascade Lake. Go to the entrance booth for directions to the large hiker-biker area, hot showers, boat rentals, and numerous hiking trails. From the state park, retrace your route back to the ferry dock. The round trip on Orcas Island, including a trip to the summit of Mount Constitution (see below), is 35.4 miles.

Mount Constitution Side Trip

The chief attraction of Moran State Park is the view from the 2,409-foot summit of Mount Constitution, located just 4.7 miles above 351-foot Cascade Lake. To say the road is steep is definitely an understatement. However, cyclists sweat their way to the summit every day. Be sure to deposit all heavy baggage at the bottom. For those without low gears, try the 4-mile hiking trail.

There are two viewpoints, one at each end of the mile-long summit, visit both to enjoy the sweeping views over hundreds of islands to the Cascade Mountains where Mount Baker is the star, the Coast Range, Vancouver Island, and the Olympics.

Inland Route: Anacortes Ferry Dock to Fort Worden State Park (35.9 Miles)

It's a short ride from the Anacortes ferry dock to Fort Worden State Park, allowing plenty of time in the morning for the long, leisurely ferry trip from Sidney or one of the San Juan Islands, and a second ferry ride from Keystone to Port Townsend. Neither of these ferries runs frequently, so expect to spend a hour at the ferry docks.

The ferry dock at Anacortes is located on Fidalgo Island, a large body of land solidly connected to the mainland. From the dock the road heads up, launching the day's ride over a long series of steeply rolling hills. The route to Fort Casey State Park travels over Fidalgo Island, across Deception Pass, and on to Whidbey Island.

Do not expect the same island feeling found in the San Juans. Like Fidalgo Island, Whidbey is securely linked to the mainland, and bustles with activity from several large towns and a naval air base at Oak Harbor.

To avoid the busy main highway on Fidalgo and Whidbey islands, most of this ride is on the back roads. Scenery varies from forest to beautiful views west over Puget Sound to the Olympics and east to the snow- and ice-capped Cascade Range.

Parks provide the chief highlights of this ride, so plan extra time between your ferry rides to enjoy them. Washington Park, near the Anacortes ferry dock, has a not-to-be-missed 2.3-mile loop road around a small headland with viewpoints of the San Juan Islands and Rosario Strait, framed by wind-sculptured trees.

Deception Pass State Park (6.2 miles south of the Anacortes ferry dock), spans Fidalgo and Whidbey islands, and has miles of trails, lakes, beaches, views, as well as picnic and camping facilities. Stop at Pass Island, a small chunk of rock in the center of the rushing, rolling waters of Deception Pass, and watch boats challenge the dangerous currents.

A small city park in Oak Harbor is a fun place to visit after a stop at the bakery. The city beach has a majestic windmill that looks as though it came straight from the Netherlands.

Fort Casey State Park is located next to the ferry dock at Keystone. While waiting for your ferry, take time to explore the old fort, or check out the lighthouse and museum. If you miss your ferry, stay in the state park campground that overlooks the ferry terminal.

If time allows, take a side trip from Fort Casey to Rhododendron Campground, a county park. In May, this forested park is bright with flowering rhododendrons. Free camping is the main attraction the rest of the year. Also within easy riding distance of Fort Casey is a Washington State game farm specializing in pheasants. Visitors are welcome.

The Keystone ferry takes you on a scenic, 35-minute ride across Puget Sound to Port Townsend, a beautifully maintained Victorian town. Settled in the 1850s, it was a thriving seaport until the mid-1890s, when Seattle became the western terminus of the Union Pacific Railroad. Today, the downtown and bluff area are a designated National Historic District with buildings dating back to the 1880s. Stop at the information center and pick up a free guide map to the historic buildings, art galleries, antique shops, and the Jefferson County Museum.

The day ends at Fort Worden State Park, which has a restored military fort, working lighthouse, marine science center, and miles of beach with views of the Strait of Juan de Fuca, San Juan Islands, and Admiralty Inlet.

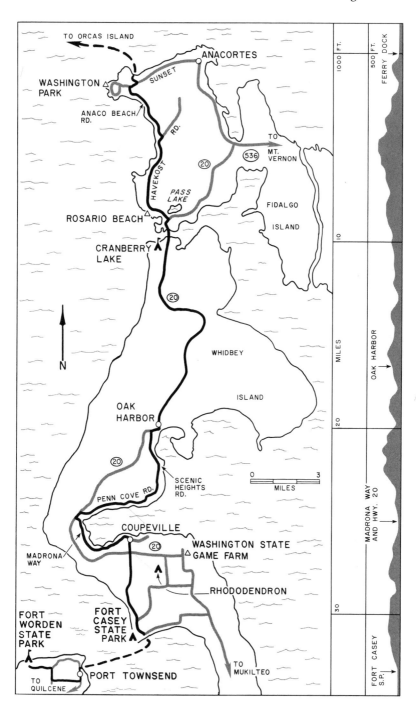

TO ORCAS ISLAND

ANACORTES

WASHINGTON PARK

SUNSET

ANACO BEACH RD.

RD.

TO MT. VERNON

20

536

HAVEKOST

PASS LAKE

FIDALGO

ROSARIO BEACH

ISLAND

CRANBERRY LAKE

20

N

WHIDBEY

ISLAND

OAK HARBOR

20

SCENIC HEIGHTS RD.

PENN COVE RD.

0   3

MILES

COUPEVILLE

20

WASHINGTON STATE GAME FARM

MADRONA WAY

RHODODENDRON

FORT WORDEN STATE PARK

FORT CASEY STATE PARK

TO MUKILTEO

TO QUILCENE

PORT TOWNSEND

1000 FT.

500 FT.

FERRY DOCK

10

MILES

OAK HARBOR

20

MADRONA WAY AND HWY. 20

30

FORT CASEY S.P.

MILEAGE LOG

0.0 Anacortes ferry dock. Follow the main stream of traffic uphill to the first intersection.

0.5 Intersection. Take a sharp right (west) on Sunset, a quiet, narrow county road. The left fork heads east 8 miles to Anacortes; tourist facilities, bike shop, and large grocery stores.

0.6 Intersection. Turn left (south) on Anaco Beach Rd. and skim through housing developments, past views, and over a few steep hills. *SIDE TRIP* to Washington State Park. Continue straight on Sunset for 0.6 mile past Anaco Beach Rd. to the park; scenic loop, restrooms, running water, picnic area, hiker-biker (primitive) site, and forested trails to viewpoints over the San Juan Islands and Olympics.

3.4 Anaco Beach Rd. ends. Go right on Havekost Rd. Follow this somewhat busy road, staying right at a large unmarked Y-intersection.

6.2 *SIDE TRIP* to Rosario Beach picnic area, part of Deception Pass State Park. Follow signs 0.5 mile to the picnic area, restrooms, and running water. There are tide pools to poke into and several trails, including a 0.2-mile loop to wide-flung views from Rosario Head.

6.7 *SIDE TRIP* to Bowman Bay picnic area and campground, another section of Deception Pass State Park. Turn right and follow the road 0.4 mile west to its end at a picnic area and campground. A trail heads south around the bay to Reservation Head, where a short, scenic loop is made around Lighthouse Point. Total hike is 2 miles.

6.8 (mp 43.0) Join Highway 20 at Pass Lake and turn right. The road narrows as it heads south off Fidalgo Island.

7.4 (mp 42.4) Deception Pass Bridge. The bridge is narrow, with a broad sidewalk for pedestrians. In the middle of the bridge lies Pass Island. Walk down the rocks to the water's edge for the best views. The rocks are slippery, so take off cleats before starting.

8.3 (mp 41.5) Cranberry Lake Campground, the main camping area in Deception Pass State Park; excellent hiker-biker facilities, hot showers, two picnic areas, a good swimming hole at Cranberry Lake, and numerous hiking trails. A small store is located just south of the park. Heading south from the park, Highway 20 widens to include broad shoulders. This is a settled area with farms, stores, and a naval airfield.

16.5 (mp 33.0) Oak Harbor; numerous supermarkets, a bakery, and a host of fast-food restaurants. Follow Highway 20 straight into town to a large intersection near the waterfront.

Lunch stop on Pass Island in Deception Pass

18.0 (mp 31.5) Follow Highway 20 as it turns right (west) and heads uphill out of Oak Harbor. *SIDE TRIP:* To visit the windmill park, turn left at the intersection and ride 1 block to the park entrance.

18.4 (mp 31.1) Turn left off Highway 20 onto Scenic Heights Rd. The road winds around Oak Harbor Bay with views of the city and, when lucky, Mount Baker above the Cascade Range. Scenic Heights Rd. follows the coastline around a headland and into Penn Cove, where the name changes to Penn Cove Rd.

24.3 (mp 26.1) Rejoin Highway 20 briefly.

24.9 (mp 25.7) Turn left off Highway 20 on Madrona Way and follow it along the south side of Penn Cove, past groves of madrona trees.

27.9 Intersection. Stay left at Broadway and descend to the quaint town of Coupeville, with its renovated Victorian harbor and small museum. Explore the beach and waterfront before heading up N. Main St.

28.3 Head steeply up N. Main St. to Highway 20.

28.9 (mp 20) Highway 20. Go straight across the highway, past a large grocery store, the last one before Fort Casey State Park. (If planning to visit Rhododendron Campground, turn left on Highway 20 and follow it 1.5 miles south.)

33.0 Fort Casey State Park; campground, showers, trail, fort, lighthouse, and museum all located near the ferry dock. *SIDE TRIP* to Rhododendron Campground and the Washington State game farm. From the fort, head back north for 0.5 mile to the first intersection. Turn right (east) on Fort Casey Rd. In 2 miles, find Patmore Rd. and go right. Cycle uphill for 0.8 mile and turn left on an unmarked gravel road, just before the group area. Walk or cycle 0.8 mile through the park to the campsites and Highway 20. To reach the game farm, ride south on Highway 20 for 0.9 mile to milepost 19. Turn left as the highway makes a sharp bend around a small airfield, where the navy practices aircraft carrier landings.

33.1 After a 35-minute crossing, the ferry lands in Port Townsend. To reach the supermarket and information center (0.7 mile to the south), go left on Water St. (also called Highway 20). The main historic area is located to the right on Water St. Fort Worden State Park may be reached by riding either right or left on Water St. Go left on Water St. for the easiest and least hilly route to the park.

33.7 Turn right on Kearney St.

34.2 Kearney St. ends; go right on Blaine St.

34.4 Blaine St. ends; turn left on Cherry St. and follow it to the park entrance.

35.9 Fort Worden State Park; hiker-biker area, youth hostel, hot showers, hiking trails, restored fort, lighthouse, and marine science center.

Inland Route: Fort Worden State Park to Potlatch State Park (67.1 Miles)

Weaving through the byways of the Puget Sound country, the Inland Route follows a mixture of quiet, rural roads and busy highways from Fort Worden State Park south to Potlatch State Park. The highlight of this section is the scenery.

Back roads are followed to Quilcene, where the route joins U.S. 101, and heads south along the west shore of the Hood Canal (an offshoot of the Puget Sound). The Hood Canal is a popular vacation area for residents of western Washington, and people flock to this area in summer months for scuba diving, clam digging, boating, and fishing. Campgrounds, trailer parks, motels, and restaurants abound.

U.S. 101 offers several access points to Olympic National Park. These are hiking accesses to wilderness sections of the park and,

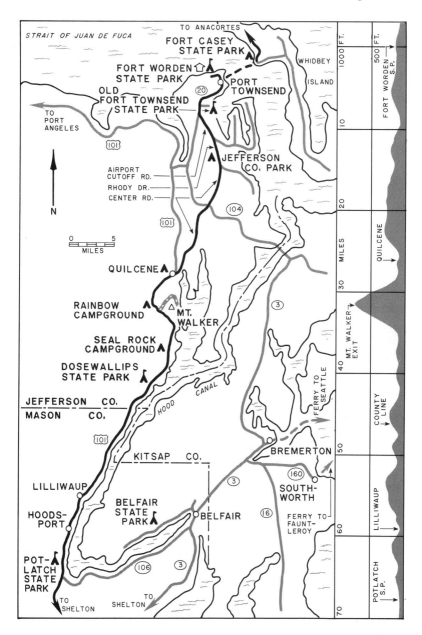

STRAIT OF JUAN DE FUCA

TO ANACORTES

FORT CASEY
STATE PARK

FORT WORDEN
STATE PARK

OLD
FORT TOWNSEND
STATE PARK

PORT
TOWNSEND

WHIDBEY
ISLAND

TO
PORT
ANGELES

101

20

JEFFERSON
CO. PARK

AIRPORT
CUTOFF RD.
RHODY DR.
CENTER RD.

101

104

N

0   5
MILES

QUILCENE

RAINBOW
CAMPGROUND

MT.
WALKER

3

SEAL ROCK
CAMPGROUND

DOSEWALLIPS
STATE PARK

JEFFERSON   CO.
MASON   CO.

HOOD   CANAL

101

FERRY TO
SEATTLE

KITSAP   CO.

BREMERTON

LILLIWAUP

3

160

SOUTH-
WORTH

HOODS-
PORT

BELFAIR
STATE
PARK

BELFAIR

16

FERRY TO
FAUNT-
LEROY

POT-
LATCH
STATE
PARK

106

3

TO
SHELTON

TO
SHELTON

1000 FT.   500 FT.

FORT WORDEN S.P.

10

QUILCENE

20

MILES   MILES

30

MT. WALKER EXIT

40

COUNTY
LINE

50

LILLIWAUP

60

POTLATCH
S.P.

70

from the cycle tourist point of view, useless. If you wish to include the park in your itinerary, now is the time to turn east towards Port Angeles and the Peninsula Route.

This section is long and challenging. U.S. 101 receives considerable commercial use as well as an abundant tourist traffic. The shoulders vary from almost wide enough to nonexistent. Hills in this section are mostly short but quite steep. However, one hill just south of Quilcene is long, and demands a heavy dose of carbos before heading up.

Potlatch State Park, at the end of the day's ride, has a pleasant location on the edge of the Hood Canal. Pick up groceries 3.7 miles north at Hoodsport.

MILEAGE LOG

0.0 Starting the day at Fort Worden State Park, cycle back to the main highway.

Native American art seen along Highway 101

0.5 Turn right on Water St. and follow it out of town. Water St. turns into Sims Way, which in turn becomes Highway 20. The shoulder starts off narrow, then widens as you leave town.

4.0 Cross a narrow bridge; no shoulder.

4.9 *SIDE TRIP* to Old Fort Townsend State Park. The park lies 1.3 miles east of Highway 20. Campsites, hiker-biker area, running water, restrooms, beach access, and hiking. Open in the summer only.

5.3 Stay left (east) on Airport Cutoff Rd. Watch for low-flying air-craft. Highway 20 branches right, towards Port Angeles.

7.7 When Airport Cutoff Rd. ends, bend left on Rhody Dr.

10.0 Pass Jefferson County Park; limited camping, water, picnic shelter, and pit toilets.

10.6 Turn right on Center Rd., and head towards the town of Quilcene. The Olympic Mountains form a dramatic backdrop as this rural road crosses open farmlands, clearcuts, and forest.

15.9 **(mp 5.2)** The road divides; stay left, continuing on Center Rd.

17.6 **(mp 6.9)** Center Rd. passes under Highway 104.

25.8 **(mp 15.1 and mp 294.5)** Go left on U.S. 101 and enter the small town of Quilcene; grocery store, campground, and fast-food outlets. Quilcene prides itself on its oysters; the largest oyster hatchery in the world is located southwest of town on Linger Longer Rd. (Note: the mileposts on this section of U.S. 101 are unusual, as the mileage increases from north to south.)

26.2 **(mp 294.9)** Another Jefferson County campground; camp-sites, picnic area, swings, water, restrooms, and a Best trac-tor.

26.4 **(mp 295.1)** Quilcene ranger station offers information on campgrounds and upcoming attractions. Open weekdays only. U.S. 101 begins a steep climb over Walker Point, wandering in and out of the Olympic National Forest. Shoulder is adequate, and logging truck drivers are adept at avoiding cyclists.

29.6 **(mp 298.3)** Falls View Campground; picnic area, water, and trail to Falls Canyon. No hiker-biker sites.

31.0 **(mp 299.6)** Rainbow Campground; another Forest Service camp area offering campsites, water, and a hiking trail. No hiker-biker facilities.

31.1 **(mp 299.7)** Summit of the Walker Point climb. It's a downhill glide for the next couple of miles. *SIDE TRIP:* From the high-way summit, a gravel forest road on the left climbs 5 steep miles to the true summit of Mount Walker and two outstand-ing viewpoints, east over Hood Canal to the Cascades and west to the Olympics. (This side trip is suitable for mountain bikes only. Cyclists on standard bicycles may reach these same viewpoints by walking a 2-mile hiking trail starting 0.2 mile from the main highway.) As considerable elevation must be gained to reach the viewpoint, set up camp at Rainbow Campground and leave all your extra gear there.

34.6 (mp 303.8) Yelvick; motels and restaurants. U.S. 101 winds along the edge of the Hood Canal, climbing in and out of small bays. When the tide is out, the beach is lined with clam diggers. Near the shore, the large sections of the canal marked off with buoys are oyster farms. With a little luck, you can spot blue herons. Enjoy the scenery, but remember to keep a sharp lookout for traffic; the shoulder varies from adequate to none.

36.8 (mp 306) Seal Rock Campground, a Forest Service area with campsites, picnicking, running water, and beach access. No hiker-biker facilities.

37.3 (mp 306.5) Brinnon, a small resort town with a general store, restaurant, and motel.

38.4 (mp 307) Dosewallips State Park has camping on the west side of the highway, and beach access and picnic area on the east. Amenities include a hiker-biker (primitive) site on the banks of the Dosewallips River, hot showers, running water, beach access, hiking trails, full hookups, extra vehicle parking, swings, sandbox—what a place!

41.7 (mp 310.3) Duckabush River Bridge. This bridge, like most of the bridges to follow, has no shoulder. Use caution when crossing. Shoulder on U.S. 101 is narrow to nonexistent.

46.2 (mp 314.6) Leave Jefferson County, enter Mason County.

50.7 (mp 319) Eldon, a very small community with a restaurant.

54.7 (mp 323) Shoulder widens to a comfortable width for riding.

57.9 (mp 326.1) Public beach access and roadside parking.

59.0 (mp 327.2) Lilliwaup; small grocery store, motel, and restaurant. The town spreads south of the main commercial area with cottages butting right up to the edge of the highway, leaving no room for a shoulder.

63.3 (mp 331.3) Hoodsport is a resort town with a market, restaurants, bakery, motels, and even wine tasting at the Hoodsport Winery. An information center for Olympic National Park and Olympic National Forest is located on the right side of the road. Pick up groceries for the night here.

65.5 (mp 333.6) Potlatch, this small town is the center of the Skokomish Indian Reservation.

66.6 (mp 334.6) Tacoma Power Plant and picnic area is a scenic location overlooking The Great Bend of the Hood Canal.

67.1 (mp 335.1) Potlatch State Park has a picnic area and beach access on the east side of the highway, and a campground on the west. Amenities include a hiker-biker (primitive) area and hot showers.

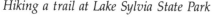

Inland Route: Potlatch State Park to Twin Harbors State Park (73.3 Miles)

This section of the Inland Route is your last chance to see the Puget Sound country before turning west and heading toward the Pacific coast. With no specific stops or side trips between Potlatch and Twin Harbors state parks, you can concentrate solely on riding.

This is a long but easy ride. The terrain is rolling, with several short, steep hills interspersed by long, level sections where the miles seem to speed away. A considerable portion of this ride is on a freeway with broad shoulders. If the ride seems too long, spend the night near Montesano at Lake Sylvia State Park. This

Hiking a trail at Lake Sylvia State Park

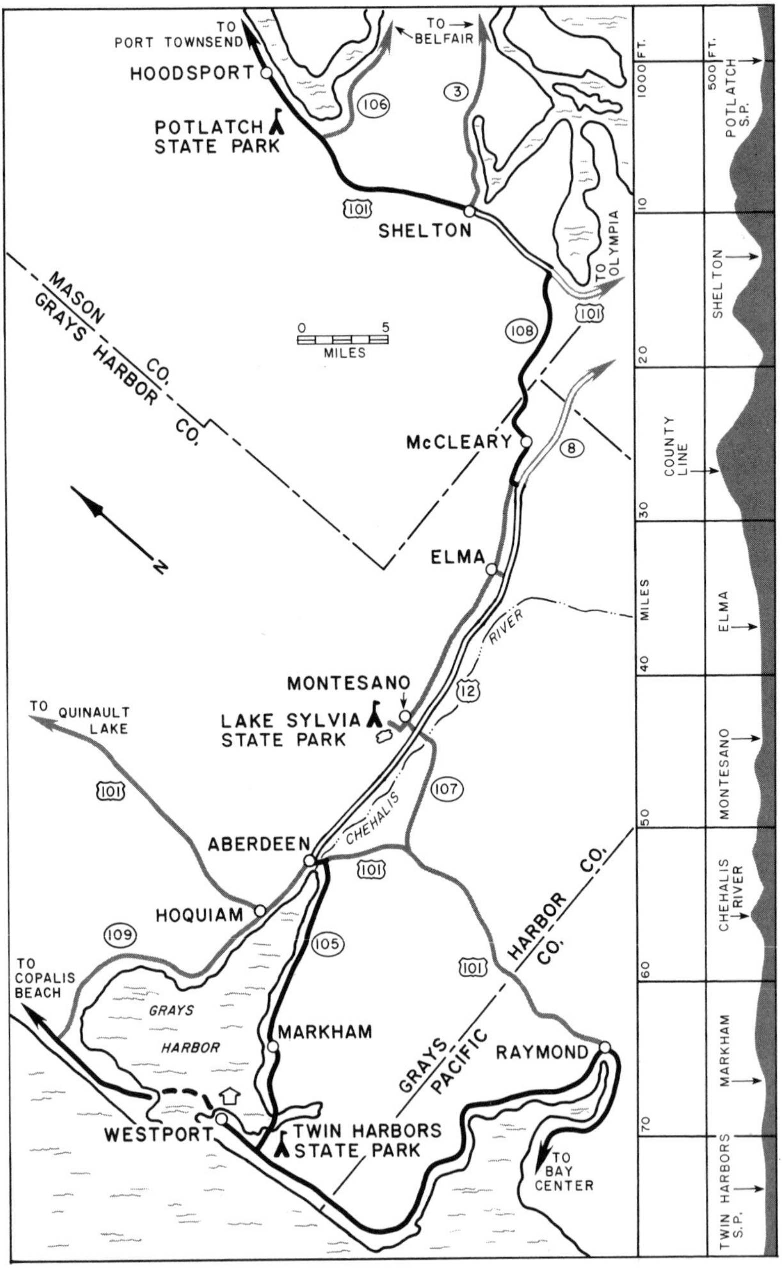

TO PORT TOWNSEND
TO → BELFAIR
HOODSPORT
106
3
POTLATCH STATE PARK
101
SHELTON
TO OLYMPIA
MASON CO.
GRAYS HARBOR CO.
0 5 MILES
108
101
McCLEARY
8
N
ELMA
RIVER
MONTESANO
12
TO QUINAULT LAKE
LAKE SYLVIA STATE PARK
101
107
CHEHALIS
ABERDEEN
101
HOQUIAM
109
105
TO COPALIS BEACH
GRAYS HARBOR
MARKHAM
101
GRAYS HARBOR CO.
PACIFIC CO.
RAYMOND
WESTPORT
TWIN HARBORS STATE PARK
TO BAY CENTER
1000 FT.
500 FT.
POTLATCH S.P.
10
SHELTON
20
COUNTY LINE
30
MILES
ELMA
40
MONTESANO
50
CHEHALIS RIVER
60
MARKHAM
70
TWIN HARBORS S.P.

will ensure that you have plenty of time to get that rented surfboard waxed just the way you want it before braving the first wave at Westport. Or, you may take a shortcut from Montesano and head south on Highway 107 and U.S. 101 to join the main route at Raymond.

Scenery along the route varies from cooling towers of a defunct nuclear power project to blue herons fishing in the mud flats of Grays Harbor. At the end of the ride is Twin Harbors State Park, located on a thin peninsula between Grays Harbor, Elk Bay Harbor, and the Pacific Ocean (which is sometimes peaceful and sometimes not, but always interesting).

The day ends near the town of Westport, a bustling resort town, and host to an endless stream of visitors during the summer. Westport is a great place to spend an hour or a day, strolling the beaches and harbor. Watch kayakers and surfers challenge the waves, and, if you are brave and very warm-blooded, rent a board (and wet suit) and catch a few waves yourself. Check out the long fishing piers, watch the fishing boats, then work your way through the ice cream shops and bakeries, and top off the day with fresh oysters, crab, or salmon purchased from a little roadside stand.

MILEAGE LOG

0.0 (mp 335.1) From Potlatch State Park, continue south on U.S. 101 paralleling the mud flats of The Great Bend of Hood Canal. The ride starts off on a 2-foot shoulder, which narrows as you go south.

2.0 (mp 336.8) Highway 106 branches off to the left, heading east to Bremerton and the Seattle ferries. This area is part of the Skokomish Indian Reservation, and grocery stores, fruit stands, and firework stands line U.S. 101.

4.5 (mp 339.5) Purdy Cutoff, an alternate access to Highway 106 and Bremerton. On the right is a turnoff to the Skokomish Valley Recreation Area. Campground and recreation facilities are a long way west of the highway. At this point, U.S. 101 climbs up from the lowlands of Hood Canal, then cruises past Christmas tree farms.

10.2 (mp 345.3) First turnoff to the town of Shelton (known as Christmas Town U.S.A. because of the large number of Christmas trees produced in the area). A large shopping center is located just off U.S. 101 on the left (east) side. Continuing south, the shoulder disappears along this busy section of highway for the next 2.4 miles. (Local cyclists will tell you that discretion is the better part of valor in this state.)

12.6 (mp 346.9) Shoulder resumes at the second Shelton exit. U.S.

Sunrise at Westport

101 is now a freeway (bicycles are allowed). Use considerable caution when crossing exits and on ramps.

18.3 (mp 353.6) Exit right off U.S. 101 and follow Highway 108 west towards McCleary. A medium-sized grocery store, the last for 10 miles, is located near the exit. Highway 108 winds west past farms and forest. The shoulder is narrow, and traffic is light. Expect an occasional logging truck.

26.3 (mp 4.3) Leave Mason County, enter Grays Harbor County.

28.5 (mp 2.1) Intersection. Still following Highway 108, turn left (south) and enter McCleary on a good shoulder.

29.4 (mp 1.2) At the center of town, turn right (west) towards Elma, past several small stores and restaurants, as well as a small city park with running water, restrooms, and old logging equipment on display.

30.4 (mp 0.2) Intersection and a choice. Highway 108 bears left 100 feet to join Highway 8, a freeway heading east to west. Highway 8 may be followed west all the way to Grays Harbor; shoulders are broad, traffic volume heavy, and the head wind frequently strong. The *ALTERNATE ROUTE* continues straight ahead on the McCleary–Elma Rd. which receives only moderate use but is narrow and shoulderless. The McCleary–Elma Rd. parallels Highway 8 through farm country. Cooling towers of the Satsop nuclear plant are visible on the hills to the south.

35.8 Highway 8 merges with Highway 12. Continue west on Highway 12.

36.2 Elma; a small town with several grocery stores, a city park (no facilities), and fairgrounds (fairs take place during the second week of August; expect considerable traffic in town at that time). If tired of the traffic on Highway 12, Elma is a good place to exit. Follow the McCleary–Elma Rd. west, straight through town, where it becomes the Elma–Montesano Rd. Beyond Elma, the shoulders are good.

38.9 Satsop; small grocery store.

43.9 Montesano; large grocery store, fast food, restaurants, and Lake Sylvia State Park. The town's chief structure is the county courthouse, visible throughout most of the area. The state park is located on a forested lake one mile above town. To reach the park, ride to the center of town. At the intersection with Highway 107, continue straight for 3 blocks, then take a right on 3rd St. and follow the signs to Lake Sylvia State Park. The park has a hiker-biker area, hot showers, lakeshore campsites, boat rentals, swimming, and hiking trails.

44.8 If you have stuck to the back roads this far, it's now time to join the freeway and continue west on Highway 12. From the center of Montesano, turn left on Highway 107 (also called Main St.) for 0.2 mile.

45.0 **(mp10.1)** Go right, up on the on ramp, on Highway 12 heading west.

50.4 **(mp 4.6)** Central Park; grocery stores.

54.4 Road narrows and shoulder disappears on the final descent into Aberdeen. Traffic is very heavy here.

54.7 Enter Aberdeen and cross the Wishkah River on a narrow bridge. Follow the U.S. 101 *South* signs, starting with a left-hand turn 2 blocks beyond the bridge.

55.0 **(mp 0.0 and mp 88.4)** Turn left on U.S. 101 and cross the Chehalis River on a wide bridge. When traffic is heavy, use the sidewalk.

55.6 **(mp 87.8 and mp 48.8)** On the south side of the Chehalis River Bridge, go straight on Highway 105 (U.S. 101 turns left here). Two large supermarkets, located on the left side of the highway at the intersection, offer an excellent opportunity to pick up your groceries for the night. Highway 105 (a Washington State Scenic and Recreational Highway) heads west through forest, paralleling the tide flats of Grays Harbor to Westport and the Pacific Ocean. The highway is narrow and shoulder-less in town.

56.4 **(mp 48.0)** Beyond a large shopping mall, the road narrows to two lanes with a wide shoulder.

66.2 **(mp 38.2)** Markham; home of Ocean Spray fruit juices. No tasting room or retail outlet. Shoulder starts to deteriorate here and soon disappears altogether.

70.6 **(mp 33.8)** Bay City; small town with a grocery store. Shoulder returns here.

73.1 **(mp 31.3)** Westport; a resort town with charter boats, salmon fishing, aquarium, museum, ocean beaches, campground, motels, restaurants, ferry to Ocean Shores, tourist shops, bakeries, kite shops, etc. Grocery stores and restaurants are located 2 miles north in the center of town. Continue straight ahead on Highway 105 for 200 feet, then turn left to reach Twin Harbors State Park.

73.3 Twin Harbors State Park; hiker-biker (primitive) area, hot showers, beach access, and hiking trails.

Twin Harbors State Park to Bush Pacific County Park (50.2 Miles)

The Peninsula and Inland routes through Washington come together at Aberdeen. From Twin Harbors State Park, a single united route heads through the southern sections of the state to the Columbia River and Oregon.

The southern coastline of Washington is broken by large bays which force the route to turn inland below Twin Harbors State Park. Cyclists can expect to ride over rolling, forested hills with only an occasional view of the Pacific Ocean or Willapa Bay as the route heads east to rejoin U.S. 101. Back on U.S. 101, the road runs south through Raymond, a mill town, and South Bend, then through clearcut forests and young tree plantations. Shoulder width varies from wide to none.

Start the day with full water bottles and plenty of extra food; few stores or restrooms are found along the route. With only a few towns and scenic beaches to break the rhythm of the ride, the miles tend to speed by. Cyclists arriving at Bush Pacific County Park may be tempted to continue south another 33 miles to Fort Canby State Park near Ilwaco. However, do not short-change the southern end of Washington. There are beautiful views and interesting places to visit along the Columbian River.

The economy in this portion of the state is based on the logging industry, so be prepared to meet logging trucks on the highways. Always give these huge trucks as much room as possible, or even get off the road to avoid being trapped in a squeeze play. Most truck drivers are very friendly to cyclists, but it's best to be on the safe side.

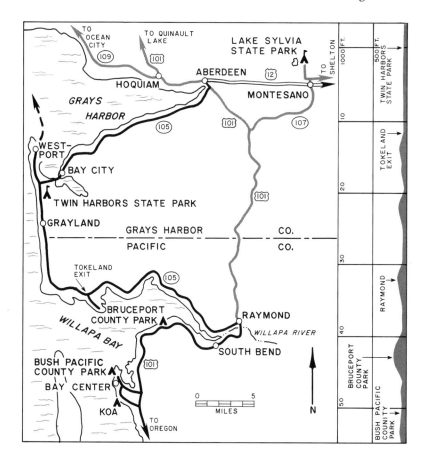

MILEAGE LOG

0.0 (mp 30.5) Head south on Highway 105 from Twin Harbors State Park. Shoulders are narrow, and traffic is moderate to light.

3.1 (mp 27.4) Grayland; a small resort town with motels, grocery store, deli, and a state park.

4.9 (mp 25.6) Turnoff to Grayland State Beach Park; water, restrooms, showers, hiker-biker (primitive) sites, and beach access. This park is oriented to the needs of campers with recreational vehicles. If you feel more comfortable surrounded by tents, stay at Twin Harbors State Park. Near the state beach is a shop which rents recumbent bicycles.

5.0 (mp 25.4) Leave Grays Harbor County, enter Pacific County.

6.8 (mp 23.6) Pass the first of several beach access points. The highway lies inland here, away from the beach. The land between the highway and the beach is all private property except for the occasional access provided by the state park.

8.1 (mp 22.5) North Cove; a very small town with a very small market. Beyond North Cove, the highway turns east heading inland to Raymond and U.S. 101. The highway broadens here to include a wide shoulder.

10.4 (mp 20.2) Highway 105 parallels the edge of Willapa Bay. The bay is very shallow, and the ebbing tide exposes miles of tideflats. To the south lies Leadbetter Point (the northern tip of the North Beach Peninsula), as well as the objective for this day's ride, Bay Center. The route skirts around Willapa Bay for the next 63 miles.

11.2 (mp 19.4) Enter the Shoalwater Indian Reservation; groceries, motels, and fireworks may be found near the turnoff to Tokeland, a small community with a fishing dock and an uninteresting historic hotel. All services are located near the turnoff.

20.1 (mp 10.6) After passing a commercial campground, the highway crosses North River, then Smith Creek. Beyond the second bridge, the shoulder disappears. Across the bay, the mills of South Bend and Raymond come into view.

30.0 (mp 0.7) Raymond; a lumber town. You will find just about everything for the touring cyclist here except a good bike shop. There are motels, restaurants, a supermarket, and camping at the county park.

31.0 (mp 0.0 and mp 59.6) Highway 105 ends; turn right on U.S. 101 and cycle across the 0.3-mile bridge over the North Fork Willapa River. If every vehicle on the road is a logging truck, the wooden sidewalk is recommended over the very narrow, shoulderless roadway on the bridge.

31.4 (mp 59.2) Pass a small city park on the left side of the highway; restrooms and running water.

32.3 (mp 58.5) U.S. 101 intersects Highway 6 on the south side of Raymond. Stay on U.S. 101 as it bends to the right (west) crossing the South Fork Willapa River, and then follow the Willapa River west. Hundreds of exposed pilings (reminders of the early 1900s, when there were 20 working lumber mills in Raymond) come into view. The shoulder along this section of the highway is very good.

35.1 (mp 55.6) Enter South Bend, a town that claims to be the oyster capital of the world. Despite this grandiose claim, South Bend is a small, charming town, first settled in 1860. Many old buildings remain. Amenities include a city park, public restrooms, grocery stores, tourist facilities, and an RV park that accepts bicycles.

Oyster processing plant on Willapa Bay near Bay Center

36.7 (mp 54.0) Pacific County Museum and information center, a small, friendly facility. Beyond South Bend, the road is level for several miles with a comfortable shoulder.

42.7 (mp 48.6) Bruceport County Park; picnic area, campground, restrooms, running water, hot showers, and special rates for cyclists. Campsites overlook Willapa Bay and are available on a first-come basis.

45.0 (mp 46.3) Historical marker relating the story of Bruceport's origin.

47.3 (mp 42.6) Palix Creek Bridge.

47.5 (mp 42.4) Turn off U.S. 101 to Bush Pacific County Park and Bay Center on Bay Center Dike Rd. Cycle along the water's edge past huge piles of oyster shells.

49.9 Bay Center, a small town with a grocery store. Turn right (north).

50.2 Bush Pacific County Park. This is a primitive park with campsites, picnic area, restrooms, and limited beach access. Generally, space can be found for all cyclists. If you prefer more amenities, try the KOA campground located just south of Bay Center on Bay Center Rd. (The KOA campground has hot showers, laundry, and store, as well as an area with tables and a shelter just for cyclists. Rates are very reasonable.)

Bush Pacific County Park to the Oregon Border (45.5 Miles)

The ride south through Washington ends at the Columbia River, a few miles east of its terminus. Here, water from the Canadian Rockies, 1,270 miles north, enters the Pacific Ocean. It's a scenic area, rich in history. Indians lived and fished here for thousands of years before European explorer Captain Robert Gray located the river in 1792. In 1805 Lewis and Clark ended their long western trek at the Pacific Ocean and wintered on the south bank of the river, near Astoria. The Hudson Bay Trading Company was

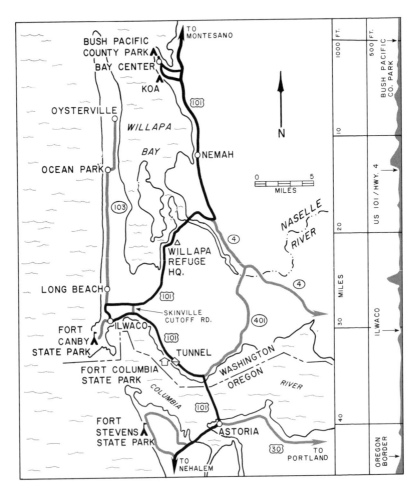

located here until forced out by settlers from the States. The entrance to the Columbia is guarded by a tricky sandbar; the river was the scene of numerous shipwrecks before lighthouses were built and the channel marked. Although tamed by numerous upriver dams and navigational guides at the mouth, the Columbia River remains an impressive sight.

The ride from Bush Pacific County Park to Oregon is an easy one, leaving plenty of time for exploring along the way. Plan to spend some time on the Long Beach Peninsula, just north of the Columbia River. The peninsula is a long, sandy spit that protects the western edge of Willapa Bay. Its most visible attractions are tourist-oriented: the "world's longest driving beach," innumerable restaurants, motels, and amusement centers. At the edge of all this activity is the Willapa National Wildlife Refuge, inhabited by migrating ducks and geese in the spring and fall, and a host of shorebirds year around. Two blinds for viewing and photographing the birds are located near the refuge headquarters.

At the southern end of the Long Beach Peninsula is Fort Canby State Park. The old fort is now the site of an excellent museum commemorating the Lewis and Clark Expedition, and exhibits lead visitors on an imaginary walking journey over the Lewis and Clark Trail. Two lighthouses, North Point and Cape Disappointment, are located within easy walking distance of the park. North Point is the most photographed lighthouse in Washington. The best photographs can be taken from the beach at the north end of the camping area, when the surf is up and the tide is in.

No campgrounds are conveniently located at the state border, so either spend the night at Fort Canby State Park or cross into Oregon and cycle another 10 miles at Fort Stevens State Park. During the summer months, a hostel at Fort Columbia State Park provides a third alternative.

MILEAGE LOG

0.0 The day starts at Bush Pacific County Park. Ride south through Bay Center and continue straight on Bay Center Rd.

3.1 (mp 41.5) Bay Center Rd. ends; head south (right) on U.S. 101. Shoulders are narrow.

8.9 (mp 35.6) Nemah. The only evidence of a town here is a small cafe that is sometimes open but often-times closed.

10.8 (mp 33.8) Cross the Middle Fork Nemah River.

14.2 (mp 30.3) Shoulder widens.

15.3 (mp 29.0) Junction of Highway 4 and U.S. 101. The bicycle route follows U.S. 101 as it turns sharply right (west). Shoulder is narrow to nonexistent. *ALTERNATE ROUTE:* Highway 4, in conjunction with Highway 401, may be used as a short cut to Astoria, Oregon to eliminate 11.1 miles of riding. No camping facilities or points of interest but the shoulder width is good for the entire distance.

17.9 (mp 26.4) Naselle River Bridge; shoulder begins. Parallel the Willapa Bay shoreline; beyond the bridge, the road is narrow and winding, with turnouts for taking in the views over the winding sloughs and scenic mud flats.

20.3 (mp 24.3) Willapa National Wildlife Refuge headquarters, on the left (east) side of U.S. 101 with information on what to see and where to see it. Take the time to check out the bird blinds.

23.8 (mp 18.7) *SIDE TRIP* to the Willapa Refuge waterfowl watching area. Turn right (north) on Jeldness Rd. just after crossing the Bear River bridge. Cycle north 1.2 miles, partly on gravel, to a gate and then walk a short 0.5 mile to the viewing area. Best time for viewing is in the winter.

28.8 (mp 15.7) Intersection of U.S. 101 and Alternate U.S. 101, called the Skinville Cutoff. The bicycle route continues straight on U.S. 101 to the Long Beach Peninsula, Ilwaco, and Fort Canby State Park. The cutoff is 0.2 mile long and eliminates 6.1 miles of riding while bypassing the Long Beach Peninsula and Fort Canby State Park.

31.1 (mp 13.4) Intersection of U.S. 101 and Highway 103 at Seaview on Long Beach Peninsula; grocery stores and complete tourist facilities. The bicycle route bears left (south), following U.S. 101. Highway 103 heads right, accessing the town of Long Beach and the northern end of the peninsula.

32.2 (mp 12.3) Enter Ilwaco, on the Columbia River; tourist facilities and grocery store. The turnoff to Fort Canby State Park, museum, and lighthouses is at the center of town. *SIDE TRIP* to Fort Canby State Park. Turn right (west) when U.S. 101 makes a sharp turn left (east) in the center of Ilwaco. Go straight until the road branches. Either branch may be followed for the 3-mile ride to the park; hiker-biker (primitive) campsites, hot showers, beach access, lighthouses, museum, and numerous trails.

34.4 (mp 10.4) Intersection of U.S. 101 and Alternate U.S. 101 (the Skinville Cutoff Rd.). Continue straight on U.S. 101 as it parallels the Columbia River through farmland. Shoulder width varies from none to 2.5 feet.

37.3 (mp 5.5) Chinook, a small town with grocery store. Beyond town, pass a county park with campsites for RVs only.

42.5 (mp 3.0) Fort Columbia State Park; picnic tables, trails, running water, restrooms, museum, and a hostel.

42.6 (mp 2.9) Pass through a short, straight tunnel. Before enter-

Clam diggers at Long Beach

ing, set off the blinking light that warns motorists that cyclists are in the tunnel.

43.2 (mp 2.3) Lewis and Clark Campsite, a small area set aside to commemorate one of the expedition's overnight stops.

45.0 (mp 0.5) Intersection of U.S. 101 and Highway 401 at the Astoria Bridge. Follow U.S. 101 south across the bridge.

45.5 (mp 0.0) Washington–Oregon border is located on the Astoria Bridge over the center of the Columbia River.

Peninsula Route: Port Angeles to Mora Campground (67.0 Miles)

The Coho ferry from Victoria takes 90 minutes to cross the Strait of Juan de Fuca and dock in Port Angeles, the starting point of the Peninsula Route through Washington State. The first ferry arrives midmorning, too late to embark on a full day of cycling, so spend the rest of the day on a side trip to one of the state's scenic

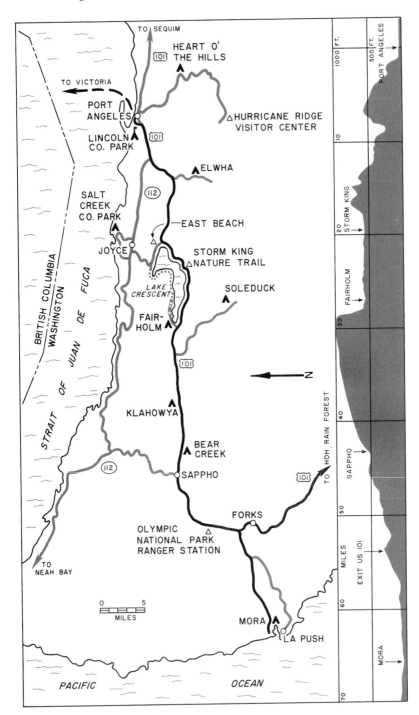

highlights, Hurricane Ridge. (Check ahead for winter ferry schedule.) The ridge is part of Olympic National Park (a designated World Heritage Park), and is the only place a cyclist may sample the alpine aspect of the Olympic Mountains. The Hurricane Ridge Rd. is long and demanding. Only strong cyclists will find pleasure in the mountain road that gains 5,300 feet in 18 miles but everyone will enjoy the view from the ridge and the ride back down.

If Hurricane Ridge sounds like too much of a challenge, check out the visitor center near the base of the climb. Spend the rest of the day exploring the Elwha or Soleduck river valley entrances to the park. The Elwha River Valley is located 9.8 miles south of Port Angeles on the route to Mora Campground. This lowland valley has campgrounds, numerous trails (including one to Hurricane Ridge), a large lake, and, if you go far enough, a hot springs. The Soleduck River Valley is located 29.7 miles south of Port Angeles and is famous for its hot springs and rain forest. A campground and hiking trails are found near the end of the road.

Heading south from Port Angeles, you will encounter the most notorious stretch of road in Washington, the 10 miles of U.S. 101 around Lake Crescent. The road around this beautiful lake is narrow and shoulderless, with blind corners, and heavy, fast auto and logging-truck traffic. If ever there was a place to install flashing lights to let motorists know when cyclists are on the road, this is it. At one time, a bicycle route was planned around the opposite side of the lake, but this turned into a scenic trail along the abandoned Spruce Railroad grade, suitable as a challenge for mountain bikes but useless for touring bikes.

Highway 112 provides an interesting but not necessarily better alternative to U.S. 101 around Lake Crescent. Starting 6.5 miles west of Port Angeles, this rural highway heads through miles of trees with an occasional view over the Strait of Juan de Fuca. The first 12 miles are relatively flat with good shoulders. The road narrows and shoulders disappear as you climb over several short, steep hills. Finally, the route crosses over a moderate pass and returns to U.S. 101 at Sappho. Campgrounds are numerous along Highway 112 but food is scarce.

At the end of the day, the route leaves U.S. 101 for a 12.9-mile trip to the Olympic National Park beaches and Mora Campground. The campground may be used as a base for many intriguing day trips and hikes. Walk or cycle the Mora Rd. to its end at Rialto Beach, and hike the beach north to Hole in the Wall and beyond, depending on the tide. Or, cycle back to the junction with the La Push Rd., and follow it down 5.5 miles to Third, Second, or First Beaches for enjoyable walks along driftwood-jammed beaches, over rocky headlands, and past lonely sea stacks—far different from the warm, crowded, sandy beaches of the south.

View south over the Olympic Mountains from Hurricane Ridge

MILEAGE LOG

0.0 Trip starts from the Victoria (Coho) ferry dock. Everyone (that includes cyclists planning to ride up to Hurricane Ridge) should turn right on Railroad St. and follow it along the waterfront. (As Port Angeles has the last large grocery stores until Forks, anyone who needs to stock up on food should take a side trip into town. Follow the signs for U.S. 101 south to the supermarkets at the upper end of town.)

0.2 The road divides; go right on Front St.

0.4 Bear right on Marine Dr. (also called W. 1st St.).

0.6 Intersection; continue straight (trucks go left).

0.7 Turn left on Tumwater St. (this is the first left after the truck route), which climbs steeply uphill for 0.3 mile; gear down.

1.0 Tumwater St. turns into W. 5th St.

1.5 Turn left on I St. and head inland.

2.3 I St. ends; go right on W. 18th St.

2.5 Take the first left on L St.

2.9 The road divides. To the left is Lincoln County Park campground; hiker-biker area, water, restrooms. A small grocery store is located right across the street. If planning to ride up Hurricane Ridge, set up camp here before heading out (see route description below). If heading south, go right on Edgewood Dr. and follow it through the twists and turns of a rural residential area for 2.7 miles.

5.6 Bend left on Laird Rd.

6.4 Intersection with State 112. Go straight across to reach U.S. 101. *ALTERNATE ROUTE* on Highway 112. The highway passes several privately operated campgrounds and Salt Creek County Park, as well as one grocery store at Joyce (10.2 miles). After following Highway 112 for 39.4 miles, go left and head inland towards Forks and Sappho. Return to U.S. 101 at Sappho in 49.4 miles (11.1 miles longer than U.S. 101). Expect considerable traffic on weekends.

6.5 (mp 242.9) Turn right and head south on U.S. 101. Terrain is rolling and shoulders are good, except on bridges.

9.8 (mp 239.5) Turnoff to Elwha River Valley and campgrounds on the left (east), and combination gas station-store on the right (west). *SIDE TRIP* Cycle up the Elwha River Valley to the national park on a narrow road which passes through cool, shady groves of trees and by quiet farms. The first campground is located 3 miles off U.S. 101; running water and limited campsites. Shortly beyond is a ranger station, then a second campground. The road is gated 4 miles from its end at Olympic Hot Springs. Bicycles may continue on to the camp area at the hot springs; pick up a backcountry permit at the ranger station if you wish to camp at the hot springs.

17.3 (mp 231.9) Turn off to East Beach, Piedmont, and Spruce Railroad Trail.

17.8 (mp 231.4) Shoulder ends as U.S. 101 leaves Olympic National Forest and enters Olympic National Park. Tighten your grip—the next 10 miles are nerve-racking.

18.0 (mp 231.2) Sign warning cyclists about hazards ahead. (Where is the sign for *motorists* to use caution over the next 10 miles?)

21.2 (mp 227.9) Barnes Point turnoff. Go right 0.2 mile to a large parking lot; restrooms, water, and 1-mile hiking trail to a hidden waterfall.

25.5 (mp 223.7) La Poel Picnic Area, on the shore of Lake Crescent; running water but no restrooms.

28.0 (mp 221.0) Fairholm Grocery; limited supplies and boat rentals. Shoulder resumes here as U.S. 101 begins a 1.5-mile climb away from the lake.

28.2 (mp 220.8) Fairholm Campground; a small area with restrooms, running water, and a nature trail. This is also the southern end of the Spruce Railroad Trail.

29.7 (mp 219.3) *SIDE TRIP* to Solduck Hot Springs begins on the left. The scenic road parallels the Soleduck River for 12 miles into the Olympic National Park to reach the hot springs. A substantial fee is charged for a soak in the waters. You may stay at the national park campground or rent a cabin (expensive) and eat at the restaurant. Take time for a 0.9-mile walk through the rain forest to Soleduck Falls.

37.0 (mp 213.9) Klahowya Campground; restrooms, and running water.

42.8 (mp 205.8) Bear Creek Campground (on the left side of U.S. 101); restrooms, running water and three short nature loops along the Soleduck River.

44.3 (mp 204.3) Enter Sappho; only facility is a small cafe.

44.7 (mp 203.8) Alternate route through Joyce rejoins U.S. 101.

45.0 (mp 203.5) Tumbling Rapids Rest Area; restrooms but no running water.

48.2 (mp 200.4) Lake Pleasant Grocery; this small store is the last before Mora Campground.

52.3 (mp 196.2) Olympic National Park Ranger Station; information on hiking trails and sights in and around the Mora Campground.

55.3 (mp 193.2) Turn right (west) off U.S. 101 towards La Push and Mora Campground. The next 12.9 miles are mostly downhill on a narrow road with little shoulder. Traffic is light but travels very fast. (Groceries may be purchased in Forks, 1.5 miles south of the turnoff to Mora.)

63.2 Junction; turn right toward Mora Campground. *SIDE TRIP* to La Push and First, Second, and Third Beaches. Go left at the intersection and descend to the beach trails or to end of the road in 5.5 miles at La Push (the center of a small Indian reservation); a private campground on the beach, cabins, and a store.

67.0 Mora Campground; restrooms and running water. *Warning:* Thievery is common at all beach trailheads. Do not leave a bicycle or even a water bottle unattended unless it is securely locked. When locking a bicycle, be sure to lock both the front and back wheels and the frame to something that does not move, like a 100-foot-tall tree.

Hurricane Ridge Side Trip

0.0 Once you have unloaded your bike at the Lincoln County Park campground, retrace your route back to the waterfront. Be sure to carry plenty of warm clothing and food for the trip.

2.5 Stay on Marine Dr., which becomes W. 1st St. Once across Lincoln St., W. 1st St. joins U.S. 101; follow it for 0.8 mile.

3.6 Turn right (south) on Race St., following signs to Hurricane Ridge. From this point, it's all uphill to the ridge. Buy groceries before leaving town.

4.6 Olympic National Park headquarters; park and weather information, restrooms, and water.

10.6 Heart o'the Hills Campground, elevation 1,957 feet. The road above Heart O'the Hills is steep and narrow, with numerous turnouts, all on the left side.

21.5 Hurricane Ridge visitor center; restrooms, water, and information. If the weather turns bad, head back immediately. The views from the top are unforgettable, extending over the Strait of Juan de Fuca, Vancouver Island, the Cascades, and Mount Olympus shining above the Olympics. The roadside meadows burst with colorful wildflowers mid-July through mid-August. A 2.5-mile trail through the meadows leads to Klahhane Ridge, where mountain goats wander through the meadows and on the slopes of nearby Mount Angeles. For your own safety, make the descent to the campground before dark.

Peninsula Route: **Mora Campground to Hoh Rain Forest Campground (44.7 Miles)**

From rugged, storm-blasted ocean beaches, the Peninsula Route heads inland, back to U.S. 101, then south 14.6 miles to the Hoh River Rd. Here, once again, the route sidetracks as it heads inland to the western edge of the Olympic Mountains and the wettest spot in the continental United States, the Hoh Rain Forest.

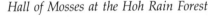

Hall of Mosses at the Hoh Rain Forest

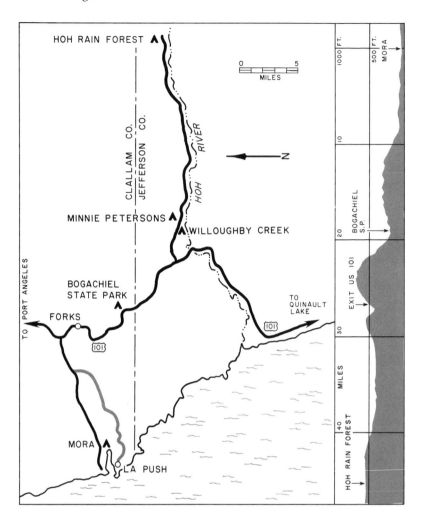

Although connotations of a rain forest have little to attract cyclists, you should not bypass the Hoh. The rain forest is a world colored in green, from the lush vegetation of the forest floor to the giant trees covered with lacy moss. Vegetation grows at fantastic rates and trees grow to record heights. Elk, deer, and a multitude of small forest animals thrive in this environment.

The day ends at a large national park campground in the rain forest. Nearby is a small, cozy information center, an excellent place to browse for an hour on a wet day. Spend a couple of quiet hours exploring the two nature trails through the rain forest.

No stores are located near the Hoh Rain Forest Campground.

The closest major store is in Forks, and the next major grocery is at Kalaloch, 21 miles south on U.S. 101.

On this ride, only U.S. 101 has a shoulder. The La Push–Mora Rd. and the Hoh River Rd. are both narrow. Terrain is moderate, with rolling hills.

MILEAGE LOG

0.0 From Mora Campground, ride back towards U.S. 101.

3.7 Mora Rd. joins the La Push Rd. Continue inland to U.S. 101.

11.7 (mp 193.2) Junction with U.S. 101. Turn right (south) towards Forks.

12.8 (mp 192.1) Enter Forks, a logging town with full tourist facilities as well as a large supermarket (located on U.S. 101 at the south end of town).

14.4 (mp 190.5) Pass a visitor information center on the left. Shortly beyond, the shoulder deteriorates.

19.1 (mp 186) Bogachiel State Park, a campground with running water, restrooms, and covered cooking areas. This is a popular fishing area.

20.2 (mp 184.7) Leave Clallam County and enter Jefferson County.

26.3 (mp 178.5) Turn left (east) off U.S. 101 on the Hoh River Rd., heading inland to the rain forest. The road is narrow and winding, a perfect road for riding if there were no cars. Use the numerous turnouts to let traffic pass or to stop for a breather. The road passes through ugly clearcuts, then peaceful forest. Wear bright, visible clothing to help motorists see you. Terrain is rolling; however, some of the short hills are steep.

29.8 (mp 3.5) Willoughby Creek Campground; 3 campsites, outhouse; no running water. The campground is located on the edge of the Hoh River.

31.0 (mp 4.7) Minnie Peterson's Campground and picnic area; water, outhouses, and river access.

32.0 (mp 5.7) Limited groceries, postcards, hamburgers, and rental cabins.

33.6 (mp 7.3) Morgan's Crossing and public fishing; no facilities.

38.3 (mp 12.0) Enter Olympic National Park. The road narrows as it passes under a canopy of dense trees.

39.0 (mp 12.7) Park entrance booth, outhouse.

41.9 (mp 15.6) Big Spruce Tree exhibit.

44.5 (mp 18.2) Turn right to campground.

44.7 (mp 18.4) Hoh Rain Forest Campground; water and restrooms. Establish camp and set out to explore the area via the nearby information center.

Peninsula Route: Hoh Rain Forest Campground to July Creek Campground (71.5 miles)

From the Hoh Rain Forest, head west, back to U.S. 101, then southwest to the coast and another section of the Olympic National Park. Plan to stop at one of the numerous beach access trails for a stroll along the coast. Each pounding wave washes in treasures—intriguing shells, weathered rocks and wood, plant life, and the occasional Japanese glass ball (used as floats on fishing nets).

Keep a sharp eye out over the water for animal life. Seals roam the coast throughout the year. Fall and spring often bring the gray whales, close to shore on their migrations to and from their breeding grounds in the south.

If relaxing is on the schedule, Kalaloch Campground, at the ocean's front door, offers an opportunity to break this section into two days. Sunbathe, swim, and walk the beach.

Leaving the national park, U.S. 101 turns southeast, heading inland through miles of forest and logging clearings. The highway is narrow, with no views or points of interest, and generally very little shoulder. This is a good section to just cover some miles.

The day's ride ends back in Olympic National Park at a campground on beautiful Quinault Lake. This is another rain forest area, less famous than the Hoh but just as exotic with lush, green forests, fern-filled canyons and moss-covered trees. Explore the nearby trails, or take part or all of a 29-mile loop ride around Quinault Lake past grocery stores, picnic areas, campgrounds, nature trails, and, above all, fantastic scenery.

MILEAGE LOG

0.0 From Hoh Rain Forest Campground, retrace your path back to U.S. 101.

18.6 (mp 178.5) Turn left (south) on U.S. 101. Shoulders are moderate, disappearing at bridges. Traffic volume is low but moves very fast. Expect a lot of logging trucks.

19.8 (mp 177.3) Turnoff to Cottonwood Recreation Area, a private campground.

21.0 (mp 176.0) Turnoff to Hoh-Clearwood State Forest (campgrounds are miles away from U.S. 101).

21.7 (mp 175.4) Small store and RV park with cabins.

27.7 (mp 169.4) Rain Forest Home Hostel; open all year. Call ahead for reservations, 206-374-2270.

29.4 (mp 167.6) Turnoff to Hoh Indian Tribal Center.

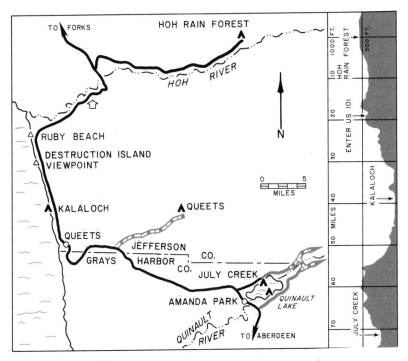

30.2 (mp 166.8) Enter Olympic National Park. The road runs through heavy forest with occasional views over the ocean.

32.4 (mp 164.5) Ruby Beach; views over the rugged Pacific Northwest coast, beach access, and pit toilets. Tide pools and sea stacks make this the most interesting of the area beaches for exploring.

33.5 (mp 163.4) Destruction Island viewpoint. A small turnout with information board relating the not-so-happy history of Destruction Island.

34.2 (mp 162.7) Beach 6; small parking lot and beach trail.

34.7 (mp 162.2) Big Cedar; a very old and abused tree located 0.3 mile off U.S. 101 on an easy-to-ride dirt road.

36.0 (mp 160.5) Beach 4; parking lot, restrooms, and path to the beach.

36.7 (mp 159.8) Beach 3; another beach access.

38.7 (mp 157.8) Kalaloch Campground; restrooms, running water, and beach access. A small grocery store can be reached by a 0.5-mile trail from the campground.

39.2 (mp 157.4) Small grocery store and cabins.

39.4 (mp 157.2) Olympic National Park ranger station; information.

40.2 (mp 156.1) Beach 2; parking area with path to the beach.

41.1 (mp 155.2) Beach 1; the last turnout, beach access, and restrooms.

41.9 (mp 154.5) South Beach Campground and picnic area. The primitive campground is an overflow area for Kalaloch Campground. Beyond the campground, U.S. 101 leaves the national park and turns inland to bypass a section of the coast owned by the Quinault Indians. The ocean is not seen again until Copalis Beach, 61.4 miles south. Terrain is mostly level. Expect some logging-truck traffic.

44.2 (mp 152.2) Queets; a very small grocery store is located on the left, off U.S. 101.

44.8 (mp 151.5) Leave Jefferson County and enter Grays Harbor County. The terrain remains almost level as the route makes its way down a narrow, tree-lined corridor. The trees hide acres of clearcuts and stumps.

48.2 (mp 148.0) Leave Grays Harbor County and reenter Jefferson County.

49.4 (mp 146.8) Shoulder disappears.

51.6 (mp 144.6) Queets Valley turnoff. Riders on mountain bikes may be interested in this 14-mile gravel road, which leads to a campground and hiking trails in Olympic National Park.

51.8 (mp 144.4) Leave Jefferson County and reenter Grays Harbor County. After a few miles, a 1- to 1.5-foot shoulder returns, allowing a little more space for logging trucks to whoosh by.

65.4 (mp 130.8) Enter Olympic National Forest.

66.3 (mp 129.9) Pass a small cafe.

67.8 (mp 128.4) Turn left (east) off U.S. 101 on North Shore Rd. A small grocery is located here. (If this store is closed, another is located 1.7 miles south.) Follow the narrow and shoulderless road into Olympic National Park.

Pacific Ocean near Ruby Beach

71.5 (mp 124.7) July Creek Campground; a walk-in-only area with restrooms and running water located on the shores of Quinault Lake. If this campground is full, try one of three others located on the south shore of the lake.

Quinault Lake Loop

If you are on a mountain bike, you may make an enjoyable loop of the entire lake by continuing east on the North Shore Rd. for 12 miles. Negotiate 4 miles of excellent hard-packed gravel as the route heads across the Quinault River and west on South Shore Rd. for 12 miles back to U.S. 101.

Peninsula Route: July Creek Campground to Twin Harbors State Park (65.6 Miles)

This ride depends entirely on a small passenger ferry that crosses the narrow mouth of Grays Harbor Bay between Ocean Shores and Westport. Unfortunately, this ferry is seasonal and in service only from the fourth week of June through Labor Day. The ferry runs on weekends *only* from the fourth week of May to the fourth week of June, and from Labor Day through the third week in September, about once every hour and a half between 11:00 A.M. and 6:00 P.M. If you have questions, call ahead to the Marina Store in Ocean Shores, 206-289-3391.

When the passenger ferry is not running, you must follow the alternate route, using U.S. 101 to reach the congested twin cities of Hoquiam and Aberdeen. At the south end of Aberdeen, the alternate route leaves U.S. 101 and heads west on Highway 105, winding along Grays Harbor Bay on narrow highway to Twin Harbors State Park. This route is 10 miles longer than the standard route, uses congested roads and passes through some very monotonous country.

No matter which route you follow, the day starts with a long stretch on U.S. 101, miles inland from the ocean. The route passes through alternating clearcut areas and bands of timber left along the edge of the highway to give the road a woodsy feel. Expect considerable logging-truck traffic and minimal shoulder for the first 22.6 miles. A short side trip to the Quinault Rain Forest offers a temporary escape from the humdrum of the ride, as well as a chance for a last look at the rain forest. A beautiful mile-long nature loop trail leads to a fern canyon, then through a grove of moss-hung trees.

At Humptulips, the suggested route leaves U.S. 101 and heads west on narrow country roads back to the Pacific Ocean at Copalis

Beach. Here, you enter a world completely different from the wilderness beaches of the national park in the north. Grocery stores, motels, RV campgrounds, restaurants, beach cabins, and tourist shops abound. Some of the beaches are open to motor vehicles. Clam digging, kite flying, and sunbathing are popular activities on the long, sandy beaches. (The alternate route continues south on U.S. 101.)

Once the route reaches the Pacific, it turns south, paralleling the ocean on a level, shoulderless road which runs through several small towns and past Ocean City State Park to reach the small passenger ferry to Westport, a small fishing and resort town. The ride continues south from Westport for another 3 miles to Twin Harbors State Park. Peninsula Route riders encounter the first showers in Washington at this park—enjoy. Twin Harbors State Park is the junction of the Peninsula and Inland routes.

MILEAGE LOG

0.0 From July Creek Campground, head back to U.S. 101 on North Shore Rd. Leaving Olympic National Park for the last time.

3.7 (mp 128.4) Head south of U.S. 101. Terrain is gently rolling, shoulders minimal.

5.4 (mp 126.9) Amanda Park; grocery store.

5.7 (mp 126.6) *SIDE TRIP* to the Quinault Rain Forest nature loop trail. Turn left (east) on South Shore Rd., follow it 1.2 miles to a junction, then go left again. In 0.4 mile, turn right to the nature loop parking lot. The loop trail leads to a fern canyon and then through a grove of moss-hung trees. Running water and restrooms are available in the parking lot. The small resort town of Quinault lies 0.3 mile further east; motels, restaurants, and a grocery store.

6.7 (mp 125.6) Pass second turnoff to a nature loop and Quinault. Enter the Quinault Natural Area.

8.9 (mp 123.4) Neilton; small grocery store.

12.1 (mp 120.1) First access road to Olympic Beaches is on the Moclips Highway. This is the backroad entry, and advisable only for mountain bikes.

14.1 (mp 118.1) Leave Olympic National Forest.

19.8 (mp 112.3) Promise Land rest area; large gazebo lets you hide from the rain or dodge the sun.

22.6 (mp 109.5) Humptulips; small grocery store.

22.7 (mp 109.4) Turn right off U.S. 101, following signs to OCEAN BEACHES. Be sure your food supplies are in good order; no towns for 12.6 miles. (See end of this log for alternate route description.)

23.1 Riverview Campground; a private facility with campsites

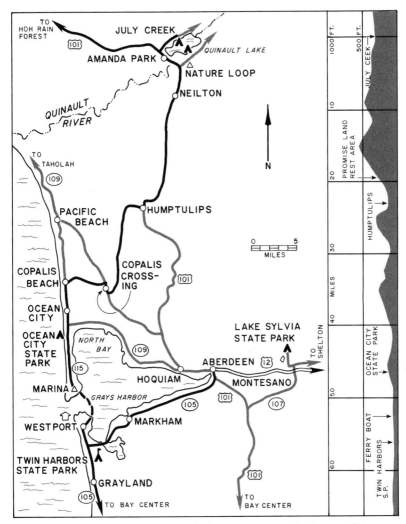

and rental cabins. Beyond the campground, the road is narrow with no shoulder.

24.1 After passing a large fish hatchery, the road heads steeply uphill.

24.8 Top of the hill; check out the view.

34.6 Enter Copalis Crossing; cafe.

34.8 Go right (north) following sign to BEACHES.

35.4 Turn left (west) towards BEACHES. Pass a small market on the right at the intersection.

40.0 (mp 21.3) Intersection. Go straight on Highway 119 into Copalis Beach; grocery store, cafe, motels, and beach access.

Westport boat harbor

40.4 (mp 20.9) Pass the first of many beach access roads. The beach, located 0.4 mile west, may be used as a highway for several miles south to Ocean City. Highway 119 is narrow and congested.

41.0 (mp 20.3) Pass a privately operated campground with beach cabins.

42.8 (mp 18.4) Ocean City; motels, grocery stores, and restaurants.

43.2 (mp 18.0) Beach access.

45.2 (mp 16.0 and mp 0.0) Intersection. Go right to Ocean Shores on Highway 115 and relax while riding along the wide shoulder.

46.1 (mp 0.9) Ocean City State Park; hiker-biker site, showers, beach access.

47.1 (mp 1.9) Highway 115 ends. Go left, following signs to PED FERRY. Enter Ocean Shores tourist area on a divided road. Grocery stores and numerous other tourist amenities.

47.8 Intersection; continue straight ahead. The divided road ends.

49.4 Intersection; continue straight on narrow and shoulderless Pt. Brown Ave.
52.3 Intersection; go right.
52.5 Ride past the Silver King Motel, then turn left into the Marina. Tickets for the 30-minute ferry ride across Grays Harbor Bay to Westport must be purchased at the Marina Store before boarding. The ferry docks at Westport, a tourist town which lies on a narrow peninsula, with the Pacific Ocean to the west and Grays Harbor Bay to the east. Near the tip of the peninsula is Westhaven State Park, a day-use area with beach access. The town is a popular resort for sport fishermen, with numerous hotels, motels, restaurants, and a grocery store. Seafood is readily available here; try a restaurant or purchase it from a roadside vendor. Westport Dorm Hostel (open March 1 to September 30) overlooks the marina at Float 17. Call ahead for information, 206-268-0949.
52.7 Once off the ferry, go left for two blocks, past the main tourist area, then turn right.
52.9 Take a left on Harbor Blvd. and ride south.
55.9 Turn left on Highway 105.
56.0 Twin Harbors State Park; hiker-bike sites, hot showers, beach access, and hiking trails.

Alternate Route

Continue south from Humptulips on U.S. 101 for 20 miles to Hoquiam. Follow U.S. 101 south through the congested downtown area. Shoulders narrow and disappear; however, traffic moves slowly through town. When crossing the Hoquiam River, cyclists may use the sidewalk on the left side of the extremely narrow, steel-grate-surfaced bridge.

Hoquiam becomes Aberdeen, with more supermarkets, tourist facilities, and stores that sell bicycles but very few parts. Continue to follow U.S. 101 South as it makes a sharp bend to the right (south) and crosses the Chehalis River on a wide bridge. On the south side of the bridge, leave U.S. 101 as it takes a sharp bend to the left at a traffic signal. Go straight on Highway 105 and head west for the next 18.2 miles. (Two large supermarkets, located on the left side of the highway at this intersection, provide an opportunity to pick up groceries for the night.) Highway 105 (a Washington State Scenic and Recreational Highway) runs through forest, skirting the tideflats of Grays Harbor. The highway is narrow, and shoulders vary from good to none.

Enter Westport 42.6 miles from Humptulips. The road skirts the edge of town; grocery stores, restaurants, and ferry to Ocean Shores are located 2 miles north at the town center. Turn left to Twin Harbor State Park.

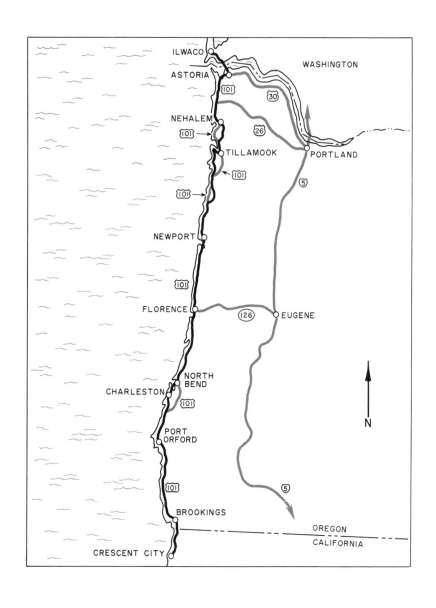

ILWACO

ASTORIA

WASHINGTON

101

30

NEHALEM

26

101

TILLAMOOK

PORTLAND

101

5

101

NEWPORT

101

FLORENCE

126

EUGENE

NORTH
BEND

CHARLESTON

101

N

PORT
ORFORD

101

5

BROOKINGS

OREGON

CALIFORNIA

CRESCENT CITY

Right, *Harris Beach near Brookings*

OREGON

The Oregon Coast Bicycle Route has 384.6 miles of spectacular ocean views, long beaches, sand dunes, wave-sculptured sea stacks and headlands, as well as quiet farmlands and forests. Food and lodging pose no problems. The coast is dotted with towns, state parks, and forest camps. The Oregon coast trip is good for everyone, from first-timers to expert tourists.

Cyclists should not just try for miles on the Oregon coast; there are too many exciting stops. Save the marathon days for a tour across the Great Plains. Riders doing the entire Pacific coast tend to reach peak physical strength in Oregon, and rush to achieve more miles, passing the scenic waysides and beaches that make this the most interesting section of the entire coast. Don't waste your time riding through this outstanding area and never seeing it. Slow down, hike, explore, or just sit and watch the sun set.

Cyclists on the Oregon coast should carry rain gear for protection against long, rainy days. Bright, visible clothing and bike lights are essential in the heavy, wet fog that can engulf the coast for days during the summer months. Fenders are a much-appreciated accessory on rainy days, protecting you and your gear from the grime of wet roads. The months of July, August, and September are the driest. Expect heavy rains October through March. Coastal winds gust up to 60 miles per hour in the summer months (most often from the northwest), and are even stronger in the winter.

The Oregon Highway Department expects the majority of riders to be heading from north to south. When the road is narrow, the southbound shoulder has been developed at the expense of the shoulder on the northbound side of the road.

Most key intersections have been marked with Oregon coast bike route signs; unfortunately, these have proven popular for home decorating, so keep a close eye on the directions and map.

The two tunnels on the Oregon coast cannot be avoided by any means less than flying. Flashing signs, activated by the cyclists before entering, warn motorists that bicycles are in the tunnels. Despite this convenience, tunnels are very hazardous, so be cautious. Strap on a light that will be visible to vehicles approaching from behind, then wait for a lull in traffic before starting out. All these precautions notwithstanding, the tunnels are nerve-racking and hazardous, so pedal fast.

The popularity of the Oregon coast extends beyond the bicycling world. People flock to the coast in the summer, many driving oversize recreation vehicles—you know the kind—with picture windows, microwaves, showers, televisions, and toilets. Drivers of these bus-size "camping" machines generally lack experience in handling large vehicles. Ride defensively and try to anticipate the problems these drivers will have when they pass. Most of all, pray that the next gas shortage will send these "campers" back to hotels.

In Oregon, the milepost signs note miles in whole numbers, starting at the Washington border and increasing to the south. In the mileage logs, mileposts are noted in tenths for increased accuracy; a milepost number of 25.7 indicates that the point of interest is located 0.7 mile past (south of) milepost 25.

State parks along the coast provide 15 hiker-biker camps for cyclists. The sites are primitive and generally tucked away from regular camping areas. Water, restroom facilities, and showers may be somewhat removed from the campsite, or nonexistent. These areas are never "full," no reservations are required, and the cost is moderate. However, since the charge is per person, groups of three or more (depending on the park) may find the regular campsites a better bargain. If a regular site is desired, be sure to get reservations ahead of time by writing to the state park and sending a deposit.

Between November 1 and mid-April, only six state park campgrounds are open. They are, from north to south, Fort Stevens, Cape Lookout, Beverly Beach, J.M. Honeyman, Bullards Beach, and Harris Beach.

Portland has the closest major airport and train access to the northern Oregon coast. The only form of public transportation from Portland to Astoria is the bus. To ride to the coast from Portland, Highway 30 (95 miles to Astoria with a good shoulder most of the way) or Highway 26 (80 miles to Cannon Beach with moderate shoulder, some freeway riding, and one tunnel) are recommended.

Neither route offers camping. Highway 30 is the easier of the two to reach from the airport, train, or bus station, and has numerous small towns with restaurants and motels along the way. To reach Highway 30 from the airport, follow Tom McCall Blvd. for 0.5 mile, then go right on busy 82 Ave. for 0.4 mile. Turn right on Lombard St., then take the first left on Alderwood. Follow Alderwood for 1.0 mile (you are on a city bike route after the first 0.5 mile). When Alderwood ends, go right on Columbia Blvd. for 0.1 mile, then turn left on Cully Blvd. for 0.3 mile. Turn right on N.E. Alberta St., following a city bike route. At 1.3 miles, the route makes a jog left on 47th Ave.; take the first right to get back on Alberta St. After 0.7 mile, the route jogs right on 33rd St.; take the first left back to Alberta St. for 2.3 miles to Concord Ave., where the route jogs right, then left, back to Alberta St. for another 0.2 mile. Go right on Denver for 0.5 mile, then take a left on N.

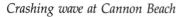

Crashing wave at Cannon Beach

Ainsworth for 0.6 mile. Turn right on scenic Willamette Blvd. and follow it for 4.0 miles. Cross the Willamette River at St. Johns Bridge, and head west on Highway 30.

From the train or bus station (located next to each other in downtown Portland), head up 5th or 6th Ave. to Olisan and turn right. In 0.6 mile, turn right on N.W. 18th. After another 0.6 mile, take a left on Raleigh and follow it for 1.0 mile, then turn right on 28th St. After 0.2 mile, go left on Thurman for 0.2 mile. Turn right on 29th St. for 0.3 mile to a major intersection. Go left here, onto Highway 30 (also called St. Helens Rd.).

Try to avoid weekends when the traffic is heavy. The city of Portland publishes a good metropolitan bicycle map, helpful if you plan to ride out of town. Write Metropolitan Service District, Transportation Department, 2000 S.W. First Ave., Portland, Oregon 97201-5398. The cost is $3.50 (as of 1989).

At the end of Oregon, riders again face transport problems. Brookings offers only a bus station, from which the trip to Portland is six hours—on the express. The alternative is to continue south 21 miles to Crescent City, California, and rent a car or take a commuter flight to larger cities inland (however, these small airlines may refuse to transport your bicycle).

Note: some cyclists have experienced difficulties in obtaining bicycle boxes in Brookings. To avoid hassles, have a friend ship you a bike box by bus.

Washington Border to Nehalem Bay State Park (43.5 Miles)

The northern coast of Oregon is ideal country for touring. The route follows U.S. 101 from the state border over a bridge high above the Columbia River, then rolls through farm country, past historical landmarks easily accessible by bicycle, to a wild and scenic coast where the road clings to a steep hillside with the surf pounding below.

U.S. 101 is busy along this section of the coast route. The shoulder is good for the first 33 miles but disappears in Oswald State Park. The first of the two tunnels on the Oregon coast is encountered in this section. Use all precautions for tunnel travel suggested in the introduction to this chapter. Strap on a light, wait for a lull in traffic, activate the warning signals, and pedal like mad.

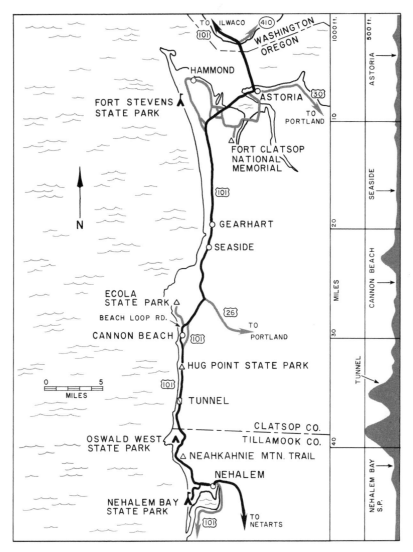

The ride is a short one, allowing time for three major side trips and two shorter ones. The first side trip is into Astoria, where a collection of photographs and memorabilia at the Maritime Museum depicts the colorful marine history of the Oregon coast and Columbia River.

The Lewis and Clark Expedition ended its westward journey in November 1805 at what is now Seaside, Oregon. Here, a few expedition members spend months boiling sea water for salt while the main body of the expedition weathered the damp winter near

Overlooking remains of the Peter Iredale, *Fort Stevens State Park*

Astoria at Fort Clatsop. The second side trip is to the site of the old fort, now a national monument.

More recent history is explored on the third side trip to Fort Stevens State Park, where the remains of the *Peter Iredale*, shipwrecked in 1906, lie just offshore. This once-mighty, four-masted British sailing ship is a reminder of the many ships that sunk trying to enter the placid-looking mouth of the Columbia River. Fort Stevens, abandoned for many years, guards the entrance to the Columbia River and is the only West Coast fort that was ever shelled.

Farther south, at Hug Point State Park, are remains of the first coast highway. Most of this early roadway was right on the beach, and drivers had to schedule their travel for low tide. One exception was at Hug Point, where a narrow, single-lane road was blasted into the side of a sea cliff.

Not to be forgotten is the tremendous scenery along the way. In Astoria, a side trip to the Astoria Column reveals sweeping views of the Columbia River, Pacific Ocean, Oregon's Coast Range, and parts of Washington. A side trip to Ecola State Park at Cannon Beach gives you a chance to enjoy a view of Tillamook Head Lighthouse (currently serving as a mausoleum) and a broad vista over Cannon Beach. Farther south, the highway climbs over a large shoulder of Neahkahnie Mountain, with breathtaking views south over Nehalem Bay to the miles of coast beyond. Leave the bicycles and hike 2 miles to the summit of the mountain for an unforgettable 360-degree view of the coast and inland.

The day ends at Nehalem Bay State Park, where long, sandy beaches provide an excellent opportunity to take a stroll while watching the sunset.

MILEAGE LOG

0.0 (mp 0.0) Enter Oregon by following U.S. 101 across the Columbia River on the 4.2-mile Astoria Bridge. The Oregon coast ride starts officially 0.5 mile from the north end of the bridge at the Washington State border.

3.7 (mp 3.7) Astoria Bridge tollgate, where cyclists pay a small fee for crossing. A few yards past the tollgate, a stoplight marks the entrance to Astoria. The bike route turns right (south), following U.S. 101. See end of this mileage log for a side trip description to Astoria Column and the Maritime Museum.

4.2 (mp 4.2) Intersection U.S. 101 and U.S. 101 Business. Continue south on U.S. 101 across Youngs Bay.

4.5 (mp 4.5) Jetty and bridge over Youngs Bay. Traffic on the bridge is heavy; however, the shoulder provides ample room for cyclists.

6.3 (mp 6.3) Leave Youngs Bay. For the next 18.4 miles, U.S. 101 passes over rolling terrain, past large pastures, and through small towns. A roomy shoulder provides relief from a constant flow of traffic.

6.5 (mp 6.5) First turnoff to Fort Stevens State Park; continue on U.S. 101.

7.0 (mp 7.0) Turnoff to Fort Clatsop National Memorial on the left (south), and to Fort Stevens State Park and campground on the right (north). The coast route continues straight on U.S. 101 towards Seaside. (For descriptions of these side trips, see end of this mileage log.)

16.1 (mp 18.3) Gearhart; grocery stores.

17.3 (mp 19.5) Seaside; bike shop, several supermarkets, and surf shop. A side trip into this resort town leads to several historical sites, such as the end of the Lewis and Clark Trail and salt mine. Directions to historical sites are well signed from U.S. 101.

22.7 (mp 25) Junction of U.S. 101 and U.S. 26. Stay right on U.S. 101 as it heads up a 2.2-mile hill. Once at the top, it's a downhill glide to Cannon Beach.

25.7 (mp 28.1) Turn right (west), leaving U.S. 101 at the Cannon Beach exit. Continue downhill on Beach Loop Rd. for a scenic tour through Cannon Beach, one of the most photographed areas on the Oregon coast. (On weekends, Cannon Beach is an extremely popular tourist area, and the roads through town are congested.)

26.1 *SIDE TRIP* to Ecola State Park. Two miles of steeply winding, narrow road through beautiful coastal forest lead to Ecola State Park, where you will be treated to fantastic views over Cannon Beach and Tillamook Head Lighthouse (located on an offshore island). Picnic tables, restrooms, and running water. It takes all day to thoroughly explore the long, sandy beaches and forested trails of the park. However, no camping is allowed in the park.

26.5 Cannon Beach, a very popular resort area with beaches, grocery stores, delis, and restaurants. At some point in town, Beach Loop Rd. becomes South Hemlock. Continue south.

29.2 (mp 31.4) Tolovana Park, a small community with a store, beach access, restrooms, and water. Return to U.S. 101 here. Heading south, the shoulders are moderate for southbound travelers, and the occasional ocean views excellent. Little to no shoulder exists on the northbound side for the next 15 miles.

30.2 (mp 32.4) Arcadia State Park; beach access, ocean views, running water, and restrooms.

Cyclist activating the warning light before entering Cape Arch Tunnel

31.4 (mp 33.6) Hug Point State Park; a short, steep descent leads to restrooms, running water, picnic tables, and beach access. Walk the beach 0.5 mile north to a waterfall and small cave, then climb over a low headland on the remains of the original coast highway. The narrow road was blasted into the rock, forcing drivers to "hug" the cliff.

33.4 (mp 35.7) Cape Arch Tunnel runs uphill and bends to the left. Before entering, activate the flashing signal by pushing the button. At the south end, a scenic turnout provides an opportunity to catch your breath while you enjoy the view. After the tunnel, the route continues to gain elevation for several miles.

33.5 (mp 35.8) Enter Oswald West State Park. The campground, picnic area, and beach access are 4.3 miles south.

34.8 (mp 37.1) Leave Clatsop County and enter Tillamook County.

37.8 (mp 39.3) Oswald West Campground (no hiker-biker campsites) is a walk-in area reached by 0.2-mile paved trail. Wheelbarrows are provided at the trailhead to help campers transport their gear to the tent sites. To reach the picnic area, walk the same trail for 0.7 mile to Short Sand Beach. Beyond the trailhead, U.S. 101 climbs steeply over a shoulder of Neahkahnie Mountain.

37.7 (mp 40.2) Neahkahnie Mountain Trail starts on the left (east) side of the highway, opposite a gravel turnout, and is marked by an unobtrusive wooden post. Once past the start of the trail, the shoulder on U.S. 101 nearly disappears as the road climbs steeply for the next mile. *SIDE TRIP:* hide the bikes in the bushes and hike the steep 2-mile trail to unsurpassed views from the summit.

38.9 (mp 41.2) Top-of-the-hill viewpoint and start of a steep downhill.

39.4 (mp 41.6) Neahkahnie Mountain Trail, south side. This trail is a longer, less scenic version of the trail on the north side.

40.7 (mp 43.2) Manzanita market; this last grocery store before Nehalem State Park is easy to miss when zooming down from Neahkahnie Mountain. The next grocery store is located 1 mile beyond the state park turnoff in Nehalem.

41.5 (mp 43.9) Turn right off U.S. 101, and follow the signs to Nehalem Bay State Park.

43.5 Nehalem Bay State Park; hiker-biker campsite, hot showers, beach access, and a short bike path to the south end of the Nehalem spit.

Astoria Side Trip

To visit the Astoria Column, the Maritime Museum of the Columbia River, the bicycle shop, or one of Astoria's grocery stores, turn left (east) and follow U.S. 30 for 1 mile into town. The road divides and becomes one way. To reach the Astoria Column, take the first left on Commercial St. to 16th St., then turn right and head steeply up to the column. A left on 17th St. leads down to the Maritime Museum and the dock of the old lightship *Columbia*. The bicycle shop is located at the eastern end of town, and markets and grocery stores are located throughout.

Fort Clatsop National Memorial Side Trip

Exit left (south) for this highly recommended side trip to the winter quarters of the Lewis and Clark Expedition. Cycle 0.3 mile to intersect U.S. 101 Business, then turn left (east). After 1.9 mile, turn right on an unnamed road for the final 1.6 miles to the fort site. A fee is charged to enter the visitor center at Fort Clatsop. At the reconstructed fort, watch the movie, then wander through the displays, which feature live demonstrations showing how the expedition survived the long winter. Amenities include a nature trail, picnic area, restrooms, and running water.

Fort Stevens State Park Side Trip

Turn right off U.S. 101 and cycle northwest 1.1 miles to Warrenton. Continue straight 2.3 miles to Hammond and a stop sign. Turn left on Lake Dr. and follow it south, past two other well-signed park roads before reaching the campground entrance at 0.8 mile. Here you will find hiker-biker sites, beach access, a nature trail, hiking trails, bike paths, and lots of mosquitoes. Explore the park, hike, bike, swim in the lake, watch the sunset over the wreck of the *Peter Iredale*, explore the old fort historic area, or browse through the military museum. Maps of the park are available at the entrance booth.

If spending the night at the park, pick up your groceries at the shopping center near the U.S. 101 turnoff or in Warrenton.

To return to U.S. 101 from the park, continue south from the campground entrance on Lake Dr. for 2.3 miles to a Y-junction. Either fork will take you back to U.S. 101 in 1.6 miles.

Nehalem Bay State Park to Cape Lookout State Park (47.4 Miles)

At Nehalem, the route leaves busy U.S. 101 and heads inland on quiet back roads, past small dairy farms and through green valleys. Returning to U.S. 101, the route continues south, following the coast around Tillamook Bay. The road is nearly level here and miles are covered quickly, leaving you plenty of time to tour the cheese factory at the outskirts of the town of Tillamook. A self-guided tour through the factory leads to a large viewing window where you can watch the cheese-making process. A museum explains the history of cheese making, and a slide show illustrates the process. Finally, a snack bar answers any remaining questions.

At Tillamook, the bicycle route turns off U.S. 101 for the second time to follow a scenic drive known as the Three Capes Scenic Route (Cape Meares, Cape Lookout, and Cape Kiwanda), with spectacular ocean views, a lighthouse, and beach trails. (U.S. 101 heads inland here to avoid the rugged coast.)

The majority of the ride from Nehalem Bay State Park to Cape Lookout State Park is on narrow, shoulderless roads. The only shoulders along this route are on U.S. 101, which is followed for 7 miles around Tillamook Bay. The inland route starting from Nehalem was developed to avoid a narrow section of U.S. 101 that has since been widened to include a shoulder, making it safe for

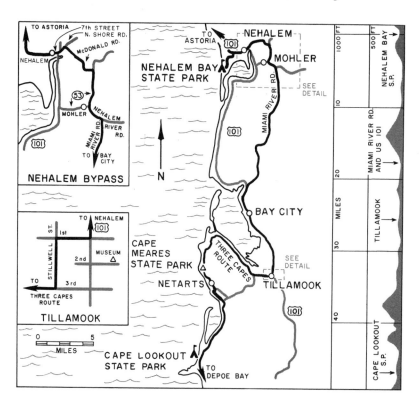

cyclists. We have retained the inland route because the riding is excellent, and the pastoral countryside is a marked contrast from the tourist meccas on the coast. Roads on the inland route are narrow, and without shoulders but also without traffic.

This is not the case on the Three Capes Scenic Route. The roads on this route are narrow, without shoulder, and very busy. However, the scenery justifies the inconvenience.

MILEAGE LOG

0.0 From Nehalem Bay State Park, pedal back to U.S. 101.

2.0 (mp 43.9) Rejoin U.S. 101 and head south. The shoulder is narrow and rough for southbound riders, and nonexistent for northbound riders.

3.1 (mp 46) Nehalem, a small town with a grocery store. U.S. 101 turns right, heading around Nehalem Bay, but the bicycle route takes a left turn and heads out of town on 7th St., a shoulderless road with little traffic.

3.4 The road divides; stay right on N. Shore Rd. (unsigned here), which parallels the N. Fork Nehalem River.

4.6 Turn right on McDonald Rd., crossing the North Fork Nehalem River.

5.8 Intersection; go right on Highway 53. Traffic volume increases here; however, there is plenty of cycling space.

7.2 Turn left on Nehalem River Rd. just before crossing a small bridge.

8.2 Bear right at Miami Rd., crossing the Nehalem River and heading back to U.S. 101 through a long, quiet, green valley dotted with small farms. This country was made for bicycle riding.

19.7 (mp 56.8) Intersection; turn left and head south on U.S. 101 along the shore of Tillamook Bay. The shoulder is adequate except at the first bridge encountered immediately after returning to U.S. 101. You may want to use a wooden sidewalk on the southbound side.

22.2 (mp 59.3) Bay City, a small town with a small market.

26.5 (mp 63.6) Tillamook cheese factory, located on the left (east) side of the highway. Signs, two busy parking lots, and a large sailing ship on the front lawn make this an easy attraction to spot. Admission is free; however, free samples are limited and the cheese is cheaper elsewhere. Check out the cheese curd, sold in small bags; it's very affordable and tastes great.

26.9 (mp 64) Tillamook; supermarkets, laundromats, bicycle shops, shopping malls, and just about anything else. Allow time for a stop at Pioneer Museum, where something new is

Fresnel lens inside Cape Meares Lighthouse

always going on. To reach the museum, pass through the first stoplight and turn left (east) at the second; the museum is located one block up on 2nd St.

28.2 (mp 65.3) Three Capes Scenic Route. At the first stoplight, turn right (west) off U.S. 101 onto 1st St., and follow the signs to the Three Capes Scenic Route.

28.4 Turn left (south) on Stillwell St.

28.5 Go right (west) on 3rd St., following it out of town past cows busy producing milk for the cheese factory. Cross a bridge over the marshes at the end of Tillamook Bay.

30.1 Turn right (west) on the Three Capes Scenic Route. The old, bumpy, shoulderless road hugs the very edge of Tillamook Bay. Keep an eye out for a wide variety of waterfowl as well as cars on the road.

33.3 Intersection; turn left for a steep, 1.5-mile climb up Cape Meares, still on the Three Capes Scenic Route. *SIDE TRIP* of

1.0 mile (level) on the right fork of the intersection leads to a unique pepple-covered beach dotted with skeletal trees.

37.3 Cape Meares State Park; picnic tables, restrooms, and water. Stop and see the Octopus Tree, a large Sitka spruce, or walk 0.1 mile down to the lighthouse and climb the stairway to the top of the tower for a firsthand look at the prisms. (The lighthouse is open daily during the summer from 11:00 A.M. to 5:00 P.M.) The park is a National Wildlife Refuge for hundreds of birds that nest on the rocks right offshore from the lighthouse. May through July are the best months for bird watching; bring your binoculars.

39.8 Oceanside State Park Beach; beach access and picnic tables.

41.8 Netarts. If spending the night at Cape Lookout State Park, this is your last chance to replenish your food supplies.

42.2 Turn right, following the Three Capes Scenic Route. Descend to the water's edge, then head south along Netarts Bay. Road remains narrow. Traffic is heavy on weekends.

42.3 Netarts Bay Recreation Area; picnic tables and restrooms.

43.6 Stop sign and junction. Continue south along the water, still on the Three Capes Scenic Route.

47.4 Cape Lookout State Park; hiker-biker campsite, hot showers, picnic area, beaches, and hiking trails. This is an excellent park to spend the night or several days. If time allows, hike the trail to the end of Cape Lookout for terrific views of the coast.

Cape Lookout State Park to Beverly Beach State Park (62.1 Miles)

The riding in this section of the coast combines great scenery with the double hazards of high winds and heavy traffic. Over half of the ride is on side roads. Start your day early to ensure you have time for a stop at Cape Kiwanda, where a short walk over sand dunes leads to one of the most photographed areas on the Oregon coast. The cape is a fascinating place. Here, boats are launched directly into the surf, hang gliders take off from the sand dunes, and surfers challenge the waves. Don't spend too much time here—some of the most scenic spots on the coast lie just ahead.

This day's ride leads to the end of the Three Capes Scenic Route, then returns you briefly to U.S. 101. Follow the coast to Neskowin, where the route leaves U.S. 101 and heads inland for another scenic tour off the highway. This route winds through an experimental forest on a little-used road, climbing over Cascade Head before switchbacking down to the town of Otis. The cool and quiet rain forest is a welcome relief from the continuous roar

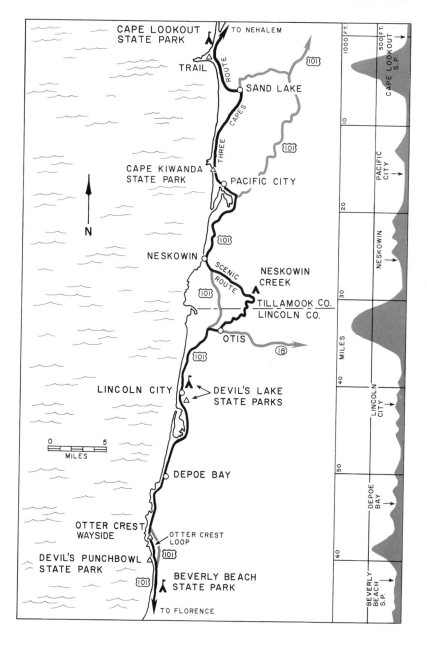

of U.S. 101. Signs are posted along the road with basic information about the forest.

The route returns to U.S. 101 to pass through Lincoln City (a very congested area) and stays on the highway through Depoe Bay (a famous whale-watching area) to reach the third U.S. 101 bypass. Here, the route follows the Otter Crest Loop over Cape Foulweather on a beautiful road which hangs on sheer cliffs over the ocean. The top of the cape may be very windy but the view is excellent over Otter Crest to Beverly Beach.

MILEAGE LOG

0.0 The day begins with a steep climb as you head south from Cape Lookout State Park on Three Capes Scenic Route. The next 2.7 miles are devoted to climbing over the cape.

1.1 Pass Andersons Viewpoint, which overlooks Netarts Spit and Bay as well as the ocean and state park.

2.7 Top of cape (elevation 550 feet) and access to Cape Lookout Trail, a 5-mile round-trip hike through lush rain forest to a beautiful end-of-the-cape viewpoint.

6.0 Junction. At the base of Cape Lookout, take the first right (south) to the community of Sand Lake and its peaceful pastures, sleepy beach homes, and one small store. The lake is visible through the trees on the west side of the road. Past the intersection, the terrain varies from level to rolling. The road is narrow and traffic moderate, except on weekends when thousands of dune-buggy riders and tourists in huge vacation vehicles invade the area.

12.1 Unmarked junction. Stay right (west), paralleling the ocean.

13.6 Cape Kiwanda State Park; running water, restrooms, and beach access. Plan to stop here. The park is the scene of constant activity: dories launched directly into the surf from the beach, hang gliders, surfers, skim boarders, kayakers, sunbathers, children and adults sliding on sand dunes, cameras clicking and whirring. Take a short hike north up the sand dune to one of the most-photographed areas on the entire coast. In fall and winter, people come from all over the world to photograph the waves as they beat against the sculptured cliffs. The summer visitor can enjoy a colorful display of layered sandstone as well as sliding on the steep sand dunes.

14.6 Intersection; the bike route turns left (east) and crosses the Nestucca River Bridge. *SIDE TRIP* to Bob Straub State Park. Turn right at the intersection and pedal 0.5 mile south to a parking lot. Beach access.

14.7 Pacific City, where several small stores allow you to stock up on food supplies. To continue, turn right (south) at the junction and follow the Nestucca River back to U.S. 101. The road is rough and narrow.

17.4 (mp 90.6) Return to U.S. 101 and head south. The traffic is heavy and the shoulders wide. After several level miles over open plain, the highway enters a small valley, climbs over a small headland, then returns to the coast. This is a very scenic but windy section.

24.5 (mp 97.8) Neskowin, a small town specializing in hotels and motels. A state park wayside gives access to a sandy beach.

26.7 (mp 99) Start of Cascade Head Scenic Route. Turn left (east) off U.S. 101 on Slab Creek Rd. Climb past small farms and pastures, then green forest as Slab Creek Rd. becomes Forest Rd. 12.

Waves breaking on sandstone cliffs at Cape Kiwanda State Park

30.9 Neskowin Campground, a small forest camp with *no* facilities.

32.2 Reach the summit of Cascade Head (elevation 704 feet) and begin an exciting descent down hairpin turns.

33.0 Tillamook County–Lincoln County line.

35.9 Junction. Turn left (south) on the Old Coast Highway.

36.6 Otis, a one-store town. Go right (west) on State Route 18.

38.1 (mp 110.5) Junction of State Route 18 and U.S. 101. Head south on U.S. 101 over rolling hills. The road is busy but has a good shoulder. Roadside development increases close to Lincoln City.

39.5 (mp 111.9) Cross the 45th parallel. You're halfway to the Equator.

39.7 (mp 112.1) Enter Lincoln City, one of the chief tourist towns on the Oregon coast. There are innumerable hotels, motels, restaurants, bakeries, curio shops, several state and beach parks, large supermarkets, and a bike shop. (Traffic is heavy in the city area, and shoulders disappear in several sections of this very built-up, 5-mile-long strip.)

40.4 (mp 112.8) Turnoff to Roads End Wayside State Park; accessed by a 1-mile road that terminates in a steep descent to picnic tables and beach access. A large supermarket is located near the turnoff, a good opportunity to shop for the night.

42.1 (mp 114.7) Devil's Lake State Park campground, on the east side of U.S. 101 above Devil's Lake. The hiker-biker area is located just past the entrance booth on the left and is divided into two levels, forest and open grass. Showers are solar heated.

Cyclist on the Cascade Head Scenic Route

42.5 (mp 114.9) "D" River Beach Wayside State Park, a popular area for kite flying. Restrooms and water. Take a quick look at "D" River, claimed to be the world's shortest.

43.2 (mp 115.5) Turnoff to Devil's Lake State Park picnic area. Picnic area, boat launch, restrooms, and water are located on Devil's Lake, 2 miles east of U.S. 101.

50.0 (mp 122.5) Turnoff to Gleneden Beach Wayside State Park. A 0.2-mile access road leads to picnic tables, restrooms, water, and a trail to a long, sandy beach. Several small markets are located along U.S. 101 near the park turnoff.

51.5 (mp 124.9) Fogerty Beach State Park; picnic area, restrooms, water, and beach access. The park has two accesses off U.S. 101, one on each side of a small creek. The two parking lots are joined by a paved path.

52.7 (mp 126.1) Boiler Bay Wayside State Park gets its name from a boiler, the remains of an old shipwreck visible in the bay at low tide. Restrooms, water, and picnic tables are available at this scenic overlook. This is a popular whale-watching area in season (see next mileage point).

53.8 (mp 126.3) Enter Depoe Bay, whose claim to fame is the world's smallest harbor. The bay is a popular whale-watching area from December through May. (Whales may occasionally be seen through the end of July.) Calm, gray days are the best for sighting whales.

56.9 (mp 129.5) Rocky Creek Wayside State Park, another popular whale-watching area; restrooms, water, picnic tables. Views from the park extend north over Whale Bay and south to Cape Foulweather.

57.1 (mp 129.7) Turn right (west) off U.S. 101 on Otter Crest Loop, a section of the Old Coast Highway which inches along the sheer rock cliffs of Cape Foulweather. The road is scenic but narrow and shoulderless. Traffic is generally light on the stiff 1.8-mile climb up Cape Foulweather. At the summit, stop at the overlook for a view south to Otter Crest. Hold on tight to bicycles—winds of up to 60 miles per hour are common at the crest. For the descent, stay on Otter Crest Loop, and ignore several opportunities to rejoin U.S. 101.

60.4 *SIDE TRIP* to Devil's Punchbowl State Park and Marine Gardens. Go right on the 0.4-mile access road to a natural punchbowl, which churns best at high tide, and a beach where shellfish gathering is prohibited to preserve the ecosystem.

61.1 (mp 133.0) End of Otter Crest Loop; return to U.S. 101.

62.1 (mp 134.0) Beverly Beach State Park campground, located on the left (east) side of U.S. 101. The campground has a hiker-biker camp (located on the hillside past the group area), hot showers, and access to long, sandy Beverly Beach. Groceries may be purchased near the park entrance.

Beverly Beach State Park to Jessie M. Honeyman State Park (59.5 Miles)

With so much to see in the next 59.5 miles, expect travel time to be long and distances between stops short.

The first stop, Yaquina Lighthouse National Wildlife Refuge, lies just 3.5 miles south of the campground. The chief attraction here is not the tall, white lookout tower on the windswept point, visible for miles up and down the coast. It's the birds, nesting on rocky offshore islands clearly visible from the viewing platform at the lighthouse. A trail from the lighthouse descends the steep cliffs to the shore where sea lions sunbathe on the rocks.

The bike route takes to the residential streets through Newport to avoid downtown congestion, then returns to U.S. 101 in time for a side trip to the Oregon State University's Marine Science Center, which features fascinating undersea displays and a tide pool stocked with a variety of sea creatures to see and touch; admission is free.

At Sea Gulch; stop and gawk at the world's largest collection of chainsaw woodcarvings. The artists at work along the side of the road are fascinating to watch.

Among the many parks and waysides along the route, Cape Perpetua is the most popular. Trails lead to the Devil's Churn, high viewpoints, tide pools, and an old Indian camping ground. A visitor center offers displays and a movie on the area's history. A steep, 1.5-mile side road near the visitor center beckons cyclists up to one of the best views on the coast.

Sea lions are common along the coast but not always easy to spot. However, south of Cape Perpetua, at Strawberry Hill turnout, you'll probably see these mammals taking their daily sun bath on rocks just 100 feet offshore.

Farther south, the route passes Devil's Elbow State Park, where the much-photographed Heceta Head Lighthouse is located. The park is near the Sea Lion Caves (even if you are not familiar with the caves, you have probably seen the bumper sticker on a car or two).

The day's ride ends at Jessie M. Honeyman State Park, located on the edge of the Oregon Dunes Recreation Area. Hours can be spent here, walking and sliding on the dunes.

This section on the coast includes some of the worst sections of U.S. 101. The road lacks a shoulder in the Cape Perpetua and Devil's Elbow areas. The second and last tunnel on the Pacific Coast Bicycle Route for southbound travelers is located here.

Sea lions sunbathing at Strawberry Point

MILEAGE LOG

0.0 (mp 134) Leaving Beverly Beach State Park, cycle south on U.S. 101 along the edge of the ocean. Moolack Beach parking area provides access to the beach. Yaquina Head Lighthouse is visible from the highway. Shoulders are wide and traffic heavy.

2.5 (mp 136.6) Newport city limits; the bike route follows a bypass route through Newport. Cyclists looking for supermarkets, bike shop, or youth hostel (located only two blocks off the bypass route on Brook St., 503-265-9816), must leave the bike route and venture into the city.

3.5 (mp 137.6) *SIDE TRIP* to Yaquina Head Lighthouse. Turn right (west) on the narrow, 1.5-mile lighthouse road. The road surface is gravel—rough but rideable. At the lighthouse, walk to the viewing platform to look for cormorants,

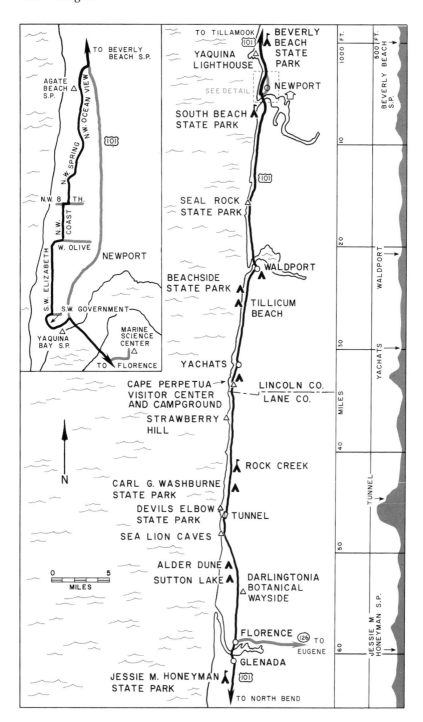

TO BEVERLY
BEACH S.P.

AGATE
BEACH
S.P.

N.W. OCEAN VIEW

N.W. SPRING

US 101

N.W. 8 TH.

N.W. COAST

W. OLIVE

NEWPORT

S.W. ELIZABETH

S.W. GOVERNMENT

YAQUINA
BAY S.P.

MARINE
SCIENCE
CENTER

TO FLORENCE

N

MILES
0   5

TO TILLAMOOK
101

YAQUINA
LIGHTHOUSE

BEVERLY
BEACH
STATE
PARK

SEE DETAIL

NEWPORT

SOUTH BEACH
STATE PARK

101

SEAL ROCK
STATE PARK

WALDPORT

BEACHSIDE
STATE PARK

TILLICUM
BEACH

YACHATS

CAPE PERPETUA
VISITOR CENTER
AND CAMPGROUND

LINCOLN CO.
LANE CO.

STRAWBERRY
HILL

ROCK CREEK

CARL G. WASHBURNE
STATE PARK

DEVILS ELBOW
STATE PARK

TUNNEL

SEA LION CAVES

ALDER DUNE

SUTTON LAKE

DARLINGTONIA
BOTANICAL
WAYSIDE

FLORENCE

126 TO
     EUGENE

GLENADA

JESSIE M. HONEYMAN
STATE PARK

101

TO NORTH BEND

1000 FT.

10

20

30

MILES

40

50

60

500 FT.

BEVERLY BEACH S.P.

WALDPORT

YACHATS

TUNNEL

JESSIE M HONEYMAN S.P.

common murres, tufted puffins, and gulls nesting on the offshore islands. Whales are occasionally spotted in the bay below. A trail descends to the shore where tide pools may be explored, and sea lions sunbathe on the rocks. Restrooms are available.

4.2 (mp 138.3) Start Newport Bypass by turning right (west) off U.S. 101 on N.W. Ocean View Dr.

5.6 N.W. Ocean View Dr. becomes N.W. Spring St. in a quiet residential neighborhood.

5.9 N.W. Spring St. ends; turn right (west) on N.W. 8th St.

6.0 N.W. 8th St. ends; turn left (south) on N.W. Coast St.

6.4 Turn right (west) on W. Olive St., which in a few blocks, becomes S.W. Elizabeth St. Head south past summer houses, motels, and small shops.

7.3 When S.W. Elizabeth St. ends, turn right (west) on S.W. Government St. and follow it into Yaquina Bay State Park; restrooms, water, picnic tables, beach access, and a lighthouse that may be toured for a small fee. Follow the road as it loops through the park, then returns to U.S. 101.

7.8 (mp 141.4) Back on U.S. 101, head south across the 0.5-mile long Newport Bridge. Use the sidewalk when bridge traffic is heavy.

8.5 (mp 142.1) *SIDE TRIP* to the Oregon State University Marine Science Center. Exit right (west) off U.S. 101. (Northbound riders also exit right, east.) Follow signs 1.5 miles to the science center; open daily 10:00 A.M. to 6:00 P.M. during the summer, and 10:00 A.M. to 4:00 P.M. the rest of the year.

9.7 (mp 143.3) South Beach State Park; hiker-biker sites, hot showers, and beach access.

13.5 (mp 147.1) Lost Creek State Park; picnicking and access to a sandy beach.

15.3 (mp 149) Ona Beach State Park; restrooms, water, and beach access. Stop and enjoy a picnic in the shade on a grassy lawn. Beyond the park, U.S. 101 runs along the coast with glimpses of sandy beaches and the ocean. Shoulder width is moderate.

16.6 (mp 150.3) Sea Gulch, the chainsaw art center, is on the east side of the highway. The detail etched into these life-sized and larger figures is incredible, and worth more than just a quick glance.

17.0 (mp 150.7) Seal Rock State Park; restrooms, water, and beach access. Walk to the cliff's edge and watch the surf pound against a giant rib of rock. Despite the name, seals are rarely spotted on these rocks.

19.2 (mp 153.2) Driftwood State Park; restrooms, water, picnicking, and a beach access.

Heceta Head Lighthouse, Devils Elbow State Park

21.5 (mp 155.2) Enter Waldport at the southern end of a 0.5-mile long bridge (when traffic is heavy, consider the sidewalk). The town offers grocery stores, tourist facilities, and a private campground.

23.4 (mp 157.1) Governor I.L. Patterson State Park; restrooms, water, and a nice sandy beach for walking.

25.3 (mp 159) Beachside State Park; a small campground near sandy beaches. No hiker-biker campsite.

26.6 (mp 160.3) Tillicum Beach Campground, operated by the U.S. Forest Service. No hiker-biker site.

29.6 (mp 163.4) Enter Yachats. In early July of each year, the world's largest smelt fish fry is held here—perfect for hungry cyclists. Much of the smelt fishing takes place in the center of town at Yachats State Park. If you miss this fish fry, there are grocery stores nearby.

29.7 (mp 163.5) Smelt Sands State Park; as the name suggests, a popular smelt-fishing area. The fishing is exciting to watch in the early months of summer.

30.9 (mp 164.7) Yachats Oceanic Wayside, a favorite beach spot for the locals; restrooms and running water. Some of the Oregon coast's most spectacular scenery and steepest hills lie just ahead. Shift to low gear and pedal slowly to enjoy every possible view. The next 20 miles are the windiest on the coast; expect gusts up to 60 or more miles per hour. The shoulder width is narrow to nonexistent for southbound riders, and even less for northbound riders.

32.5 (mp 166.3) Cape Perpetua.

33.0 (mp 166.8) Devil's Churn Wayside. At high tide, rushing waves are forced into a narrow channel where they churn into a white foam. Trail to the churn starts on the right (west) side of U.S. 101.

33.1 (mp 167.0) Cape Perpetua Campground and *SIDE TRIP* to Cape Perpetua Viewpoint. The campground is run by the Forest Service and has restrooms, running water, and walk-in campsites, as well as trails to the viewpoint, a visitor center, and beach. The side trip to Cape Perpetua Viewpoint involves a very steep 1.5-mile ride to the top of the cape, where you are treated to a spectacular panoramic view over 150 miles of coast. The viewpoint may also be reached by a hiking trail from the campground or visitor center. (If you don't wish to tackle the steep road up to the viewpoint, check out the excellent photographs at the visitor center.)

33.4 (mp 167.3) Cape Perpetua visitor center, a highly recommended stop. Open 9:00 A.M. to 5:00 P.M. daily. The visitor center has many displays, including a 15-minute movie explaining the natural history of the area. Trails lead to viewpoints and tide pools.

33.7 (mp 167.6) Leave Lincoln County, enter Lane County.

34.6 (mp 168.5) Neptune State Park; restrooms, water, and picnic tables.

35.4 (mp 169.3) Strawberry Hill turnout. View sea lions and harbor seals on rocks just a few feet offshore.

36.1 (mp 171.0) Commercial campground and small market.

36.6 (mp 171.5) Stonefield Beach Wayside; picnic area and beach access. As the name implies, an intriguing stone-covered beach.

40.3 (mp 174.3) Rock Creek Campground; run by the Forest Service and open during the summer months only. Exit left (east) to reach the hiker-biker sites. No hot showers.

41.3 (mp 175.3) Muriel O. Ponsler State Park, one of many scenic wayside stops with beach access.

42.0 (mp 176.0) Carl G. Washburne State Park. Exit left (east) off U.S. 101 for camping and hot showers.

44.1 (mp 178.1) Devil's Elbow State Park; picnicking, restrooms, water, and beach access. Descend a short, steep road to the park, then walk the scenic path to the much-photographed Heceta Head Lighthouse.

44.2 (mp 178.2) A short, shoulderless, uphill bridge with no sidewalk.

44.3 (mp 178.3) Enter Cape Creek Tunnel, the second and last tunnel on the coast route. The tunnel has an uphill grade, so strap on a bicycle light and activate the warning signal before entering. After the tunnel, the highway narrows, climbing steeply over a barren, windswept headland. Shoulder is narrow on the southbound side and nonexistent northbound. Check out the scenic turnouts with views north to Heceta Head Lighthouse.

45.1 (mp 179.1) Sea Lion Caves. Bumper stickers for this pay attraction are seen up and down the coast. Admission fee covers the cost of an elevator ride down to a large cave inhabited by a sea lion colony. Past the caves, the road winds over a second headland, then glides downhill for several miles with sweeping views south over the coast.

49.4 (mp 183.4) Alder Dune Campground; a Forest Service area with restrooms and water but no hiker-biker sites.

51.0 (mp 185.2) Sutton Lake Campground, a Forest Service facility with restrooms and water but no hiker-biker sites. U.S. 101 widens to include a bike lane.

51.2 (mp 185.4) Darlingtonia Botanical Wayside; picnic tables, restrooms, and water. Approximately 100 yards left (east) off U.S. 101, a short path leads to a small marsh, where the rare and unusual California pitcher plants (*Darlingtonia californica*) flourish. These plants thrive in nutrient-deficient soils by devouring insects.

51.7 (mp 185.9) Indian Village; will this be the next bumper sticker craze?

53.8 (mp 188) Florence; supermarkets large enough to feed the hungriest of cyclists are located here, as well as a bike shop for those in need of repairs. Expect considerable traffic.

56.0 (mp 190.2) Junction of U.S. 101 and State Route 126 (to Eugene and points east). Continue straight on U.S. 101.

56.4 (mp 190.6) Turnoff for Harbor View Park, a city park with beach access.

57.0 (mp 191.2) Bridge with a slippery steel-grate decking. Cyclists are advised to use sidewalk.

57.2 (mp 191.3) Glenada, the last chance to purchase groceries before Jessie M. Honeyman Memorial State Park.

59.5 (mp 193.6) Jessie M. Honeyman Memorial State Park; hot showers, hiker-biker camp, a small lake for swimming, and access to the sand dunes. The hiker-biker area is located about 1 mile from the regular campground, so register and shower before setting up camp.

Jessie M. Honeyman Memorial State Park to Cape Arago State Park (57.4 Miles)

The Oregon Dunes National Recreation Area spans the coast from Florence to North Bend. Miles of soft sand contoured by the wind and accented with systematic ripple marks are the chief feature of this section. Lie on it, walk through it, run over it, or slide down it; no matter how, take time to get to know this beautiful area.

Very little of this fascinating sea of sand can be viewed from U.S. 101, so plan one or more short side trips out into the dunes. The easiest accesses by bicycle are at Jessie M. Honeyman Memorial State Park and Oregon Dunes Overlook. For foot access into the dunes, try one of several short trails starting from Carter Lake, Tahkenitch or Eel Creek campgrounds. These trails are particularly attractive in April and May, when the native rhododendrons are in bloom.

The monotony of U.S. 101 is broken by a brief, scenic tour at Winchester Bay, where backroads lead you past a busy marina, Umpqua Lighthouse, a state park campground, and picnic area. The bicycle route leaves U.S. 101 for a second time at North Bend for a tour of Coos Bay, Charleston, and Cape Arago, then remains on backroads for the next 30 miles. This route is extremely scenic

Sand dunes near Tahkenitch Campground

and highly recommended over the congested and shoulderless U.S. 101 in the Coos Bay area.

Cape Arago provides a magnificent ending for the day with three state parks along a 2.5-mile stretch of scenic coast. The first is Sunset Bay Campground, situated near a narrow bay with hiking trails to overlooks of Cape Arago Lighthouse. The second is the Shore Acres Botanical Gardens, formerly part of a lumber baron's private estate, with formal gardens and overlooks from sculptured sandstone cliffs. Last is Cape Arago, a picnic area with hiker-biker camping. Numerous trails lead to nearby beaches and coves. Picnic tables overlook jagged Simpson Reef, home for much of the year to a large colony of sea lions.

MILEAGE LOG

0.0 (mp 193.5) From Jessie M. Honeyman Memorial State Park, U.S. 101 travels south through forested countryside. Shoulder varies in width from two to three feet.

3.3 (mp 196.8) Tyee Campground, a Forest Service area with restrooms and running water but no special hiker-biker facilities.

4.6 (mp 198.1) Turnoff to Siltcoos Dunes and Beach Area access, a popular dune buggy area. The Siltcoos Dune Rd. passes a Forest Service campground with a short nature loop trail through the dunes, 2 miles west of U.S. 101.

5.1 (mp 198.6) Carter Lake Campground, a Forest Service area situated on a deep-blue lake. A trail leads through the dunes to the beach.

5.5 (mp 199.0) East Carter Lake Campground, another Forest Service area.

7.2 (mp 200.8) *SIDE TRIP* to Oregon Dunes Overlook; a 0.3-mile road leads to viewpoint overlooking the dunes, berm, and ocean. If time for dune exploration is limited, this is a choice spot. Hike a trail through the dunes to the ocean, or, take the entire 4-mile loop hike or just take off your shoes and wander through the dunes. The overlook has restrooms, water, and picnic tables.

10.0 (mp 203.6) Tahkenitch Campground, A Forest Service area with a 1-mile trail through rhododendron forest to the dunes.

14.8 (mp 208.4) Gardiner, a small town with a grocery store and large International Paper Company plant. The road levels as U.S. 101 winds inland around Winchester Bay, a popular clam digging area.

16.6 (mp 210.2) Smith River is crossed on a narrow bridge. Cyclists choose between a narrow sidewalk or a narrower shoulder.

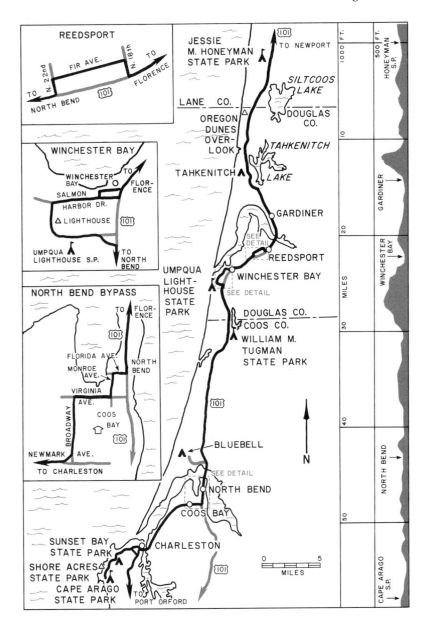

Sunset Bay State Park

17.4 (mp 210.9) Historical marker dedicated to Jedediah Smith.

17.5 (mp 211) Umpqua River Bridge. Cyclists may use the sidewalk for 0.3-mile ride into Reedsport.

17.8 (mp 211.3) Reedsport; grocery stores, small shops, and headquarters of the Oregon Dunes National Recreation Area (located on the right-hand side of the highway at the first stoplight after the Umpqua River Bridge), with displays of dune formation and habitat. U.S. 101 goes straight through the center of this small, congested town. Cyclists are encouraged to follow the city bike route around the worst section.

18.8 (mp 212.4) Start Reedsport city bike route; turn right (north) on N. 18th Ave. for one block, then turn left (west) on Fir Ave. for four blocks. At N. 22, turn left (south) and return to U.S. 101.

19.2 (mp 212.7) Return to U.S. 101. Beyond Reedsport, the road climbs a long, forested hill then sweeps down to the town of Winchester Bay. Shoulder width varies from two to eight feet.

22.3 (mp 215.8) Winchester Bay; small grocery store.

22.4 (mp 215.9) Start Winchester Bay scenic tour. Turn right (west) off U.S. 101 on State Route 251, also called Salmon Harbor Dr. Cycle the shoulderless, level road past the marina and Windy Cove County Park campground. The park has a nice tent area at the west end.

23.3 Take the first left (south) off Salmon Harbor Dr. and head uphill towards Umpqua Lighthouse State Park, past Umpqua Lighthouse and a Coast Guard museum. Near the lighthouse is a view over the breakwater and harbor entrance. Note how the surf is higher in the harbor entrance than on the surrounding beaches.

24.3 Umpqua Lighthouse State Park Campground; hiker-biker area, hot showers, a small lake for swimming, beach access, and picnic area.

24.6 Beyond the park, the road heads steeply uphill to an intersection. Take the right (uphill) fork.

24.8 (mp 216.8) Return to U.S. 101 and continue climbing to the top of a forested hill, then cruise down past Clear Lake.

29.0 (mp 221) Leave Douglas County and enter Coos County.

29.3 (mp 221.3) Pass William M. Tugman State Park campground on the left (east) side of U.S. 101. Hiker-biker camp to the left of the entrance booth; hot showers, picnicking, and swimming in North Tenmile Lake. Nearby food supplies are very limited.

29.5 (mp 221.5) Lakeside; a small tourist town with a small grocery store and commercial campground.

30.3 (mp 222.3) Eel Creek Campground; a Forest Service area with a trail to the dunes and beach, restrooms, and running water. Beyond the campground, U.S. 101 runs past a series of small lakes captured between large, forested sand dunes. The road levels at about milepost 230 and swings inland around Coos Bay, where large mud flats attract hundreds of clam diggers.

40.9 (mp 232.9) *SIDE TRIP* to Horsfall Dunes and beach access, the southern end of the Oregon Dunes National Recreation Area. It's a 2-mile side trip to the Forest Service's Bluebell Campground, and 3 miles to a long, sandy beach. The area is scenic and very popular for dune-buggy riding.

41.5 (mp 233.3) Coos Bay Bridge. Ride with caution; the bridge is narrow, traffic is heavy, vehicles are large, and crosswinds are often fierce. When traffic is heavy, consider using the narrow sidewalk. When crosswinds are strong, consider walking.

42.5 (mp 234.3) South end of Coos Bay Bridge and entrance to North Bend. No shoulder here, so ride with caution. Several lumber mills offer tours during the summer months in North

Bend and its sister city, Coos Bay. Amenities include bike shops and supermarkets.

42.9 (mp 234.7) Tourist information, Pioneer Museum, and a city park lie on the right (west) side of U.S. 101. Running water and restrooms.

43.4 (mp 235.2) Turn right (west) off U.S. 101 at Florida Ave. Cycle one block uphill, halfway around a large road circle, then continue down Florida Ave.

43.6 Turn left on Monroe Ave.

43.7 Go right on Virginia Ave., a broad road without a shoulder. Watch for road signs to Charleston and state parks. Several large grocery stores are passed in this section.

44.3 Turn left (south) on Broadway for 0.9 mile.

45.2 Go right (west) up a freeway-type ramp to Newmark Ave. A bike lane starts in 0.5 mile when the road enters the town of Coos Bay.

47.0 At the end of Newmark Ave., turn left (south) on Empire and follow it to Charleston. Bike lane is good in this section.

51.9 Cross South Slough on a narrow bridge. On busy days, cyclists may choose to use the sidewalk.

52.2 Charleston; two small grocery stores, the last until Bandon, 20 miles south.

52.4 Leaving Charleston, the road climbs a short, steep hill to an intersection. Stay right for Cape Arago. The left fork climbs steeply up towards Seven Devils and Bandon. (You will return to intersection in the next section.)

53.8 Turnoff to Bastendorf County Park; campsites, hot showers, and beach access.

54.6 The bike lane ends and road narrows—travel with caution.

54.9 Sunset Bay State Park campground; picnicking on a narrow bay nearly enclosed by rock walls, hot showers and hiking trails. The hiker-biker area is 2.5 miles south at Cape Arago State Park.

56.0 Shore Acres State Park; botanical gardens, scenic overlooks of the coast, picnicking, running water, and restrooms.

57.0 Simpson Reef Viewpoint. A magnificent view of the reef and sea lions sunning on the rocks and sand.

57.4 Cape Arago State Park at road's end. The hiker-biker camp access is a gated dirt road three-quarters of the way around the turn-around loop. Walk uphill 1,000 feet to the primitive campsite, which only offers running water. Restrooms are in the picnic area below, and showers are at Sunset Bay. For the best scenery, walk at least 100 feet down the north beach trail from the picnic area to the tables on the edge of the bluff overlooking the surf, an outstanding backdrop to any meal, with sea lions on nearby Simpson Reef providing a nonstop live orchestra.

Cape Arago State Park to Humbug Mountain State Park (58.8 Miles)

Scenic backroads start the day from Cape Arago State Park. Away from the coast, the route rolls along ridgetops with sweeping views of Oregon's coastal forest and South Slough Estuary, with only an occasional intrusion from passing cars. Deer and other wildlife are common. Leaving the ridgetops, the route sweeps back down to sea level and returns to U.S. 101 after 21.4 peaceful miles—but not for long.

The bike route follows U.S. 101 for just 2.7 miles before branching off for a scenic ride along the coast at Bandon, where the beaches are dotted with sea stacks of all shapes and sizes. There are overlooks, state parks, and numerous access points to this unusual beach.

Beyond Bandon, the bike route returns to U.S. 101 and follows it inland over rolling, grassy hills. This is prime rangeland for cows,

Authors overlooking the sea stack–studded beach at Bandon

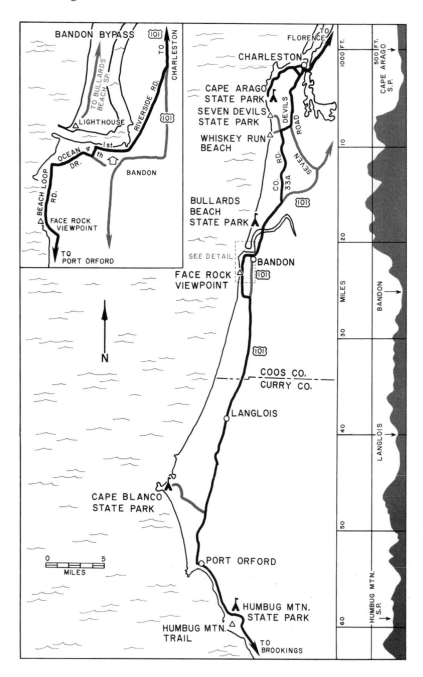

BANDON BYPASS 101 TO CHARLESTON

TO FLORENCE

TO BULLARDS BEACH S.P.

CHARLESTON

RIVERSIDE RD.

101

CAPE ARAGO STATE PARK

LIGHTHOUSE

SEVEN DEVILS STATE PARK

SEVEN DEVILS ROAD

1st

OCEAN DR.   4th

WHISKEY RUN BEACH

CO. RD.

BANDON

33A

101

BEACH LOOP RD.

BULLARDS BEACH STATE PARK

FACE ROCK VIEWPOINT

101

TO PORT ORFORD

SEE DETAIL

BANDON

FACE ROCK VIEWPOINT

101

N

COOS CO.
CURRY CO.

LANGLOIS

CAPE BLANCO STATE PARK

0   5
MILES

PORT ORFORD

HUMBUG MTN. STATE PARK

HUMBUG MTN. TRAIL

TO BROOKINGS

1000 FT.

500 FT.

CAPE ARAGO S.P.

10

20

MILES

BANDON

30

40

LANGLOIS

50

HUMBUG MTN. S.P.

60

horses, sheep, goats, and even llamas. It's also excellent riding country, and miles fly by without the distraction of waysides and scenic overlooks.

Humbug Mountain State Park, the destination for this section, has a treat for saddle-sore cyclists—a 2.5-mile hiking trail up Humbug Mountain. The trail is an excellent afternoon walk to a high vantage point with views south along the coast. Or, if the Humbug Mountain Trail seems too much, try walking north from the park on an abandoned portion of the Old Coast Highway. The road climbs up a small hill to a viewpoint of the coast and U.S. 101, a great place to watch the sunset.

If you have any spare time during the day, consider a stop at Bullards Beach State Park, a tour of the old town of Bandon, or a visit to the cheese factory. The state park features a lighthouse and museum located on a long, sandy spit at the mouth of the Co-quille River, and excellent views south to Bandon and the fishing marina. The old section of Bandon has a delightful selection of tourist shops designed to please a starving cyclist, such as a bakery, fudge factory, and restaurants. The cheese factory, the Coquille Valley Dairy Coop, is located on the north end of Bandon at 680 U.S. 101 (2 blocks north of the old town), and is open to vis-itors from 8:00 A.M. to 5:00 P.M., Monday through Friday.

If you have lots of extra energy, take a side trip (5 miles each way) out to Cape Blanco State Park and lighthouse. It's a beautiful, secluded area; once there, you may be tempted to stay.

MILEAGE LOG

0.0 Leaving Cape Arago State Park, retrace the route north to-wards Charleston.

5.0 At the intersection just above Charleston, turn right (east) on Seven Devils Rd. (County Road 208). The road is steep for the first mile, steeper than most in Oregon, after which it levels off on a rolling ridgetop.

10.0 South Slough National Estuarine Reserve; interpretive cen-ter, views, nature trail, estuary trail, restrooms, and water. The South Slough cannot be properly explored without spending time hiking or boating the area; however, for an overview, check out the interesting displays illustrating the ecology and history of the area at the interpretive center.

11.4 Pass a gravel road, not recommended for bicycles, to Seven Devils Wayside.

15.8 Junction with unnamed road signed to Whisky Run Beach and Seven Devils Wayside. Turn right (west) and begin an exhilarating descent.

18.6 Junction with County Rd. 33A. The bike route turns left (south) heading back to U.S. 101. *SIDE TRIP* to the right (north) County Road 33A goes 2 miles downhill to Seven Devils Wayside; restrooms, running water, picnic tables, and a long, lonely beach. *SIDE TRIP.* Straight ahead (west), an unnamed road descends 1 mile to Whisky Run Beach. No facilities here, just a sandy beach for strolling and beach-combing. Huge wind turbines can be seen perched on a hill above the beach. Just before the beach, a narrow dirt road branches off on the right leading 0.2 mile to a small interpretive center and viewpoint. (Unless you have a mountain bike, it's best to skip the interpretive center.)

21.4 (mp 257.4) Junction of County Road 33A with U.S. 101. Turn right (south) on U.S. 101 and start a long glide to Bandon. Shoulders are wide, making the brisk ride enjoyable.

23.3 (mp 259.3) Bullards Beach State Park; camping, hot showers, hiker-biker area, trails, beach access, and lighthouse with a museum featuring pictures of local shipwrecks (open summer months only). The nearest grocery stores are 1 mile south, at the north end of Bandon on U.S. 101, off the bike route.

23.4 (mp 259.4) Narrow shoulderless bridge over the Coquille River.

24.1 (mp 260.1) Start Bandon scenic route. Turn right (west) off U.S. 101 on Riverside Rd.

24.7 Bandon. For grocery stores or a visit to the cheese factory, stay on Beach Loop Rd. to the marina, then return to U.S. 101 and go left (north). Sea Star Traveler's hostel is located on 2d St., just off U.S. 101.

Battle Rock Historical Wayside at Port Orford

25.6 Turn right (west) on 1st St. and cycle past the marina. Views extend across the Coquille River to the lighthouse at Bullards Beach State Park.

26.1 Follow the road as it bends left (south) and climbs steeply uphill for one block.

26.3 Turn right (west) on 4th St. and ride through a quiet residential area. Fourth St. becomes Ocean Dr. and then after a few blocks, it bends left, and becomes Beach Loop Rd. again.

27.7 Face Rock viewpoint; restrooms and running water. Large sea stacks decorate the beach below. A trail leads to the beach, inviting exploration of these gigantic monoliths.

29.3 State park beach access with picnic tables and ocean view.

29.8 State park beach access; picnic tables and running water.

30.0 State park picnic area. No running water.

30.1 **(mp 277.6)** Junction, Beach Loop Rd. and U.S. 101; small market, stock up for the long haul to Langlois. Turn right (south), leaving the coast behind and exchanging the smell of salt for the scent of pine and grass. The shoulder is narrow but adequate.

38.2 **(mp 285.8)** Leave Coos County and enter Curry County.

40.0 **(mp 287.6)** Langlois; a small market.

42.6 **(mp 290.2)** Denmark; commercial campground but no other facilities.

48.7 **(mp 296.4)** *SIDE TRIP* to Cape Blanco State Park and lighthouse. The park is 5 miles west of U.S. 101 on a steep, narrow, rough road. The campground, situated on a scenic windblown bluff overlooking Cape Blanco Lighthouse, has hot showers as well as a hiker-biker area. Because of the park's isolation, buy food in Langlois or Port Orford. A small market at Sixes, 0.3 mile before the turnoff, can supply the basics when open.

52.0 **(mp 299.7)** Port Orford. If spending the night at Humbug Mountain State Park, buy food here.

53.3 **(mp 301.0)** Battle Rock Historical Wayside; ocean views, beach access, and picnicking. An information board explains the history of the area.

58.8 **(mp 307)** Turn left off U.S. 101 to Humbug Mountain State Park; hiker-biker sites, hot showers, hiking trails, and beach access. (The hiker-biker site is in the forest—very cool, and full of bugs. If the park is not already full, you may want to join up with other bicyclists and share a regular campsite.) The trail up Humbug Mountain, an energetic but highly recommended afternoon jaunt, starts from the southwest corner of the park in the lower camping loop. The Old Coast Highway Trail, an excellent place to watch the sunset, starts to the right of the pay booth.

Humbug Mountain State Park to the California Border (55.9 Miles)

The Oregon ride ends with some of the most breathtaking scenery of the entire Pacific coast; long, sandy beaches, rocks carved into graceful arches by the ocean, jagged sea stacks, and sheer rock cliffs. U.S. 101 is etched on the coast, traversing wind-blasted hillsides dotted with viewpoints, parks, and beach accesses. Highly recommended stops are Arch Rock, Thunder Rock Cove, Natural Bridge Cove, Whalehead Beach, and Harris Beach State Park. Azalea State Park is recommended in late spring and early summer, when the flowers are in bloom.

The ride is relatively easy, with only one steep climb over Cape Sebastian. You'll have more trouble with the level areas, which tend to be windy in the afternoons. Early morning starts are recommended to avoid the winds, logging trucks, and tourist traffic.

Make the most of the two (short) opportunities to escape the

Take a friend with you when you go touring

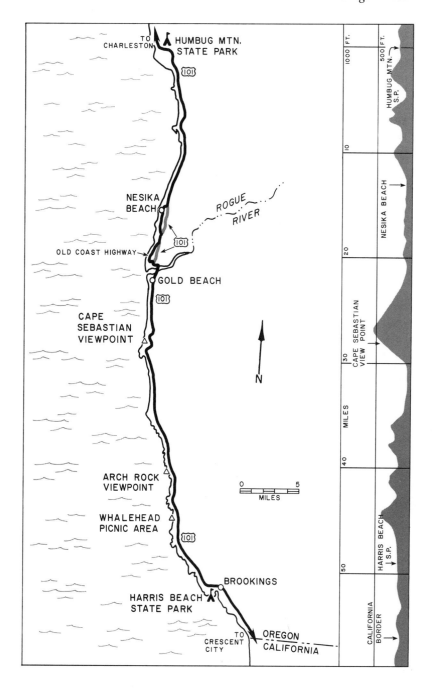

noise of U.S. 101. The first escape is a road paralleling U.S. 101 through the small community of Nesika Beach. The second is on a section of the Old Coast Highway. This narrow and rarely used road winds along the coast through scenic farms and a small beach community.

Brookings, 6 miles north of the California border, is the logical end-point for Oregon coast bicycle tours. The chief source of transportation out of town is Greyhound bus. All bicycles must be boxed for shipping, and the local cycle shop (Escape Hatch Sports Cycle) is kind enough to sell them.

Cyclists continuing south will find Harris Beach State Park a convenient and beautiful spot for camping. The next campground lies 27 miles south of the California border.

MILEAGE LOG

0.0 (mp 307) From Humbug Mountain State Park, return to U.S. 101. The road is narrow and winding as it heads inland over a shoulder of Humbug Mountain. Watch for rocks on the shoulder. Northbound cyclists have little shoulder in this area.

0.7 (mp 307.7) Humbug Mountain State Park picnic area; restrooms, tables, and running water.

3.0 (mp 310) U.S. 101 turns toward the ocean, with views of the broken coastline. Humbug Mountain dominates the northern horizon.

4.7 (mp 311.7) Shoulder ends, marking the start of a slide area. For the next 5 miles, the shoulder will appear and disappear several times.

6.2 (mp 313.2) Dinosaurs leer at travelers from the side of the road, heralding a commercial campground and the Prehistoric Gardens. Admission is charged.

11.9 (mp 318.9) Ophir rest area; beach access, restrooms, and running water.

13.8 (320.8) Start of the first U.S. 101 escape. Turn right (west) towards Nesika Beach, a small community with grocery store and commercial campground. The road has no shoulders but receives only moderate use.

15.0 (mp 322) Return to U.S. 101.

15.2 (mp 322.2) Geisel Monument State Park; a small wayside built to commemorate the burial site of the Geisel family, four of whom were massacred by Indians. Restrooms, running water, and picnic tables.

17.1 (mp 324.1) Watch closely, or you may miss the start of the second U.S. 101 escape. Turn right (west) on Old Coast Highway. The road is narrow, little-used and very scenic.

Harris Beach State Park

Pass several beach access trails and cross two cattle guards. Imagine what it was like when this was the main route along the coast.

19.9 (mp 326.3) Return to U.S. 101 at the small community of Agate Beach.

21.1 (mp 327.5) Cross the Rogue River on a shoulderless bridge. Cyclists may use the narrow sidewalk.

21.4 (mp 327.8) Gold Beach, best known as the starting point for tours on the Rogue River. Billboards advertising jet-boat rides assault the senses as you approach town. Other features include an attractive boat harbor, a large grocery store at the south end of town, and the Curry County Museum featuring local history. Beyond Gold Beach, U.S. 101 starts its climb over Cape Sebastian. This is a slide area, and shoulder width varies from none to 2.5 feet. Northbound travelers have even less shoulder.

27.1 (mp 333.5) Summit of Cape Sebastian (elevation 712 feet).

28.4 (mp 334.8) Cape Sebastian Historical Marker describes the origin of the name.

28.5 (mp 334.9) Turnoff to Cape Sebastian Viewpoint. The viewpoint, reached by a very steep 0.5-mile access road followed by a short trail, has an outstanding overlook of the coast. If the energy is there, the view is worth the struggle.

30.5 (mp 336.9) Myers Creek, crossed on a short bridge with no shoulders or sidewalk. Use caution when crossing this and the following bridges. U.S. 101 is once again near sea level, and great sea stacks dot the shoreline.

32.4 (mp 339.2) Pistol River State Park; beach access but no facilities.

37.2 (mp 344) Boardman State Park. This long, narrow park has three picnic areas, numerous viewpoints, beach accesses, and pullouts.

37.7 (mp 344.5) Arch Rock Viewpoint.

37.9 (mp 344.7) Arch Rock picnic area; views of the arch, picnic tables, and toilets. No water or beach access.

38.5 (mp 345.3) Thunder Rock Cove; the cove is awesome.

38.6 (mp 345.4) Natural Bridges Cove. Water enters this cove through rock arches. The area is exceptionally pretty when the tide is coming in.

41.0 (mp 347.8) Cross Thomas Creek on the highest bridge of the Oregon coast, rising 345 feet. At the south end is a turnout and bridge viewpoint.

41.6 (mp 348.4) Indian Sand Trail Viewpoint. The viewpoint is overgrown; the trail starts north of this area.

42.4 (mp 349.2) Whalehead Beach picnic area; reached by a steep 200-foot descent; restrooms, picnic tables, running water, and beach access.

Cyclist near Pistol River

44.3 (mp 351.1) Turnoff to House Rock Viewpoint.

45.2 (mp 352) Cape Ferrelo viewpoint access.

45.8 (mp 352.6) Lone Ranch picnic area, reached by a very steep 0.3-mile descent; restrooms, water, and tables. The scenic picnic area is located next to a sandy beach. The ocean is peppered with sea stacks.

47.0 (mp 353.8) Rainbow Rock Viewpoint.

48.5 (mp 355.3) Brookings, a very long town whose commercial section lies 1.5 miles south.

48.8 (mp 355.6) Turn right (west) for Harris Beach State Park and left (east) for the Oregon tourist information center and rest area. The state park has complete facilities for day use and camping. The hiker-biker area is located behind the trailer dump station; the showers are really hot. A visit to the beach is a must. There are sea stacks of all sizes to climb, explore, and sit on while watching a lingering sunset. The closest stores are 0.8 mile south in Brookings.

50.1 (mp 356.9) Commercial section of Brookings; large supermarkets, bike shop, and bus station. The cycle shop is located on the east side of U.S. 101, across the highway from the Redwoods Theater. The bus station is 0.2 mile north, on Pacific St.

50.8 (mp 357.7) Azalea State Park turnoff; picnic area, restrooms, water, and azalea garden. To reach the park, turn left (east) off U.S. 101 at North Bend Rd. and follow the signs.

50.9 (mp 357.8) U.S. 101 crosses the Chetco River Bridge, which marks the start of 5 nearly level miles through open farm country on an excellent shoulder.

55.9 (mp 362.8) California.

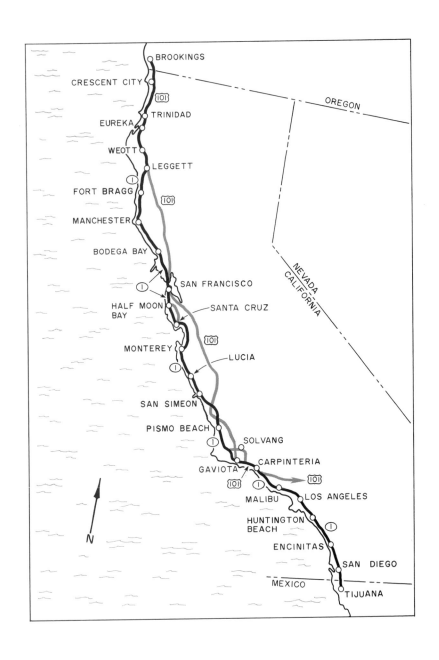

BROOKINGS

CRESCENT CITY

101

OREGON

TRINIDAD

EUREKA

WEOTT

LEGGETT

1

FORT BRAGG

101

MANCHESTER

BODEGA BAY

1

SAN FRANCISCO

HALF MOON BAY

SANTA CRUZ

MONTEREY

101

1

LUCIA

SAN SIMEON

PISMO BEACH

1

SOLVANG

CARPINTERIA

GAVIOTA

101

1

101

MALIBU

LOS ANGELES

HUNTINGTON BEACH

1

ENCINITAS

SAN DIEGO

MEXICO

TIJUANA

NEVADA

CALIFORNIA

N

Right, *cyclist on the Monterey coast*

CALIFORNIA

The California coast covers 1,025.9 miles, over half the length of the Pacific Coast Bicycle Route. California is rich in variety, from the cool redwood forests of the north to the gigantic cities and sunny beaches of the south. Some sections of the coast are ideal for riding and the miles will fly by; however, the coast is dotted with historic missions, lighthouses, marinas, and beaches, and you will spend as much time exploring as riding.

The California coast ride is divided into three sections: north, middle, and south. The northern section follows U.S. 101 (referred to as the Redwood Highway) for 200.3 miles south from the Oregon border to Leggett. Much of the riding is inland in beautiful redwood forests. Average yearly rainfall is high, up to 70 inches at Crescent City. September and October are usually the wettest months. Rain gear and fenders are recommended. Temperatures are moderate along the northern portions of the coast, warming towards Leggett. The north has several sections of hazardous highway—fast, busy, and shoulderless—as well as long, steep hills; this portion may be best left to experienced cyclists.

The middle section of the California coast follows Highway 1 for 491.8 miles from Leggett to Pismo Beach. Except for a one day's ride through the San Francisco Bay area, it is typified by lonely stretches of two-lane highway etched into the cliffs along the coast. The highway is steep, the riding demanding, the countryside beautiful, and the views outstanding—all in all, some of the best cycling on the entire coast. Traffic on Highway 1 is generally light, composed principally of vacationers. Starting at first light helps to avoid traffic for several hours each morning. The chance of rain is minimal in the summer months of June, July, and August. Temperatures may rise to the 70s or low 80s on a warm, summer day. The middle section of California is recommended for cyclists who have previous touring experience and who are in good shape.

The southern section of the coast is a must for anyone looking for the California mystique—beach boys, bikini-clad girls, surfers, suntans, palm trees, large cities, Mexican food, and Spanish architecture. The coast route loses its country flavor as it enters a long series of resort towns and sprawling cities south of Pismo Beach. The terrain levels and the need for strength is replaced by a need for navigational skills through a network of city streets. Bicycles are a common mode of transport here, and motorists are the most courteous on the coast. Weather conditions for riding are good from April to mid-November. This 333.8-mile section of California coast can be completed by all bicycle tourists.

Dense, wet blankets of fog may cover large sections of the California coast for days at a time. All riders should have bright, visible clothing and carry lights.

The Bicentennial Route is followed most of the way through California. Caltrans (California Transit) has signed most of the key intersections throughout the state; however, many of the signs have been stolen, so do not count on them. A detailed route map, published by Caltrans, is a great help for negotiating through the complex maze of the larger cities. This map is no longer being published, so check with friends and fellow cyclists to see if you can locate one.

Mileposts in California show the miles from the nearest county line. The numbers decrease from north to south, reaching zero at the south end of the county. Each milepost notes at least three points of information: the route number, the county name (abbreviated), and the mileage to the hundredth.

Almost every winter, huge sections of road slide away, making California's Highway 1 the most costly road in the country to maintain. Caltrans sets up alternate routes whenever this occurs, creating very scenic but sometimes long detours. If in doubt about the route, contact the California Highway Patrol. The best source of information is other cyclists and tourists traveling up the coast in cars. Ask around.

The California coast has only one tunnel, and it's for north-bound cyclists only. The tunnel, on U.S. 101 north of Gaviota State Park, is 0.3-mile long, with an uphill grade and an 18-inch shoulder; expect a strong head wind.

The state and county park systems provide 46 hiker-biker camps for cyclists. They are generally small, and may be very crowded. No reservations are required; you will never be turned away. Large groups (eight or more cyclists) should reserve regular sites ahead of time. Contact the state parks for details.

Most state parks on the coast remain open year-round. Only Mill Creek Campground in Del Norte Coast Redwoods State Park, the farthest north, is closed after Labor Day. Future budget cuts may result in more closures; if planning an off-season tour, check ahead.

Campgrounds are not spaced evenly along the coast. In the northern and southern sections, long distances are covered between public campgrounds. The strength of an individual or group should be the deciding factor as to whether it's too far between campgrounds. Plan ahead, and use one of the many hostels, hotels, motels, and privately operated campgrounds along the coast if necessary.

South of Santa Barbara, transients pose a major problem at all the state park campgrounds. As of 1989, the state parks were in the process of adopting policies to discourage transients from taking over the hiker-biker sites. Some parks changed the location of the site every night. Other campgrounds eliminated the site altogether. If you arrive in a campground that has closed its hiker-biker site, you will not be turned away; however, you may be required to pay full price for your site or end up sharing a site with the campground hosts.

The closest city to the northern California border is Brookings, Oregon (located 6 miles north of California). The only form of public transportation to Brookings is Greyhound bus, from Portland, San Francisco, or Eugene. Crescent City (21 miles south of the California–Oregon border), is the first major city on the California coast. It can be reached by Greyhound bus or small commuter airplane. Eureka is the first city with train access.

An easy escape from the maze of city streets that make up southern California is the Los Angeles International Airport (LAX). The bike route passes right by the end of the runway.

At the true southern end of California, San Diego International Airport and the Amtrack station lie right on the bike route, and the bus station is only a few blocks away.

Oregon Border to Prairie Creek Redwoods State Park (53.3 Miles)

Entering California is like entering a foreign country. The agricultural inspection station at the border looks suspiciously like customs. However, instead of pulling out a passport, you are required to pull out all fruit and vegetables from your touring bags and pockets. Any produce that might contaminate the native crop will be confiscated.

Once past the inspection station, the bicycle route abandons U.S. 101 in favor of the quieter rural roads, and for the next 20 miles to Crescent City, you will pedal past open fields, cattle ranches, a state penitentiary, and dense forests. (U.S. 101 is very busy and has little to no shoulder in this section.)

At Crescent City, plan a stop at the Redwood National Park visitor center for an introduction to the country ahead, home of some of the tallest trees in the world. If time allows, visit the Crescent City Lighthouse, accessible at low tide only, and the fishing docks, where, if lucky, you can watch fishermen unload the heavily laden fishing boats.

Grazing elk at Prairie Creek Redwoods State Park

South of Crescent City, ocean views give way to tall trees as the road climbs 1,100 feet over the triple summit of the Crescent City Hills. The road is narrow, truck traffic heavy, and shoulders non-existent. Early mornings and weekends are best for traveling. As if to add a little melodrama to the ride, the hill seems to be perpetually swathed in fog, making this one of the most hazardous sections of road on the entire Pacific Coast Bicycle Route. Dress brightly and ride with a great deal of caution and courtesy.

Zooming down from the last summit of the Crescent City Hills, glide south past the Trees of Mystery, where an oversized Paul Bunyan and Babe, his giant blue ox, welcome the visitors to the world's largest collection of redwood carvings.

After several short miles of level travel, the highway climbs steeply over another hill, gaining nearly 900 feet in elevation. U.S. 101 remains narrow, very busy, and shoulderless as it passes through majestic redwood groves. When traffic is annoying, stop and take a relaxing stroll or admire one of these magnificent trees.

The day ends at Prairie Creek Redwoods State Park, where a herd of Roosevelt elk graze year round in plain sight of the highway and campground; occasionally wandering through the hiker-biker site. The elk may be there any time of day, but are best viewed in the early morning and late afternoon when they are grazing. The park also has numerous hiking trails leading through the Redwood forest, short trails to fern groves, longer trails to some of the world's tallest trees, and a 4-mile trail to a fern-covered canyon on the coast.

MILEAGE LOG

0.0 (mp 46.49) Oregon–California border. Enter Del Norte County on U.S. 101.

0.2 (mp 46.29) California fruit inspection. Cooperate, and help protect California agriculture.

0.8 (mp 45.8) Take the first left after the fruit inspection on Ocean View Dr. (County Road D5). Shoulders are nonexistent, but traffic is light and travel pleasant.

6.3 Cross U.S. 101 and continue straight on Sarina Rd. The road is nearly level as it winds its way past small cattle ranches and large lily fields.

6.8 Intersection; bend left onto 1st St.

7.7 Enter the small community of Smith River and turn right on Fred Haight Dr. (County Road D4). Smith River is the heart of Del Norte dairy country and is also known as the Easter lily capital of the world. The surrounding fields produce over 90 percent of the nation's Easter lily bulbs. In July, a festival celebrates the harvest.

10.8 Turn right (south) on U.S. 101. Cross the Smith River on a short, shoulderless bridge then take the first right.

11.2 **(mp 36.00)** Exit U.S. 101 right (west) on Lake Earl Dr. (County Road D3) past a small gas station and grocery store on the right. Follow Lake Earl Dr. to Crescent City. Traffic is light, and there is a good shoulder for over half the distance.

11.6 The route bends left at an intersection near an old barn.

12.6 Cycle through the one-store town of Fort Dick.

14.0 Begin wide shoulder.

20.5 Intersection; turn right (south) on U.S. 101 and enter Crescent City; supermarkets, campground, motels, and restaurants. Traffic can be very heavy through town, and shoulders are narrow or nonexistent. If traffic becomes annoying, go right (west) for one block and work your way through town on the city streets. *SIDE TRIP* to Redwood National Park visitor center and lighthouse. Exit right off U.S. 101 on 2d St, for two blocks to K St. to find the visitor center, restrooms, and running water. To reach the lighthouse, turn right on 1st St. and follow it to the end, then turn left on A St. for one block to the parking lot. When the tide is out, the lighthouse is open. Admission charged.

22.0 **(mp 25.44)** Turnoff to the Citizens Dock. Go right (west) on Citizens Dock Rd. to the dock. When the fish are running, the area bustles with activity. U.S. 101 widens to include a shoulder as the highway leaves the downtown area.

22.2 **(mp 25.4)** Turnoff to Under Sea World. Exit right (west) on Anchor Dr. An admission is charged to see the wonders that lurk beneath the sea.

23.9 **(mp 23.54)** Base of the Crescent City Hills. Shift low, grip your handlebars, and grit your teeth. The next 17.5 miles are over some of California's most hair-raising terrain. Fog often engulfs these hills, so wear bright clothing and strap on a light that is visible to cars coming up from behind. Southbound travelers have two lanes (no shoulder) on the climb; northbound travelers have only a single lane.

26.0 **(mp 21.44)** Turnoff to Mill Creek Campground. A steep 2.2-mile road descends over 600 feet to a quiet campground nestled beneath a grove of redwoods; hiker-biker sites and hot showers. Food supplies must be brought from Crescent City. This campground is open only in the summer.

28.4 **(mp 19.00)** Summit of the first and highest Crescent City Hills, at approximately 1,200 feet. Southbound traffic merges here into a single lane. The passing lane reappears when the road begins to climb. Glide a short distance down, then start climbing the second summit.

29.7 **(mp 17.70)** Summit of second hill; only one more to go.

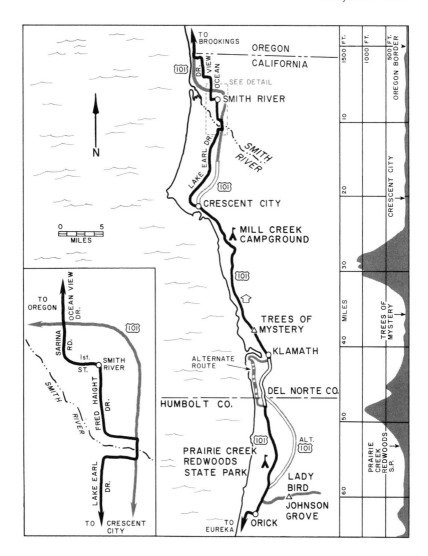

31.1 (mp 16.22) Top of the last summit. It's all downhill for the next 3.5 miles.

32.2 (mp 17.32) Halfway point of the Pacific Coast Bicycle Route from Powell River to San Ysidro.

34.7 (mp 12.53) Southern end of the Crescent City Hills is marked by a nice picnic area and sandy beach for relaxing. On the left side of the highway is the Redwoods Hostel (AYH). A narrow shoulder begins as the road skirts around a bay.

35.4 (mp 11.88) Coastal Trail access; restrooms and running water. The trail follows the coastline through this part of Redwood National Park.

36.4 (mp 10.86) Trees of Mystery and Klamath city limits. Good, rideable shoulders begin as you enter the city limits of Klamath; grocery stores and fast foods are just ahead.

40.7 (mp 5.36) Klamath shopping center lies off U.S. 101 on the left side of the highway. This is the best food selection for miles.

41.7 (mp 4.42) Golden Bear Bridge. Two golden grizzly bears, California's state symbol, stand guard at the entrance of a pair of shoulderless bridges over the Klamath River. After the second bridge, the good shoulders return as U.S. 101 climbs over the second major set of hills for the day. *ALTERNATE ROUTE:* Cyclists touring on mountain bikes may be interested in a scenic 14-mile tour along the coast (8 miles are gravel). The road starts at the southern end of the Klamath River bridges and follows the river to the coast, then swings south to loop back to U.S. 101.

44.8 (mp 1.20) Top of the first summit, approximately 500 feet in elevation.

46.0 (mp 0.0 and 134.89) Leave Del Norte County and enter Humboldt County. Across the county line, the highway climbs uphill for several more miles to an elevation near 900 feet. Shoulders are good. (In 1988 a new road was being built around Prairie Creek Redwoods. When this road is completed, it will divert a large percentage of the commercial traffic; the bicycle route will continue to use the road through the state park.)

46.6 (mp 134.29) Alternate route (Coast Road) returns to U.S. 101.

46.7 (mp 134.19) Enter Prairie Creek Redwoods State Park. Continuing uphill, shoulder narrows as the heavily shaded highway passes through towering redwood groves.

47.3 (mp 133.67) Top of the hill. It's all downhill to Prairie Creek Campground, Don't go too fast, as the road passes numerous memorial redwood groves with short (0.5-mile or less) trails into the forest. Stop at least once to look at the trees.

52.5 (mp 128.40) Cork Screw Tree turnout. Follow a short path to a twisted and deformed tree still standing tall and proud.

53.0 (mp 127.96) Big Tree. Exit left (east) off U.S. 101 to parking lot and walk to a tree over 300 feet tall and 17.7 feet in diameter.

53.3 (mp 127.24) Prairie Creek State Park Campground; hiker-biker sites, warm showers, roaming elk, visitor center, and trails through the redwoods and beach. The hiker-biker site has a bar to hang food out of reach of bears and raccoons. If time allows, take an extra day to explore the park. The trail to the beach and fern canyon is a must. Elk may be seen on the beach in the morning and late afternoon.

Prairie Creek Redwoods State Park to Eureka (46.5 Miles)

With the first major set of California hills behind you, it's a short and relatively easy ride from Prairie Creek Redwoods State Park to Eureka. This should leave you plenty of time for side trips, exploring, or bicycle maintenance at the excellent repair shops in Arcata or Eureka.

This section sees the evolution of U.S. 101 from a narrow country road into a busy 4-lane freeway. It is legal to ride on the

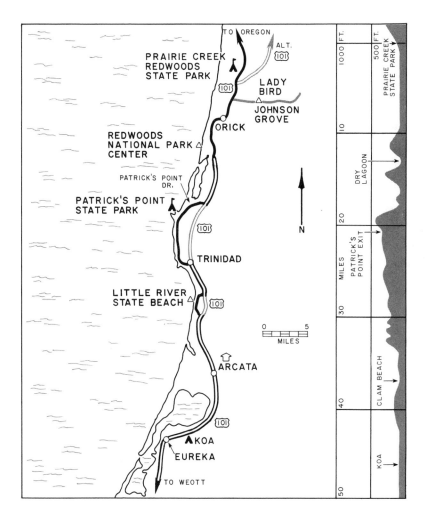

freeway (unless otherwise signed), and, thanks to a wide shoulder, it's also safer. However, the noise and dirt is fatiguing, so be sure to take advantage of the two scenic escape routes off the freeway, and all the side trips.

The first suggested side trip is just 5.4 miles south of Prairie Creek, where a narrow road climbs up to the beautiful Lady Bird Johnson Grove. The grove has a mile-long loop trail through a forest of ferns and mammoth redwoods. The access road to the grove is steep; leave the touring bags at the bottom, if possible.

The second stop of the day is just south of Orick, at the Redwoods National Park center. The displays are interesting, the building well-heated, and the local population of banana slugs is simply amazing.

As U.S. 101 heads around Stone Lagoon and Dry Lagoon (part of Humboldt State Park), the road narrows and the shoulder disappears. This is an extremely scenic section of highway, too narrow to be enjoyed. Use caution, ride quickly, and concentrate on being visible.

Giant redwood trees

Near Patrick's Point, U.S. 101 widens into a freeway with wide shoulders and noisy traffic. After a couple of miles on the freeway, the bike route escapes to backroads which parallel the coast to Trinidad and lead to the next "must" stop at Patrick's Point State Park. The park is situated on a rugged point overlooking the ocean. Trails crisscross the bluffs and climb to breathtaking views from sheer cliffs. Beaches are covered with driftwood and fun to explore. Seals live on offshore sea stacks; their constant barking echoes throughout the park.

In Trinidad, visit the Trinidad Memorial Lighthouse with its giant two-ton fog bell, then head south on U.S. 101 to more excellent views of the coast.

Leave the freeway (U.S. 101) for a second time at Little River State Beach, and cycle along the beach road for a peaceful 1.8 miles before returning to the hectic rush of the highway. When riding on the freeway, use extra caution at the busy exits and entrances as you near Arcata and Eureka.

The day's ride ends a couple of miles north of Eureka at the KOA, the only campground in the area with a special site just for cyclists. A discount camp fee is offered to cyclists (it still isn't cheap). To date the campground managers claim they have never turned away a cyclist. The other campgrounds in the Eureka area are designed for trailers; the managers do not like to take in tenters. Alternate options include hotels, bed and breakfasts, and the Arcata Crew House Hostel in Arcata.

MILEAGE LOG

0.0 (mp 127.24) Head south on U.S. 101 from Prairie Creek Campground. Elk can be spotted grazing in the open fields or resting under crab apple trees in the morning.

2.8 (mp 124.8) Prairie Creek Fish Hatchery. Exit east (left). A huge salmon sculptured out of redwood is the most eye-catching attraction. Visitors are welcome to wander around ponds containing finger-size salmon. Just south of the hatchery is the southern end of the new road which will bypass Prairie Creek Redwoods State Park.

5.4 (mp 122.2) *SIDE TRIP* to Lady Bird Johnson Grove; restrooms. Turn left (east) off U.S. 101 and cycle 2.3 miles up a narrow and very steep road to the 1-mile nature loop trail. This side trip is a must in May, when the rhododendrons are in bloom.

5.8 (mp 121.87) Enter the town of Orick. Grocery stores (the last before Patrick's Point State Park), restaurants, motels, and an assortment of tourist shops.

8.5 (mp 119.25) *SIDE TRIP* to the Redwoods National Park center and picnic area. The center, located 0.2 mile off the highway, has heated restrooms, warm water, beach access, and information. Beyond the park center, U.S. 101 returns to its typical up-and-down motion, with little to no shoulder. The highway crosses a narrow sandspit between the ocean and Freshwater Lagoon, where the county provides a large parking area on the west side of the road. Camping is allowed here; no water.

10.2 (mp 117.38) Turnoff to Stone Lagoon Primitive Campground, part of Humboldt State Park. Campground space is limited; no water.

12.2 (mp 115.50) Humboldt State Park visitor center, a small building with information about camping in the park. The tables outside offer an opportunity to picnic along the shores of Stone Lagoon.

13.1 (mp 114.50) Turnoff to Dry Lagoon State Park area; beach access, restrooms, and lots of driftwood; no water. The park is located 1 mile west of U.S. 101. Beyond the state park, U.S. 101 climbs over two small hills, then descends to parallel Big Lagoon before widening into a four-lane freeway with good shoulders.

17.7 (mp 108.32) Big Lagoon Beach County Park exit; scenic campsites near the beach, water, and restrooms. No hiker-biker campsites.

20.6 (mp 106.50) Exit U.S. 101 on Patrick's Point Dr. The road is narrow and shoulderless but has less traffic than U.S. 101. Keep a wary eye open for sections of rough road and occasional short, steep pitches. After passing motels and an RV campground, the road slips along steep, open hillsides overlooking the ocean.

20.8 Patrick's Point State Park entrance; hiker-biker sites, hot showers, beach access, and hiking trails. *SIDE TRIP:* To visit the park, take a right at the entrance and descend to the toll booth. Purchase an inexpensive map of the area, then follow the road towards Agate Beach. (To reach the hiker-biker site, take a left turn off the Agate Beach Rd. towards Wedding Rock, and follow that road to its end.)

29.9 Trinidad, a small town with a grocery store and fast-food restaurants. *SIDE TRIP:* Before returning to U.S. 101, make a short 0.5-mile side trip to Trinidad Memorial Lighthouse. Follow Main St. to its end, then turn left on Trinity St. for 0.2 mile. A state beach with picnic tables and beach access is located 100 feet right (north) on Trinity St.

30.0 (mp 100.26) Return to U.S. 101, a freeway, at Trinidad. Shoulders disappear on bridges.

33.9 (mp 97.13) Exit U.S. 101 to Little River State Beach for the second scenic escape. This is a confusing exit; watch for the truck weight station, then take the road that goes above it. At the end of the exit, go right and follow the state park road which parallels U.S. 101 for 1.8 miles, offering numerous points of beach access. Return to U.S. 101 at Clam Beach County Park; restrooms, no water.

35.7 (mp 95.50) Little River State Beach Rd. returns to U.S. 101. This is also the start of an official *ALTERNATE COAST ROUTE.* This route continues straight, passing under the freeway then heading south for 4.2 miles. At the south end of McKinnia, the route turns right on School Rd. for 0.8 miles back to the freeway. There are no discernible advantages to this route unless you are desperate for a supermarket.

36.9 (mp 94.38) Vista Point overlooking the Clam Beach–Little River area; no facilities, and no access for northbound travelers.

41.3 (mp 89.77) Mad River Bridge; little shoulder and no sidewalk.

42.1 (mp 89.00) Arcata. U.S. 101 hurries riders through town. Those wishing to visit stores, a bike shop, Humboldt State University, or simply to view some well-maintained Victorian buildings must exit the freeway. The Arcata Crew House Hostel is located on 14th and I St.; call ahead for reservations, 707-822-9995.

43.7 (mp 87.20) Humboldt State University and City Center exit. Once past the center of Arcata, U.S. 101 swings around Arcata Bay. The road is level in the open country along the edge of the bay. Be prepared for strong winds.

46.5 (mp 83.40) The KOA campground lies just off the left (east) side of U.S. 101, requiring a hazardous crossing of this busy highway. Be patient and wait for a break in the traffic. The campground has a small store, endless hot water for showers, small cabins to rent if the weather is bad, and laundry facilities.

Eureka to Marine Garden Club Grove (53.2 Miles)

Eureka is a beautiful old Victorian town with carefully restored homes. The bike route runs through a quiet, residential section of town, past fifty or more of these Victorian masterpieces. If that's not enough, you can take a short side trip to the ornate Carson Mansion and some of the outstanding buildings found in Old Town.

At the southern end of Eureka, take time to visit Fort Humboldt and wander through the excellent indoor and outdoor logging mu-

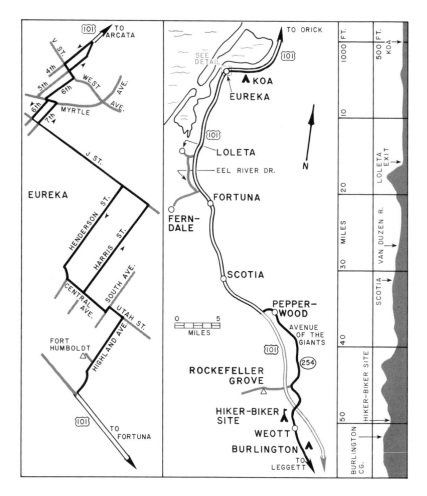

seum. Beyond Eureka, the route returns to U.S. 101. Riding is easy on the wide shoulder of the freeway, and miles speed by.

If freeway riding is not your idea of a good time, take advantage of two opportunities to ride the back roads. A loop off the freeway through the town of Loleta provides the first escape, as well as a chance to sample some cheese at the Loleta cheese factory. The little town of Scotia provides the second escape. While in Scotia, visit the Pacific Lumber Company Museum and pick up a free pass for a self-guided walking tour through the lumber mill and factory, which takes you on a catwalk overlooking the operation of the largest redwood mill in the world (open weekdays only).

Leave the freeway for the last time at the start of the Avenue of the Giants, a section of the Old Coast Highway which winds through a narrow corridor of awesome redwood trees. Explore the numerous groves, hike the trails, and spend some time pondering these magnificent trees. The avenue is narrow and generally deeply shaded. Wear bright, visible clothing.

The day ends at the Burlington Campground hiker-biker site, located 1.8 miles south of main camp area among the giant redwoods of the Marine Garden Club Grove. The site is primitive, without hot water or showers, but the scenic layout more than compensates for any inconveniences. (Showers may be taken at the campground.)

MILEAGE LOG

0.0 (mp 83.40) The first challenge of the day is to return to the west side of the freeway. Once across, head south on U.S. 101 over a level plain. Riding is easy on the wide shoulder.

2.2 (mp 81.30) Enter Eureka on the edge of Arcata Bay.

3.4 (mp 80.10) The narrow bridge over Eureka Slough, with sidewalks but no shoulders, marks the entrance to downtown Eureka. Once across the bridge, the freeway ends and the bike route bypass of Eureka begins. Eureka has a supermarket and bike shop located on the bike route at the south side of town.

3.9 (mp 80.60) Turn left (east) of V St. for 2 blocks to 6th St., starting the Eureka bypass route. *SIDE TRIP* to Carson Mansion and Old Eureka. Take 6th St. to M St. and head right (west) for three blocks to the mansion. Cyclists must be content with viewing the structure from the outside; the mansion is now an exclusive men's club. You can begin a tour of the old town from the mansion. Cycle west on 2nd St. to C. St., go left for one block, and head back up 3rd St. to M St.

4.6 Turn left off 6th St. at J St. for 1 mile to Henderson St.

5.6 Go right on Henderson St. for 1.1 miles through a commercial section of town. Look for the bike shop here. Eureka has spent time and money making this road appealing to cyclists; a bike triggers the stoplights as easily as a car.

6.7 When Henderson St. bends, take a left on Central Ave.

7.0 Jog left to Utah St. for 0.1 mile.

7.1 Turn right on Highland Ave. and continue straight to U.S. 101.

7.6 Fort Humboldt State Historic Park, a highly recommended stop. Restrooms, running water, picnic tables, as well as an indoor/outdoor logging museum and excellent views of Eureka from the old fort site.

7.7 Go left on U.S. 101 (known as Broadway through this section of Eureka).

8.3 (mp 75.3) Freeway resumes with a good shoulder as U.S. 101 leaves Eureka and passes through open country along Humboldt Bay. Use considerable caution when cycling past the exits and entrances to this busy freeway.

11.2 (mp 72.3) Fields Landing exit. East of U.S. 101 is the first of several small commercial centers where you can buy groceries.

12.9 (mp 70.6) College of the Redwoods exit.

15.4 (mp 68.2) First Loleta exit, and the first chance to briefly escape the freeway. The exit marks the start of a 1.4-mile hill, where the freeway broadens into three lanes with no shoulders. *ALTERNATE ROUTE* through Loleta. At the end of the off ramp, turn right (west) on Hookton Rd., then take the first left on Eel River Dr. If the Loleta cheese factory is on your itinerary, turn off Eel River Dr. at Main St., and ride through the center of town. Go left on Loleta Dr. and ride over the railroad tracks. The alternate route returns to the freeway at the Ferndale exit.

16.8 (mp 66.8) Top of the hill; freeway narrows to two lanes, with a shoulder on the southbound side. The northbound corridor widens to three lanes without shoulders.

18.9 (mp 64.59) Ferndale exit. Ferndale, 5 miles southwest of U.S. 101, is a beautiful Victorian town. Church and houses are in excellent condition. Small recreational vehicle campground and several grocery stores.

21.6 (mp 62.0) Fortuna exit. U.S. 101 passes through the western edge of town; the supermarkets are approximately 1 mile off the freeway.

25.5 (mp 58.1) Alton exit.

26.6 (mp 57.0) Van Duzen River Bridge marks the start of the gradual ascent inland to the redwood forests. The bridge is narrow, with little shoulder and no sidewalk.

29.1 (53.80) Rio Dell exit; an easily accessible market is located on the east side of the freeway.

31.2 (mp 50.9) Scotia exit, the second chance to briefly escape the freeway. Scotia is a company town. Its main feature is the Pacific Lumber Company mill, which claims to be the largest redwood mill in the world. Summer visitors may tour the mill and factory, or browse through the logging museum (weekdays only, closed daily from 10:30 A.M. to 1:00 P.M.). Off-season visitors may view the outdoor park section of the museum, and stock up on food at the grocery store. Parallel the freeway north, cycling past the lumber yard, and return to the freeway when the road enters Pacific Lumber land.

35.7 (mp 47.0) Vista Point exit. Gaze over the Eel River Valley and the redwoods from a large parking area.

36.7 (mp 46.0) Exit U.S. 101 and go left to ride the Avenue of the Giants, a narrow and winding road with no shoulder,

Carson Mansion, Eureka

through the redwood forests of Humboldt State Park. Traffic varies from moderate to heavy. *SIDE TRIP* to the Pacific Lumber demonstration forest and picnic area; water, restrooms, picnic tables, and nature trail. At the base of the freeway exit, go right for 0.2 mile to the parking area. This is a great chance to compare a logged redwood forest with the trees on the Avenue of the Giants.

36.8 Humboldt Redwoods State Park. Don't strain your neck looking up at all the trees.

38.7 Enter Pepperwood; small tourist shops but no grocery store. Just south of town two short nature trails, Drury Trail and Percy French Loop, lead through the redwood groves.

41.8 Immortal Tree, growing on the east side of the highway, shows marks of floods, fire, ax, and wind. The tree is a testimonial to the incredible ability of redwoods to survive.

43.3 Redcrest; a small tourist town whose principal attraction is the Eternal Tree House, a hollowed-out stump. Restaurant but no grocery store.

47.3 Avenue of the Giants brushes along the edge of U.S. 101. *SIDE TRIP* on Bull Creek Flats Rd., which branches right and ducks under the freeway. This road offers an excellent ride through tall stands of ivy-wrapped trees. At 1.3 miles is Rockefeller Grove and a loop trail, a good turnaround point.

47.5 Turnoff to Founders Grove. The grove and 0.5-mile nature loop are located just 200 feet left (east) of the Avenue of the Giants. They provide an excellent introduction to the life of the forest. Giant specimens of redwoods, notably the Foundation Tree and Dyerville Giant, are located only minutes from the road.

49.8 Marine Garden Club Grove of Humboldt State Park and hiker-biker camp; picnic tables, running water, restrooms, tall trees, and great swimming holes in the Eel River. A grocery store is located 0.1 mile south in the small town of Weott. Showers and registration booth for the camp are located 1.7 miles south at Burlington Campground.

50.0 Weott. To reach the grocery store, go left for 0.1 mile. Note the pictures of the 1964 flood inside the store.

51.5 Burlington Campground and Humboldt State Park visitor center. Pay for hiker-biker site and take your shower here.

53.2 Return to Marine Garden Club Grove. It's very easy to sleep late in this quiet, dark grove.

Marine Garden Club Grove to Standish–Hickey State Park Recreation Area (47.3 Miles)

Heading south from Marine Garden Club Grove, cycle the second half of the Avenue of the Giants, passing tourist towns with "attractions" such as a drive-through tree and one-log house. In addition to the man-made wonders, are beautiful stands of redwood, such as the Garden Club of America Grove, where you may quietly enjoy nature's handiwork.

At the end of the Avenue of the Giants, the route returns to U.S. 101 and follows the narrow South Fork of the Eel River Valley south. Redwood groves are replaced by dry, open hillsides. Temperatures soar, rising as much as 15 degrees as you leave the protective shade of the redwoods. Be sure water bottles are full and sunglasses handy.

The Avenue of the Giants is not the end of the redwoods. Just 14 miles south lies Richardson Grove State Park, a narrow band of redwoods in an area otherwise bare of the tall trees. Trails in the

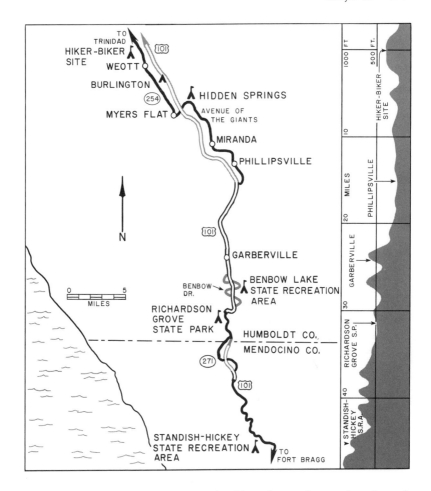

park are uniquely intriguing, climbing from the cool redwood groves to sun-dried ridgetops and open viewpoints. For a quick introduction to the park, the short nature trail provides insight to the life cycle of the redwoods and their ability to survive through infestation, fire, and flood. If planning to walk only one nature trail in the redwoods, put this one at the top of the list.

Two alternate routes offer relief from the humdrum of U.S. 101. The first follows an abandoned road through part of the Benbow Lake State Recreation Area for a peaceful, quiet journey along the South Fork of the Eel River, rejoining U.S. 101 in 3.9 miles (recommended for mountain bikes only). The second alternate route follows Percey Cook Valley Rd. (Highway 271) for 5.7 miles, paralleling the hot and dry U.S. 101 under the partial shade of deciduous trees.

This short day ends at Standish–Hickey State Park Recreation Area, a delightful place to spend an afternoon swimming, hiking, or exploring redwood groves.

Throughout this section, U.S. 101 is very busy, with an endless stream of trucks, cars, and oversized tourist vehicles. For most of the distance, the highway is wide—almost a freeway—with broad shoulders. Unfortunately, the road narrows in several sections, and four lanes of traffic squeeze onto an appallingly narrow and winding two-lane road without shoulders. Trucks and cars rarely slow down for these short sections, and cyclists are forced to fend for themselves. To be on the safe side, start this ride early in the morning and ride defensively; when you see that you will have to share the road with large vehicles in both lanes, take the coward's way out and live to tell about it.

MILEAGE LOG

0.0 From the hiker-biker camp at the Marine Garden Club Grove of Humboldt State Park, cycle south on the Avenue of the Giants.

1.7 Pass Burlington Campground on the left (east).

3.5 Garden Club of America Grove; restrooms and running water. A short path and a bridge lead across the South Fork of the Eel River to a large redwood grove.

4.7 Williams Grove day-use area; picnic tables, restrooms, running water, giant trees, and river access. Open in summer only. Williams Grove has free admission for cyclists (but not for cars). Overnight camping is allowed here—if you happen to be traveling in the company of a self-contained RV.

5.4 Myers Flat. Like all the towns located throughout the redwoods, this one is a touch of tinsel in a rustic setting. Myers Flat's main attraction, besides grocery stores, cafes, and laundromats, is a drive- or ride-through tree. Admission is charged.

6.6 Turnoff to Hidden Springs Campground; hiker-biker area, hot showers, and trails through the redwoods. Open in the summer only.

11.4 Leave Humboldt Redwoods State Park.

11.7 Miranda; groceries and fast food.

15.2 Franklin K. Lane Grove; a picnic area under cool, shady trees, running water, and restrooms.

15.4 Phillipsville; grocery store and restaurants. If intrigued, visit a house made from a single log.

18.2 End of Avenue of the Giants (Highway 254); return to U.S. 101, a wide 4-laner. Shoulders vary from several feet wide to nonexistent for the next 10 miles as the highway climbs two distinct hills. Northbound cyclists exit U.S. 101 here (mp 17.5) to follow the Avenue of the Giants.

24.5 (mp 11.29) Garberville exit; grocery stores.

27.2 (mp R8.58) Benbow Lake *ALTERNATE ROUTE.* This scenic alternate route is closed to motor vehicles due to a slide at the southern end. In 1988 touring bicycles with narrow tires could be pushed over the short, rough section of road. Mountain bikes should be able to handle the entire distance. Turn off U.S. 101 at Benbow Lake State Recreation Area Exit. Go left under the freeway, and follow the river south on Benbow Dr. At 1.1 miles, pass Benbow Lake Campground; hiker-biker campsites, running water, swimming, and hiking trails. No hot showers.

28.4 (mp R5.22) Benbow Lake Alternate Route rejoins U.S. 101. Southbound cyclists must cross the freeway without the aid of a traffic light, but gaps in traffic are common. U.S. 101 nar-

South Fork of the Eel River

rows from a four- to a two-lane highway here. Shoulders soon disappear.

32.3 (mp 2.03) Enter Richardson Grove State Park, a welcome refuge from the hot, dry surrounding countryside. U.S. 101 narrows a bit more.

32.6 (mp 1.73) Richardson Grove State Park campground entrance; hiker-biker area, hot showers, hiking trails, nature loop, small store, and swimming holes in the South Fork of the Eel River. A small grocery store is located 1 mile south.

33.1 (mp 1.18) Leave Richardson Grove State Park and the shaded coolness of the redwoods as U.S. 101 returns to a wide, fast-moving four-lane highway. Shoulders return to a comfortable size, but not for long.

33.6 (mp 0.68) Pass a private campground and small grocery store.

34.0 (mp 0.35) Percey Cook Valley *ALTERNATE ROUTE:* Exit U.S. 101 on Highway 271 and pedal south 3.4 miles along the South Fork of the Eel River. When the road divides, go left under the freeway then right for another 2.3 miles before returning to U.S. 101.

34.3 (mp 0.0 and 104.2) Leave Humboldt County and enter Mendocino County.

37.4 (mp 102.1) Highway 271 passes under U.S. 101, providing a second access to the alternate route.

39.8 (mp 101.5) Highway 271 returns to U.S. 101 as it prepares to enter a steep, narrow river valley which is subject to rock and mud slides. The road narrows again, and most of the shoulders have been carried off downhill somewhere. (Comfortable riding shoulders do not reappear until approximately 0.5 mile before Standish–Hickey State Park Recreation Area.)

42.3 (mp 99.45) Confusion Hill. Strange magnetic forces cause unexplained mysteries. For a small fee you can view these phenomenal things.

42.7 (mp 99.0) Tree house and small cafe. Last chance to see a hollowed-out, but still living, redwood tree.

44.9 (mp 96.42) Frankland and Bess Smith Redwood Grove; running water and restrooms. A small oasis of cool shade in an otherwise hot river valley.

46.1 (mp 94.02) Eel River Redwoods Hostel; sauna, river access, laundry, free use of swim tubes, bikes to rent and rooms for couples.

47.3 (mp 94.00) Standish-Hickey State Park Recreational Area. Everything for the cyclist—hiker-biker campsite, hot showers, a lake for swimming, and trails for hiking. Groceries are available at the small store and deli across U.S. 101, or 1 mile south in Leggett.

Standish-Hickey State Park Recreation Area to MacKerricher Beach State Park (40.7 Miles)

Just south of Standish–Hickey State Park Recreation Area, the route turns off U.S. 101 to follow California's famous Highway 1 back to the coast. The road starts out by climbing over the much-maligned Leggett Hill, which, at nearly 2,000 feet, is the highest point on the Pacific Coast Bike Route. Cyclists talk about Leggett Hill up and down the coast, increasing its proportions as they go. Contrary to popular rumor, abandoned touring bags do not line the road, nor are there graves of cyclists who did not make it. Although long, Leggett Hill is by no means the steepest climb on the coast.

From the summit of Leggett Hill, gaze out over miles of forested

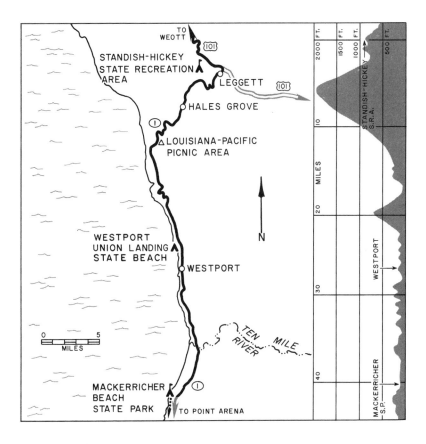

Leggett Hill

hills and deep valleys. Spot U.S. 101 rushing south towards San Francisco. To the west lies the Pacific Ocean, sometimes shimmering but frequently shrouded in a thick cover of fog.

The descent from Leggett Hill is exhilarating and much too short. The road almost reaches sea level before beginning another steep climb over 690-foot Rockport Hill. The descent of this second hill leads to the ocean and stunning viewpoints over a rocky coastline studded with offshore sea stacks.

The day ends at MacKerricher Beach State Park, an interesting place to explore. On the beach check out the fascinating tide pools, or watch the harbor seals sunbathing on offshore rocks. A small lake is excellent for swimming, and an abandoned log-haul route provides a scenic access to the grocery stores and restaurants of Fort Bragg.

Standish–Hickey State Park Recreation Area` to MacKerricher Beach State Park is a section of changes. When the coast bike route leaves U.S. 101, it also leaves behind the drier inland climate, where temperatures average from 80 to 100 degrees in the summer. (On the coast, temperatures average between 50 and 60 degrees.) Vegetation changes from forest to windswept grasslands. Once U.S. 101 is left behind, the amount of commercial traffic reduces dramatically. The only thing that does not change is the quality of the road; it remains winding with little or no shoulder.

Riding on narrow, winding roads is hazardous. It's important to stay in single file and to the right side of the road. Never climb by switchbacking. Wear bright clothing and be conscious of the motorists coming up from behind.

Between Standish–Hickey State Park Recreation Area and MacKerricher Beach State Park stores and restaurants are few, so plan food stops ahead. Small grocery stores may be found in Leggett, Westport, and just before MacKerricher Beach State Park.

MILEAGE LOG

0.0 (mp 93.87) Leave Standish–Hickey State Park Recreation Area on U.S. 101. The two-lane highway is narrow with a variable shoulder of up to two feet. Terrain is rolling, mountainous, and dry.

1.5 (mp 91.20 and mp 105.21) Exit U.S. 101 onto Highway 1.

1.6 (mp 105.11) Leggett; the grocery store is located 0.1 mile left (south) on Drive Through Tree Rd.; 0.2 mile south on the same road is the Drive Through Tree. Admission is charged. After Leggett, Highway 1 descends rapidly 0.3 mile to cross the South Fork of the Eel River.

2.1 (mp 104.61) The ascent of Leggett Hill begins at 1,100 feet.

5.6 (mp 101.10) Leggett Hill summit, elevation 1,950 feet, with views out over miles of forest to the Pacific Ocean. The descent begins with a nearly level 0.8-mile traverse, then the road drops steeply, winding through heavy forest.

9.4 (mp 97.32) Hales Grove. The road levels for a mile, then resumes its descent.

15.2 (mp 90.87) Highway 1 takes the name of the Shoreline Highway as it heads south.

15.4 (mp 90.60) Cottoneva Creek marks the end of Leggett Hill.

17.0 (mp 88.95) Louisiana–Pacific picnic area; tables, restrooms, and a small demonstration forest with a short nature walk.

18.2 (mp 87.85) Recross Cottoneva Creek and pass through the abandoned community of Rockport, hidden in the forest at the base of Rockport Hill. Beyond the creek, the road climbs steeply. Pavement is narrow, and the road winds through dark forest. Expect some logging traffic from Rockport Hill south to Fort Bragg.

20.2 (mp 85.88) Summit of Rockport Hill, elevation 690 feet. No views or turnouts, just a wonderful descent down this narrow, winding road.

22.1 (mp 83.79) Cross Hardy Creek, marking the end of Rockport Hill.

23.9 (mp 81.05) Small gravel turnout, the first of many spectacular vantage points overlooking the Pacific Ocean. Sea stacks, arch rocks, nesting birds, and barking seals may be seen and heard. Shortly after returning to the coast, the road broadens to include a two- to three-foot shoulder.

24.3 (mp 80.70) Westport Union Landing State Beach and vista point; restrooms, picnic tables, ocean views, camping, and water (not potable). The state beach parallels the highway for the next mile.

26.1 (mp 78.85) Shoulder ends, marking the start of a 16-mile section of narrow, winding road. On foggy or rainy days, wear bright clothing and use blinking lights to increase your visibility.

27.3 (mp 77.71) Westport, a small coast town with grocery store and restaurant. Beyond town, Highway 1 traverses grassy hillsides that overlook the ocean. The highway remains shoulderless as the hills give way to steep cliffs. The route continues to cling to the scenic coastline, exposed to the wind and elements, occasionally dipping into small coves and then climbing steeply back up to the open cliffs.

35.1 (mp 69.9) Ten Mile River Bridge and a 0.5-mile section of good shoulder.

40.4 (mp 64.87) Two small grocery stores, the last before MacKerricher Beach State Park and Fort Bragg.

40.7 (mp 64.57) MacKerricher Beach State Park; hiker-biker site, running water, and hot showers. From December through April, this is an excellent place to watch the migrating gray whales. Large grocery stores are available 2.7 miles south in Fort Bragg, which is reached by a scenic ride along the coast. Ride down to the lake and beach. Follow the road through an underpass, then take an immediate right up a dirt access road to the paved haul road (abandoned). At the third gate, leave the haul road and return to Highway 1 to cross Pudding Creek and enter Fort Bragg.

MacKerricher Beach State Park to Manchester State Beach (41.8 Miles)

The day starts with a ride through Fort Bragg, a lumber town whose main attraction is the famous Skunk Railroad. This charming railroad winds its way east to the inland town of Willits, through farmlands and redwood country that can only be seen from its tracks. Its not-so-charming name is due to the smell of the original engines. If you have some extra time, a ride on the Skunk Railroad is a great way to see the countryside.

Fort Bragg also has a large logging museum, tree nursery, and Noyo Harbor, the largest working harbor between Eureka and San Francisco. During the 4th of July weekend, the harbor is home of the world's largest salmon barbecue.

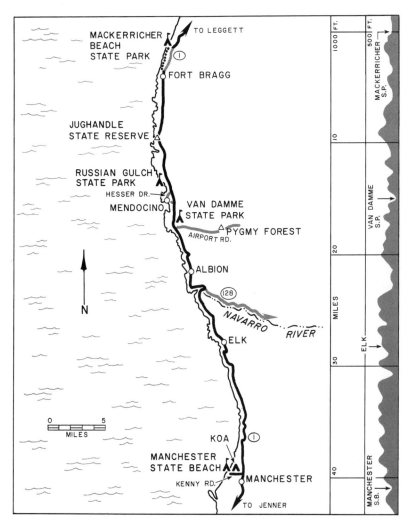

A few miles south at Jughandle State Reserve, you can study a half-million years of the earth's history by walking a nature trail up an ecological staircase with five distinct terraces, each about 100 feet higher and 100,000 years older than the last. From the ocean's edge, the nature trail heads inland through changing vegetation, starting with north coastal prairie, moving into coast redwood and Douglas fir forests, and ending near a pygmy forest. The entire 500,000 years is covered in a 5-mile round trip. A shorter 0.5-mile loop covers the most recent history—about 100,000 years worth.

The route passes Mendocino, which is perched on a cliff over-

Rugged coast north of Elk

looking the Pacific Ocean. The town has the architecture and charm of a New England village. Very little seems to have changed since it was founded in 1852.

Russian Gulch and Van Damme state parks south of Fort Bragg offer camping with hiker-biker sites, trails to a couple of waterfalls at Russian Gulch, and a pygmy forest at Van Damme. The pygmy forest, where 60-year-old trees are barely knee-high, can also be reached by bicycle.

This is a scenic ride along the broken coastline. The ride is short but physically demanding as the road climbs in and out of numerous narrow canyons. Many portions of the road are without shoulders. Traffic is generally light, except on midsummer weekends.

MILEAGE LOG

0.0 (mp 64.87) Leaving MacKerricher Beach State Park, do not return to Highway 1. Instead, descend towards the beach, past the small lake. Cycle under an overpass, then immediately turn left and head up a gravel access road which leads to an old logging haul road. Go straight ahead on the haul route past two gates. The road is rough, but the views are excellent as you parallel the coast for the next 2 miles.

2.7 (mp 62.12) At the third gate, go left, back to Highway 1, and descend to cross Pudding Creek and enter Fort Bragg. The large lumber mill located in town explains the thundering truck traffic. The largest attraction in Fort Bragg is the Skunk Railroad. Ride the open railway cars of this steam-billowing train one-half or a whole day. For rates and schedules, turn right (west) on Laurel St. to the station. The redwood museum (free) is adjacent to the Skunk Railroad. A large supermarket and well-stocked bike shop are located at the southern end of town, one block left (east) of Highway 1.

4.3 (mp 60.48) Noyo Harbor; to the left (east) of Highway 1.

5.8 (mp 59.08) Mendocino Coast Botanical Gardens. For a fee, you may walk down paths lined with rhododendrons and through a fern canyon.

8.1 (mp 56.65) Jughandle State Reserve; restrooms, picnic tables, beach access, and nature trail through the ecological staircase. Hard to spot from the road; the reserve is located south of the Highway 20 junction and just north of the Caspar exit.

9.2 (mp 55.5) Vista point with coastal view and Caspar Creek Bridge. This bridge, like most others on Highway 1, has no shoulder.

11.1 (mp 53.6) Russian Gulch State Park; hiker-biker sites and hot showers. A 2.5-mile bicycle path up the narrow gulch leads to a 1.5-mile loop hiking trail to the Russian Gulch Falls.

12.1 (mp 51.50) Mendocino State Park exit and start of a scenic *ALTERNATE ROUTE* along the ocean's edge through the state park and the tourist town of Mendocino. Exit Highway 1, then turn right in 0.5 mile on Hesser Dr. for a quiet ride along the rocky cliffs. The wide-open state park makes a nice lunch stop; watch for seals bobbing in the surf. Continue to follow the coastline back to Highway 1, through the quaint New England town of Mendocino with its grocery stores, delis, bakeries, craft shops, art galleries, and book stores.

13.0 (mp 50.6) Mendocino State Park scenic alternate route rejoins Highway 1.

13.2 (mp 50.37) Big River State Beach; beach access only.

13.7 (mp 49.84) Vista point. This is the best place to savor the New England flavor of Mendocino.

15.2 (mp 48.34) Town of Little River; grocery stores.

15.5 (mp 48.05) Van Damme Beach State Park; hiker-biker sites, water, beach access, and trail to a fern canyon and pygmy forest. (The forest may also be reached by road as described below.) To reach the park, you must make a left (east) turn across Highway 1.

16.0 (mp 48.55) Highway 1 becomes narrow and winding;

shoulders are also narrow, occasionally disappearing altogether. *SIDE TRIP* to pygmy forest. Exit left (east) off Highway 1 on Airport Rd. A moderately steep climb of 2.7 miles leads to a nature loop, located on the left (north) side of the road.

19.3 (mp 44.07) Albion; last grocery stores for 10 miles. Highway 1 heads through open coastal grasslands. At about 22 miles, the route descends steeply, with some tight corners, along the canyon walls of the Navarro River.

23.1 (mp 40.29) Intersection of Highway 1 and Highway 128. Turn right on Highway 1 and cross the Navarro River (Highway 128 heads east to Cloverdale and U.S. 101). Shift to your lowest gear and wish for a lower one. The mile-long ascent out of the river valley is steep and hot. A sign along the road reading NARROW WINDING ROAD FOR THE NEXT 21 MILES indicates the conditions ahead.

28.7 (34.15) Enter the town of Elk, the last chance to pick up groceries before Manchester State Beach. Beyond Elk, the road descends to cross a small creek, then climbs back up with a series of tight, steep switchbacks. Take heart; this short climb is probably the steepest on the entire Pacific coast.

37.3 (mp 25.32) Vista point with ocean views.

41.1 (mp 21.4) Manchester State Beach turnoff. Follow Kenny Rd. right (west) past a private campground with hot tub, swimming pool, and hot showers.

41.8 Manchester State Beach; hiker-biker camp, water, 4.5 miles of beach, and views of the ocean and Point Arena Lighthouse from the windswept bluff. No showers. Nearest grocery store is in Manchester, 1 mile south on Highway 1.

Manchester State Beach to Bodega Dunes State Beach (65.4 Miles)

Rolling, grassy hills, miles of wooden fences, surf-battered cliffs, sheltered coves, and a wide array of weathered sea stacks provide an awe-inspiring backdrop for the ride between Manchester State Beach and Bodega Dunes State Beach.

And, as if the scenery weren't enough of a distraction, the Salt Point State Park provides numerous access points to isolated beaches. One of the highlights of the state park is the Kruse Rhododendron Reserve, which lures riders off their bikes for

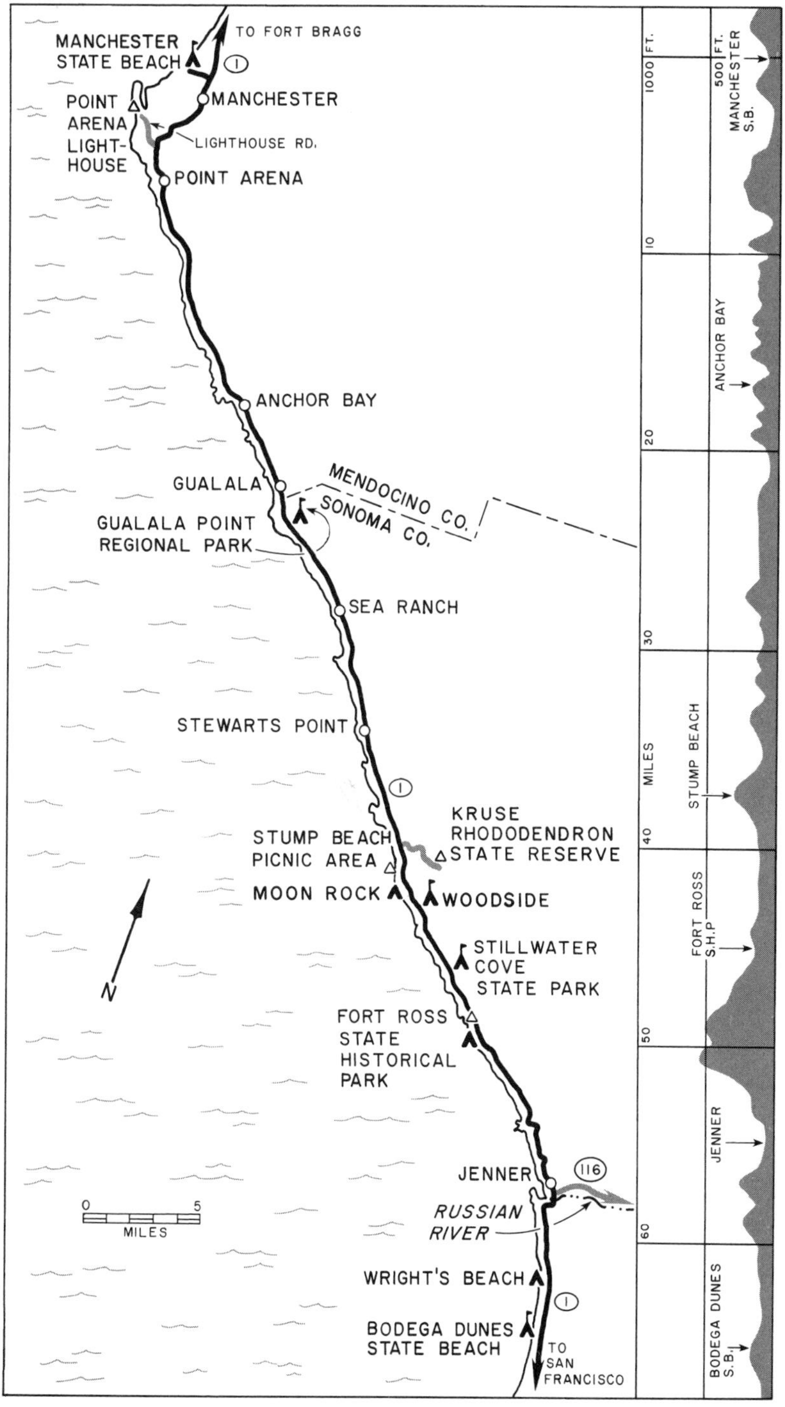

MANCHESTER
STATE BEACH

TO FORT BRAGG

①

MANCHESTER

POINT
ARENA
LIGHT-
HOUSE

LIGHTHOUSE RD.

POINT ARENA

ANCHOR BAY

GUALALA

MENDOCINO CO.

SONOMA CO.

GUALALA POINT
REGIONAL PARK

SEA RANCH

STEWARTS POINT

①

KRUSE
RHODODENDRON
STATE RESERVE

STUMP BEACH
PICNIC AREA

MOON ROCK

WOODSIDE

STILLWATER
COVE
STATE PARK

FORT ROSS
STATE
HISTORICAL
PARK

JENNER

⑪⑥

*RUSSIAN
RIVER*

WRIGHT'S BEACH

①

BODEGA DUNES
STATE BEACH

TO
SAN
FRANCISCO

N

0   5
MILES

1000 FT.

10

20

30

MILES

40

50

60

500 FT.
MANCHESTER
S.B.

ANCHOR BAY

STUMP BEACH

FORT ROSS
S.H.P

JENNER

BODEGA DUNES
S.B.

quiet walks through fern canyons, tall timber, and in the spring, beautiful, flowering rhododendron trees. Farther south, bikes will again be set aside for a long, leisurely tour of Fort Ross Historical Park. This small park provides an interesting glimpse into a little-known part of American history. The fort was built and occupied by Russians and Eskimos, sent from Alaska to grow grain to support the Russian settlements located there. The fort has been reconstructed with displays depicting its history. The visitor center provides a slide show and historical notes describing the fate of these pioneers. Picnic tables, restrooms, and a nearly constant stream of skin divers in and out of the bay below the fort, are an additional reason to linger.

The day ends at Bodega Dunes State Park. This is a large park set on Bodega Bay, at the edge of the sand dunes. Hours can be spent here, wandering through the dunes.

The ride from Manchester State Beach to Bodega Dunes State Beach is long and demanding. The road is narrow, winding, and steep. Traffic is light, except on summer weekends. The most serious hazards of this section are the sheep and cattle which wander on and off the roadway.

Cattle guards add a challenge to the 5-mile section from Fort Ross south. It is best to approach the guards straight on, at a moderate pace. Some riders prefer to walk across when the cattle guards are wet and slippery but this is not always necessary.

If you find you would like to linger in this section, do so. Numerous campgrounds dot the coast in this area, making it easy to stop and explore. Beyond Bodega Dunes, campgrounds are few and far between, and the pace becomes hectic as the route heads into the Bay Area.

MILEAGE LOG

0.0 From Manchester State Beach, go left on Kenny Rd., returning to Highway 1.

0.6 (mp 21.40) Head right (south) on Highway 1.

1.0 (mp 20.90) Manchester city limits; two grocery stores. Beyond Manchester, the road continues to be steep and narrow. Sheep and cows graze on the open, grassy hills, and occasionally wander out onto the road.

4.8 (mp 17.00) Pass a commercial campground. *SIDE TRIP* to Point Arena Lighthouse and museum. The lighthouse, located 2.3 miles out on the lighthouse road, has a distinctive, tall, slender tower visible for many miles along the coast. The lighthouse is now a museum and open to the public from 11:00 A.M. to 2:30 P.M. on weekdays and 10:00 A.M. to 3:30 P.M. on weekends. Admission is charged. Even if you don't go inside, the ride is rewardingly scenic. Once at the lighthouse, you are standing at the closest point on the West Coast to Hawaii.

5.6 (mp 16.20) Point Arena; complete tourist facilities, including grocery stores.

6.5 (mp 15.30) Coastal access, no facilities. Highway 1 parallels the coast with occasional views.

16.4 (mp 4.70) Anchor Bay, a minute-sized town with a small all-purpose grocery, private campground, and restaurant.

19.5 (mp 1.31) Gualala; many amenities dear to the heart of a touring cyclist—grocery stores, delis, restaurants, ice creameries, and motels. Watch out, or you may ride completely through this town while trying to figure out how to pronounce it.

20.9 (mp 0.00 and 58.68) Leave Mendocino County, enter Sonoma County at Gualala River Bridge.

21.3 (mp 58.20) Gualala Point Regional Park. The campground is on the east side of Highway 1; hiker-biker area, running

Crossing a cattle guard near Fort Ross State Historical Park

water, no showers. The day-use area on the west side of Highway 1 has a visitor center with restrooms, running water, and beach access. A small wind turbine near the visitor center provides electricity for the park. Past the park, Highway 1 enters Sea Ranch, a long rambling community of expensive beach houses. The area is generally quiet all week until Friday afternoon, when there is a mass migration up from the San Francisco Bay Area. On Sunday afternoon, the process is reversed as everyone dashes south. All roads through Sea Ranch are private. The state park system has set up four coastal access points where you can leave your bike and walk to the beach; restrooms but no water.

29.6 (mp 49.54) Leave Sea Ranch and return to the undeveloped cow- and sheep-dotted landscapes.

31.2 (mp 48.1) Stewarts Point; a small tourist-oriented community. The grocery store is open daily from 8 A.M. to 6 P.M. Beyond Stewarts Point, the road remains narrow, winding, and steep, with several short, tantalizing sections of shoulder. After several miles, the road enters Salt Point State Park.

36.2 (mp 42.75) *SIDE TRIP* to Kruse Rhododendron State Reserve. Turn left (east) off Highway 1 and cycle up Kruse Ranch Rd. to the end of the pavement and an intersection. Walk or ride the right fork 0.4 mile to the reserve. Trails vary from 0.2 mile to 5 miles in length.

36.3 (mp 42.63) Fisk Cove; restrooms, beach access, and picnic tables.

37.7 (mp 41.22) Stump Beach picnic area; restrooms and access to a sandy cove. No running water.

38.9 (mp 39.90) Moon Rock Campground; campsites, beach access, and running water. Hiker-biker site is located 50 feet south on the left side of the road at Woodside Campground.

39.0 (mp 39.89) Woodside Campground; hiker-biker site, water, and many miles of trails to the beach, along the bluffs, up the hills to vista points, and to a pygmy forest behind the park. No showers.

40.7 (mp 38.2) Ocean Cove; a tourist community with a very small grocery store.

41.6 (mp 37.02) Stillwater Cove State Park, a small park popular for skin diving; hiker-biker site, hot and cold running water, and beach access. No showers.

44.8 (mp 32.63) Fort Ross store; limited groceries.

45.3 (mp 32.10) The first of eight cattle crossings found in the next 5 miles.

45.4 (mp 32.00) Fort Ross State Historical Park; an old fort, visitor center, slide show, historical displays, restrooms, water, picnic facilities, and a grassy bluff for strolling. Fort Ross marks the start of 10 strenuous and scenic miles as Highway 1 winds steeply over headlands and drops sharply into deep coves.

46.1 (mp 31.37) Campground. A new facility, with restrooms only, as of 1988.

51.6 (mp 26.19) Long, moderate ascent leads to the top of a 520-foot hill and the end of the cattle guards. Highway 1 sweeps back to sea level in a long switchback descent.

53.1 (mp 24.40) Russian Gulch Bridge. The end of the descent and the start of another steep, though lesser, climb.

55.6 (mp 21.9) Jenner, a small town perched on a steep hillside overlooking the Russian River and a long sandspit. Groceries may be purchased at the gas station on the left side of the road; Jenner visitor center is located across Highway 1.

57.3 (mp 20.9) Junction of Highway 1 and Highway 116. Highway 1 continues south, while Highway 116 heads east to California's famous wine country.

57.4 (mp 20.00) Cross Russian River on a very narrow bridge. The grocery store on the south side of the river is the last before Bodega Dunes State Beach. There is a private campground here.

58.3 (mp 18.6) Turnoff to Goat Rock State Beach, the first of a series of Sonoma Coast state beaches spanning the coast from Russian River to Bodega Head. Goat Rock State Beach has two access roads. The first access descends 0.8 mile, the second is a steep 2-mile descent. Restrooms and water at both access points.

59.2 (mp 18.2) Shell Beach; tide pool exploration and surf fishing. No facilities.

60.6 (mp 16.77) Wright's Beach, a small recreational vehicle campground; restrooms and running water. No showers or hiker-biker sites.

61.1 (mp 16.35) Duncan's Landing Beach, famous as a loading area for old coastal ships and for its rocky headland, which earned the name of Death Rock among sailors.

62.7' (mp 14.68) Portugese Beach, a popular day-use area. No facilities.

63.0 (mp 14.33) Schoolhouse Beach; restrooms and tide pools to explore.

64.4 (mp 12.90) North Salmon Beach; sandy beaches, surf fishing, and restrooms. The road in this section is lined with ice plant.

65.4 (mp 11.67) Bodega Dunes State Beach campground; hot showers, restrooms, and a sandy hiker-biker area. A hiking trail through the dunes leads to a sandy beach. The nearest grocery store is 1.2 miles south in Bodega Bay.

Bodega Dunes State Beach to Samuel P. Taylor State Park (40.6 Miles)

Several large bays interrupting the coastline south of Bodega Bay to San Francisco are bypassed by heading inland over rolling hills. After avoiding the first bay, Estero Americano, the route skirts along the edge of Tomales Bay, then turns inland again, this time to skirt the Marin Headlands, heading towards San Francisco Bay.

The main attraction on this section of the coast is the Point Reyes National Seashore, a beautiful 64,000-acre park with over 70 miles of coastline. The park is divided from the mainland by the San Andreas Fault and Tomales Bay, and left in its natural state to

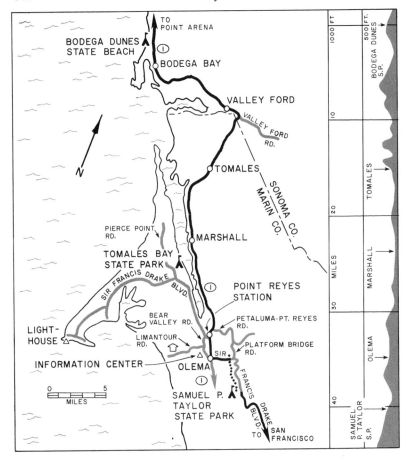

protect the habitat of the several hundreds of species of birds and seventy kinds of mammals that live there. Trails are the only access to many of the beaches, sand dunes, and lakes. Easily accessible to the cyclist are the visitor center with displays, slide show and film of the area, a special nature trail exploring the rift area of the San Andreas Fault, and an authentic replica of a native Indian village. Several days can be spent exploring this area, hiking the trails, and riding the paved roads to the lighthouse and seashore. Camping is permitted at a hiker-biker site in Tomales State Park (adjoining the national seashore) or a youth hostel in the park. If touring on a mountain bike, you can take advantage of the park's backcountry campsite system, accessed by well-maintained, double-track trails.

Beyond Tomales Bay, the route turns off Highway 1 and heads inland to the San Francisco Bay Area. Although Highway 1 appears tempting on the map, it's considered extremely hazardous south of Olema—narrow, winding, shoulderless, and busy.

Inland from coast breezes, the temperatures rise–quite a surprise, especially to those with empty water bottles. But that is not the end of the surprises; once past the first set of hot, dry hills, the route abandons the road in favor of a well-shaded bicycle path through the redwoods, ending at Samuel P. Taylor State Park.

Samuel P. Taylor State Park was one of the first areas in the United States where outdoor camping was promoted as a recreational pursuit. Trails lead to a fire lookout and to the foundations of a paper mill, where the first square-bottomed paper bags were made in the late 1800s.

If there is enough time in the day and energy in the legs, pass up Samuel P. Taylor State Park in favor of a fantastic campsite 30 miles south at Marin Headlands National Recreation Area. This extraordinary hiker-biker site has a stunning view of San Francisco and the Golden Gate Bridge. Space is limited and advance reservations are required, so call ahead to the visitor center from the state park (415-331-1540). (If you are certain of your plans, call several days ahead.)

To reach Marin Headlands National Recreation Area, it is necessary to negotiate a fair amount of city traffic, a very slow process, and a long, steep hill at the final approach to the park. See the next chapter for details.

MILEAGE LOG

0.0 From Bodega Dunes State Beach, head south on Highway 1.

0.3 (mp 11.37) Fast-food haven next to the campground, an excellent spot to fill those empty stomachs.

1.2 (mp 10.47) Town of Bodega Bay has adequate facilities to feed the hungriest cyclist, as well as motels, restaurants, grocery store, and a laundromat. From the center of town, look across Bodega Harbor to the large fishing fleet. Keep an eye out for brown pelicans and other aquatic life. Beyond Bodega Bay, the shoulders are excellent as Highway 1 heads inland, climbing over grass-covered hills.

9.4 (mp 2.10) Valley Ford; grocery stores, restaurants. Shoulders end here.

11.3 (mp 0.20) Junction of Highway 1 and Valley Ford Rd. Turn right (south) on Highway 1. The Valley Ford Rd. heads inland to Petaluma and U.S. 101.

11.5 (mp 0.0 and 50.5) Leave Sonoma County and enter Marin County. The terrain is open as the highway rolls over short, steep hills. Shoulders are narrow and infrequent, traffic light to moderate. Cattle ranches appear. Redwood groves give way to groves of eucalyptus trees.

15.9 (mp 46.00) Tomales; limited groceries, a few bed-and-breakfast houses. Leaving town, Highway 1 descends, twisting with little shoulder, to parallel Tomales Bay for the next 19 miles.

23.2 (mp 38.41) Marshall; restaurants and a grocery store.

28.2 (mp 33.65) Coastal access; parking lot, restrooms, and bay access.

32.4 (mp 29.28) Junction of two possible routes. The suggested route turns right and follows Highway 1 towards Point Reyes Station, past two grocery stores and the turnoff to Point Reyes National Seashore. *ALTERNATE ROUTE* uses back roads to bypass some hills. To follow this route, go left (east) on the Petaluma–Point Reyes Rd. for 3 miles. At the stop sign, turn right on Platform Bridge Rd. for 2.5 miles, then go right (uphill) on Sir Francis Drake Blvd. for 50 feet. Go right again on the bike path, rejoining the main route. This alternate route is recommended by the California Bicentennial; however, mileage for the two routes is about the same, and it bypasses Point Reyes National Seashore.

32.7 (mp 28.94) First turnoff to Point Reyes National Seashore; do not turn here.

32.9 (mp 28.77) Point Reyes Station; purchase groceries for the night here. This small town has numerous restaurants and coffee shops.

34.7 (mp 26.95) Turnoff for Point Reyes National Seashore. (For side trip details, see end of this mileage log.)

34.9 (mp 26.76) Olema; limited groceries. Turn left (east) off Highway 1 and cycle up Sir Francis Drake Blvd. The road climbs over a steep hill, then descends into a narrow valley.

37.1 (mp 20.54) Just before crossing a short bridge over Lagunitas Creek, go left on the Marin Bicycle Trail. Descend on an

San Andreas Fault line in Point Reyes National Seashore

abandoned road, then go right on the paved bicycle trail. The trail follows an abandoned railroad grade, crossing under Sir Francis Drake Blvd. The road heads up the east side of the Lagunitas Creek Valley; the bicycle trail heads up the west side.

38.5 Jewell Trail branches off to the right. Continue straight, paralleling the creek into the state park.

40.6 Cycle through the camp area to an intersection. Go right, crossing the creek to reach the entrance booth for Samuel P. Taylor State Park and register; hiker-biker site and hot showers, under the deep shade of the redwood forest.

Point Reyes National Seashore Side Trip

Turn right (west) on Bear Valley Rd. At 0.5 mile, go left to the information center for a park map, movie, slide show, restrooms, water, picnic tables, San Andreas Fault Trail, trails to the Indian village and the beach, and backcountry campsite reservations. To reach the hostel, it is necessary to ride up Limantour Rd. (2.1 miles north of the information center), gaining 1,400 feet before descending back to sea level. The hiker-biker campsite at Tomales State Park is a pleasant place to stay, and very easy to reach. Cycle north from the information center on Bear Valley Rd., which merges with Sir Francis Drake Blvd. At 8.2 miles, go right (north) on Pierce Point Rd. for 1 mile to the park. Follow the signs to the hiker-biker site (the only camping allowed in the park). If you ride the entire 21.1 miles to the end of Sir Francis Drake Blvd. you'll reach the famous Point Reyes Lighthouse. Visitors must descend 300 steps to the light and an impressive view of the surrounding coast, including sea lions on the offshore rocks.

Samuel P. Taylor State Park to Half Moon Bay State Beach (56.7 Miles)

Between Samuel P. Taylor State Park and Half Moon Bay State Beach sprawls San Francisco and a dozen satellite cities of the Bay Area. This is the first major urban center on the Pacific Coast Bike Route since Vancouver, British Columbia. If your bike is experiencing any mechanical problems, this is the time to take care of them.

The San Francisco Bay area is excellent for cycling, if taken at a leisurely pace. Bike paths crisscross the cities, connecting parks, viewpoints, and beaches. However, if you are planning to cross this large metropolitan area in a single day, you'll have little time for exploration. Winding through city streets, stopping for lights and stop signs makes for slow going, requiring any number of extra hours.

The route through the Bay Area is delineated by green and white bike-route signs and a rare Bicentennial marker. Some people find it easiest to buy a city street map, and trace the route on it before starting. Another helpful idea is to make a copy of the mileage log and keep it handy.

Roads are busy and sections of the route hazardous. Some directions suggested differ from the Caltrans Bicentennial Route in order to avoid dangerous stretches.

The route through San Francisco is very scenic, with views over San Francisco Bay to Alcatraz, a ride across the Golden Gate Bridge, residential areas, the Pacific beaches, and Devil's Slide. Close to but not on the route are the famous Marin Headlands, Fort Point, and Golden Gate Park. Marin Headlands is a national recreation area with a magnificent view of San Francisco, Golden Gate Bridge, Fort Point, and the Pacific Ocean. Fort Point is a classic brick fortress that was outdated almost before it was completed in 1861. The Golden Gate Park is a beautiful island of green in the middle of San Francisco with lakes, botanical and Japanese gardens, a buffalo paddock, museums, the Academy of Science, and quiet groves of trees.

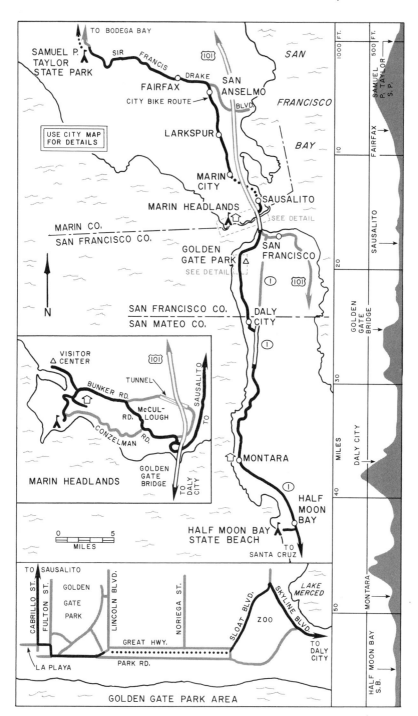

TO BODEGA BAY

SAMUEL P.
TAYLOR
STATE PARK

SIR FRANCIS

DRAKE

FAIRFAX

SAN
ANSELMO

CITY BIKE ROUTE

BLVD.

101

SAN

FRANCISCO

BAY

LARKSPUR

USE CITY MAP
FOR DETAILS

MARIN
CITY

MARIN HEADLANDS

SAUSALITO

SEE DETAIL

MARIN CO.
SAN FRANCISCO CO.

N

GOLDEN
GATE PARK

SEE DETAIL

SAN
FRANCISCO

1 101

SAN FRANCISCO CO.
SAN MATEO CO.

DALY
CITY

1

VISITOR
△ CENTER

101

TUNNEL

BUNKER RD.

McCUL-
LOUGH
RD.

RD.

TO SAUSALITO

CONZELMAN RD.

MARIN HEADLANDS

GOLDEN
GATE
BRIDGE

TO
DALY
CITY

MONTARA

HALF
MOON
BAY

0   5
MILES

HALF MOON BAY
STATE BEACH

TO
SANTA CRUZ

TO SAUSALITO

CABRILLO ST.

FULTON ST.

GOLDEN
GATE
PARK

LINCOLN BLVD.

NORIEGA ST.

SLOAT BLVD.

ZOO

SKYLINE BLVD.

LAKE
MERCED

GREAT HWY.

PARK RD.

TO DALY
CITY

LA PLAYA

GOLDEN GATE PARK AREA

FT. FT.
1000 500

SAMUEL
P. TAYLOR S. P.

FAIRFAX

10

SAUSALITO

20

GOLDEN
GATE
BRIDGE

30

DALY CITY

MILES

40

MONTARA

50

HALF MOON BAY
S.B.

Cyclists spending time in San Francisco can stay at any number of places in or near the city—on the Marin Headlands (hiker-biker campsites and a 300 person hostel), in San Francisco at the International Hostel (east of the Golden Gate Bridge), or at the Montara Lighthouse Hostel (20 miles south of San Francisco and on a main bus route to town). Reservations are necessary for all of these facilities during summer months.

If planning to end your ride down the coast at San Francisco, check at the end of the mileage log for routes to the airport and railway station. Plot the routes out on a detailed city map before you head into town.

Highway 1 is prone to sliding in the Devil's Slide Headland area, south of San Francisco. Plan to arrive in this area early enough to handle any detour, or check road conditions by calling the San Francisco branch of Caltrans (California Transit) while in the Bay Area.

MILEAGE LOG

0.0 Leave Samuel P. Taylor State Park, heading southeast on Sir Francis Drake Blvd. The road has no shoulders and is narrow, winding, shaded by dense foliage, and full of potholes.

0.5 Pass day-use area for the state park.

1.7 Leave Samuel P. Taylor State Park.

2.5 Lagunitas, a small town with a grocery store.

3.1 Forest Knolls, a sprawling residential community with a small store. The road widens to include a shoulder and remains good for the next 5 miles. Use caution, however, as you descend the steep hill into Fairfax; large water drains make riding on the shoulder hazardous.

8.3 Fairfax, the first of a long string of Bay Area cities, it will be 35 miles before you're off city streets.

9.4 Turn right on Broadway Blvd. The turnoff is easy to miss, so watch for a stucco church with a bell tower on the left (east) and Fairfax regional library on the right, just before the turn.

10.2 Jog right on Lansdale.

10.5 Jog to the right again on San Anselmo Ave., following bike-route signs through the quiet residential streets.

11.1 Go left on Hazel Ave., which makes a sharp bend then parallels Center Blvd.

11.3 Intersection; go right, back to San Anselmo Ave.

11.8 At the end of San Anselmo Ave., go left on Bolinas Ave.

11.9 Turn right, returning to Sir Francis Drake Blvd. for 1.2 miles. This is a busy, shoulderless road; be sure you are visible.

13.1 Go right at College Ave. Follow it as it turns into Magnolia

Ave. at the Larkspur city limits. Note Mount Tamalpais, the birthplace of mountain biking.

15.7 Turn left down Redwood Ave., a major thoroughfare. After one block, Redwood Ave. bends sharply right, leading into Tamalpais Dr. Continue straight for 0.5 mile.

16.3 At the second to the last stoplight before the U.S. 101 freeway entrance, take a right on Casa Buena Dr. Climb a steep hill while paralleling U.S. 101.

17.3 At the top of the second of two steep rises, the road bends sharply uphill. Go straight ahead on an unmarked bike path, paralleling the freeway.

17.7 The bike path ends on Lomita Dr. Follow Lomita Dr. as it bends to the right, and stay with it until reaching an old elementary school (in 1988 used as a small business center).

18.2 When Lomita Dr. bends left, go straight ahead on a narrow bike path. In 200 feet, turn left on a wide bikeway.

18.7 Bikeway crosses Blithedale Ave. Continue straight. Follow the bikeway over a marsh, past a small lagoon, under U.S. 101, and then along the boat harbor.

21.0 Bikeway ends (this is a confusing area; if you suddenly find yourself on a sidewalk, go back to the last intersection). Cross Bridgeway (a busy four-laner). Stay on Bridgeway until it ends.

23.4 At the end of Bridgeway, turn right and pedal up Richardson St. At the first intersection, turn left on 2nd St. and follow it through a congested area of small shops, then up a steep hill.

23.6 As 2nd St. ends, turn left on South St.

23.7 South St. bends right and becomes S. Alexander Ave.

23.8 Descend right off S. Alexander Ave. on a freeway-type exit, crossing under the street to emerge on East Rd. East Rd. enters an Army Reserve Center that must be passed through before 7:00 P.M. Views extend over the bay to San Francisco and the bay islands, including Alcatraz. Follow the shoreline road and then pedal up an extremely steep hill under the Golden Gate Bridge.

25.3 There are two entrances to the bridge. The first branches off East Rd. near the top, and crosses the bridge on the west side. This entrance is open weekends only. To use the other (weekday) entrance, cycle up to Conzelman Rd. Turn right and ride through a large parking lot, then use the pedestrian underpass to cross to the opposite side of U.S. 101 and the Golden Gate Vista Point, where there are restrooms and water to go with the view. (The underpass is very difficult, with steep ramps. You may have to unload here and take two trips, or find another touring cyclist to help push you up the ramp.) Head across the Golden Gate Bridge on the bike lane,

Residential area of San Francisco near Golden Gate Park

taking time to enjoy this classic bridge, beautiful in sun, fog, or smog. The Marin Headlands National Recreation Area side trip starts near the Golden Gate Bridge. For details, see the end of this mileage log.

25.7 Leave Marin County, enter San Francisco County.

27.3 Southern end of the Golden Gate Bridge; if you cross on a weekday, bypass the city bike-route sign and take the first road (narrow) on the left. Follow this road as it bends to the right, cycle under U.S. 101, and go right, following a bicycle route through a large paved area on Merchant Rd. If you cross on a weekend, follow the bike-route signs to Merchant Rd., joining the weekday route. Follow the bike-route signs along Merchant Rd. to intercept Lincoln Blvd. *SIDE TRIP* to Fort Point. Go the east side of U.S. 101 and ride out to Lincoln Blvd., then go left (east) for 0.5 mile to the fort access road. The fort has been turned into a museum, open to the public.

27.7 Turn right on Lincoln Blvd.

28.5 Bakers State Beach turnoff; restrooms, picnic tables, water, and a sandy beach.

29.0 Lincoln Blvd. becomes Camino Del Mar. Continue straight for three more blocks.

29.2 Turn left on 28th Ave. and ride through the densely built and beautifully maintained residential San Francisco.

30.1 Go right at Cabrillo St. (If you are heading for the Amtrak station, check the directions at the end of this log.)

31.2 Take a left on La Playa at the end of Cabrillo St. In one block, turn right on Fulton St., followed by a left on the busy Great Highway. On the left is Golden Gate Park, distinguished by two windmills facing the Pacific Ocean. The park is an excellent side trip and lunch stop.

31.6 Start of Oceanfront Promenade bike path, which parallels Park Rd. (In 1988 the bike path on southbound side was not complete. Watch for construction and detour signs.)

33.9 Bike path ends (as of 1988). Cross Park Rd. and cycle left (east) up Sloat Blvd., paralleling the San Francisco City Zoo.

34.3 Go right as Sloat Blvd. runs into Skyline Blvd. and cycle around Lake Merced.

35.0 Park Rd. joins Skyline Blvd. (Highway 35) from the right, marking the start of a broad bicycle lane.

36.0 Fort Funston on the right; beach access.

36.3 Leave San Francisco County, enter San Mateo County.

36.8 **(mp 31.00)** Daly City; fast-food and supermarkets.

38.1 **(mp 29.80)** Leave Highway 35 at Westmoor Ave. Go right one block, and then bear left on Skyline Dr. Pedal up a steep hill through a residential area, then descend steeply; enjoy the views south over the coast. (If heading to the San Francisco International Airport, leave the bike route here. Details at the end of the mileage log.)

39.9 While still descending steeply, watch for a school on the right, then take the first left on Crenshaw Dr. In one block, go right on Palmetto Ave. and stay on it as it parallels Highway 1, past freeway entrances and a shopping center.

42.3 Go left on Clarendon at the end of Palmetto Ave., then immediately left on Lakeside Ave.

42.5 Lakeside Ave. exits onto Francisco Blvd. Continue south past Sharp Park on the right; picnic tables, restrooms, and water.

43.0 Francisco Blvd. turns into Bradford Way; continue straight. Pass a Moose lodge, then take the first left. Just before you reach Highway 1, go right up a very steep bike path, paralleling the freeway.

43.6 **(mp 42.50)** Bike path ends; continue on the shoulder of Highway 1.

45.1 **(mp 41.00)** Lind Mar rest area; a parking lot with restrooms

Cyclist approaching the Golden Gate Bridge

and beach access but no water. No easy access from the northbound lanes.

45.2 (mp 40.90) *SIDE TRIP* to Sanchez Adobe. The adobe is a traditional home of the 1848 period, located 1.0 mile east of Highway 1; open Wednesday and Sunday, 10:00 A.M. to 12:00 P.M. and 1:00 P.M. to 4:00 P.M.

46.2 (mp 39.63) Highway 1 climbs steeply and shoulder ends as the road enters the Devil's Slide area. Scenery is excellent, but pay considerably more attention to the road than the view.

47.3 (mp 38.4) Devil's Slide Headland, an old military installation perched on a rugged haystack, commands an extensive view of this spectacular section of coast. A short, exposed trail leads up to the installation.

49.5 (mp 36.0) Enter Montara, a coastal tourist town with grocery stores. Shoulders are good and remain so for the rest of the day.

49.6 (mp 35.8) Beach access, restrooms, but no water. Pass Montara Lighthouse Hostel.

50.6 (mp 34.8) Enter the small coastal town of Moss Beach; no grocery stores near Highway 1. Pass the turnoff to Fitzgerald Marin Reserve, where you can explore the marine habitat in the tidal reefs.

52.1 (mp 33.4) El Granada; a small grocery store is one block left from Highway 1.

53.1 (mp 32.7) Half Moon Bay city limits. This strangely shaped city is passed through quickly here, then returned to farther down the coast.

53.7 (mp 31.8) Miramar, a small town with grocery stores.

54.6 (mp 30.6) Access to Dunes Beach, a horse park.

56.2 (mp 28.80) Junction of Highway 1 and Highway 92; major shopping center and bike shop are located on the east side of the highway. Highway 92 heads east to Half Moon Bay and Highway 35.

56.5 (mp 28.50) Turnoff to Half Moon Bay State Beach and campground; turn right (west) on Kelly Rd., opposite a small food store.

56.7 Half Moon Bay State Beach; beach access, restrooms, cold outdoor showers, and a hiker-biker site at the far end of the camping area.

Marin Headlands National Recreation Area Side Trip

At the southern end of East Rd. (the weekday entrance to the Golden Gate Bridge), turn left and head up the steep grade of Conzelman Rd. Viewpoints are numerous and, in good weather, so are the automobiles. At 1.2 miles, the road splits. Cyclists looking for views should stay left and continue up the final mile to the summit. To reach the hiker-biker camp or hostel, head right (down) for 1 mile to Bunker Rd. and go left. Follow Bunker Rd. 1.2 miles to a Y-intersection. If the hostel is the destination, stay left on Field Rd. for 500 feet, then turn uphill, following signs. If the hiker-biker camp is your destination, continue on Bunker Rd. for another 0.8 mile and register at the visitor center. Once formalities have been completed, return to Field Rd. and pedal up 1.3 miles. Immediately after passing two yellow buildings, turn left. In 0.1 mile, turn into the parking lot just before a picnic area. Walk down a short road to the Bicentennial campground.

Be prepared to put up with some inconveniences at the campground—no showers, no running water—and enjoy the tremendous views. You must call ahead to the Marin Headlands National Recreation Area visitor center for reservations. (Running water is available nearby; talk to park officials about it when calling in to reserve the campsite.)

Amtrak and the Oakland Airport

San Francisco does not have an Amtrak station. The nearest station is located across the bay in Oakland; the best way to get there

Highway 1 in the Devil's Slide area

is by BART (Bay Area Rapid Transit). Follow the route through San Francisco for 30.1 miles to Cabrillo St. Go right on Cabrillo St. to 43rd Ave., then turn left and ride through Golden Gate Park on Chain of Lakes Dr. to Lincoln Way. Go left for four blocks, then take a right on 37th Ave. At Yorba St., go left, then right on Sunset Blvd., which will turn into Lake Merced Blvd. At John Daly Blvd., go left and ride this busy thoroughfare until it crosses over a major freeway. Exit and go left (north) to BART Station No. 1. Bicycles are allowed on BART from 9:30 A.M. to 3:30 P.M. Monday through Friday, and all day on weekends and holidays. Once there, take the elevator or stairs down to the station. Look for a station agent to let you through the gate. If you cannot find an agent, buy your ticket, go through the gate, and lift your bike over the four-foot barrier.

San Francisco International Airport

To reach the airport, follow the route through San Francisco for the first 38.1 miles. When the bike route returns to the city streets in Daly City, stay on Highway 35 and follow it all the way to San Bruno Ave., then head east. Near the airport, you'll cross over U.S. 101. Continue straight until San Bruno Ave. ends, then go right and follow the busy frontage roads to the terminal.

Half Moon Bay State Beach to New Brighton State Beach (53.8 Miles)

The coast from San Francisco south to Carmel is a popular vacation getaway. During the summer, this section of the coast overflows with tourists from around the world. On weekends, fishermen, surfers, sunbathers and beachcombers from the Bay Area mob this relatively limited area. Despite its popularity, the coast is remarkably unspoiled, with only a few towns marring the open grasslands and sandy beaches. Where the highway parallels the ocean, an observant cyclist may spot sea lions basking in the sun or otters playing in the surf.

A stop at Año Nuevo State Reserve is highly recommended. From December through April, elephant seals breed and raise their young here. During the summer, they can be spotted sunning themselves on the offshore rocks.

Tide pools are excellent in this area. Some of the richest pools are at Bean Hollow State Park and Natural Bridges State Park. If you have never explored a tide pool, take this opportunity to do so. The variety of life that survives in the precarious and ever-changing environment of these small pools is amazing.

In Santa Cruz, the route divides. The standard route heads straight through town, while the alternate route parallels the coast, past the scenic Natural Bridges State Park, then follows the beach road to the Santa Cruz pier.

Riders tired of the coast or the fog may be attracted by one of two alternate routes which leave the coast and climb up into the Santa Cruz Range to views, sunshine, and cool redwood forests. Both of these routes are steep, demanding, and scenic—recommended for strong cyclists only. The Skyline Boulevard Alternate Route is the longest. It starts from Half Moon Bay and returns to the coast at Santa Cruz. The Cowell Redwoods Alternate Route is much shorter. It heads inland at mile 38.1 to the town of Felton and Henry Cowell Redwoods State Park, and returns to Highway 1 at Santa Cruz.

Highway 1 has a good shoulder throughout most of this section, and riding is generally very enjoyable—a marked contrast to riding in San Francisco. One note of caution: before leaving Half Moon Bay, be sure to check your food and water supplies. The first water stop is at 27.7 miles, and the first grocery store is 37 miles south.

MILEAGE LOG

0.0 From Half Moon Bay State Park, follow Kelly Rd. back to Highway 1.

0.2 Kelly Rd. ends at Highway 1. The Pacific Coast Bike Route heads south towards Santa Cruz. The Skyline Boulevard Alternate Route heads left (north) to the junction with Highway 92. For route details, see end of this mileage log.

10.7 (mp 18.05) San Gregorio State Beach; beach access, chemical toilets, no running water.

12.3 (mp 16.49) Pomponio State Beach; beach access, chemical toilets, no running water.

14.1 (mp 14.65) Pescadero State Beach; beach access, chemical toilets, no running water. Translated, Pescadero means "the fishing place," and is well-known for surf fishing. In the next mile, two more Pescadero state beaches are passed.

15.0 (mp 13.54) Turnoff to Butano State Park campground, located several miles inland from the coast. The park has neither hiker-biker sites nor showers.

16.8 (mp 12.00) Bean Hollow State Beach, also known as Pebble Beach, beach access, tidal pools, and a mile-long, self-guided nature trail along the bluff. Pebble Beach gets its

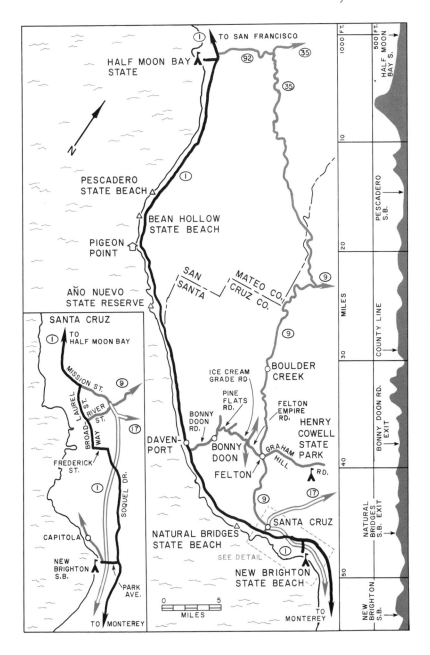

Tide pool

name from the thousands of tiny, multi-colored pebbles. Don't mine the beach; leave it for others to enjoy.

17.6 (mp 11.20) A second Bean Hollow State Beach; restroom, southern end of the nature trail, and beach access.

20.7 (mp 8.00) Turnoff to Pigeon Point Light Station and hostel. This beacon, the second tallest in the nation, is visible from great distances, by land or sea. If spending the night at the hostel, take a walk along the beach to look for whale bones, common here, or watch for the living whales at sea, on their annual migration.

22.8 (mp 5.89) Cazos State Beach; beach access, chemical toilets, no water.

27.7 (mp 0.94) Turnoff to Año Nuevo State Reserve, the first watering hole since Half Moon Bay. In winter, this is a very popular area for viewing gray whales and elephant seals. In summer, explore the tide pools, while watching for sea otters and harbor seals in the surf.

28.5 (mp 0.0 and 37.5) Leave San Mateo County and enter Santa Cruz County.

29.5 (mp 36.45) Big Basin Redwoods State Park entrance and Walden Beach. Walden Beach is located on the right (west); no restrooms or running water. Big Basin Redwoods State

Park lies to the left (east) side of Highway 1. No facilities here; only the tip of the park is touched by Highway 1. The main entrance is from Highway 9. The shoulder remains good as Highway 1 rolls past miles of artichoke and Brussels sprout farms.

37.1 (mp 28.7) Davenport. At long last—food. The solitary store in this tiny community is very popular among bicyclists.

38.1 (mp 27.7) Cowell Redwoods Alternate Route turnoff. For details, see end of this mileage log.

45.2 (mp 20.42) Santa Cruz; supermarkets, bike shops, beaches, fishing piers, tide pools, and lots of people. Some tricky navigation is needed to plot a course through this small metropolis; however, Santa Cruz is a college town, and bicycles are an accepted mode of transport.

46.1 (mp 19.62) Start Santa Cruz *BYPASS ROUTE.* Turn right off Highway 1 and follow the signs 1 mile to Natural Bridges State Park; sandy beach, tide pools, butterfly trees (wintering spot for Monarch butterflies), restrooms, picnic tables, and running water. After visiting the beach, head west along W. Cliff Dr., passing Santa Cruz's most popular surfing waters and scenic overlooks. To return to the main route, turn left (north) on High St. (at the Santa Cruz pier) and go right on Laurel St. at the start of the Santa Cruz city bike route.

46.9 (mp 18.82) If you are still on the standard route, exit Highway 1 at Laurel St. and join the Santa Cruz city bike route.

47.8 Laurel St. becomes Broadway. Both alternate routes through the Santa Cruz Mountains and redwoods rejoin the coast route here.

49.0 Broadway ends; turn left on Frederick St.

49.3 Frederick St. ends. Turn right on Soquel Dr. and follow it for the next 4 miles to the New Brighton State Beach turnoff. Purchase food for the night along this section.

53.3 Turnoff to New Brighton State Beach. Go right on Park Ave. (turn was not signed in 1988; watch carefully).

53.8 New Brighton State Beach; hiker-biker site (a one-night limit), hot showers, and beach access. *SIDE TRIP.* After you set up camp, cycle west on Park Ave. to the town of Capitola for a walk on the beach, then follow East Cliff Dr. back to Santa Cruz and the famous Boardwalk Amusement Park. If leaving your bicycle for even a moment, be sure it is locked.

Skyline Boulevard Alternate Route

From the end of Kelly Rd., turn left (north) on Highway 1 and follow it 0.3 mile back to the Highway 92 junction. Cycle Highway 92 for 7 miles to Highway 35, Skyline Boulevard. Follow this hilltop route south 26 miles, taking time to enjoy the views west to the Pacific Ocean and east over the Santa Clara Valley. When Highway 35 ends, turn west and follow Highway 9 down through Felton for 27 miles to Santa Cruz. No groceries or campgrounds along Highway 35; however, both can be found on Highway 9. This trip is for the strong, experienced cyclist only.

Cowell Redwoods Alternate Route

At the Felton turnoff, head left (east) up Bonny Rd. for this mountainous journey into the redwoods. The road is steep and narrow with light traffic, except on weekends. Head uphill for 3.5 miles to the small town of Bonny Doon; grocery stores. Pass the Bonny Doon Elementary School, then turn right on Pine Flats Rd. In a little over a mile, turn right onto Ice Cream Grade Rd. After 1.5 miles, cross Empire Grade to Felton Empire Rd., and follow it 3.5 miles to a junction with Highway 9 and Graham Hill Rd. at Felton.

Taking a break

(The Skyline Boulevard and Cowell Redwoods alternate routes join here.) Food and other necessities are available in this area.

Henry Cowell Redwoods State Park campground is located a hilly 2.5 miles past Felton on Graham Hill Rd.; hiker-biker camp, showers, bike paths, and hiking trails through the redwoods. A day-use area is located on Highway 9 just south of Felton; picnicking, hiking trails, restrooms, water, and a train ride through the redwoods (fee charged).

Highway 9 descends 7 miles to Santa Cruz, ending at a junction with Highway 17 and River St. Cross Highway 17 and follow River St. to the Santa Cruz city bike route (where Laurel becomes Broadway). Turn right (south) on Broadway.

New Brighton State Beach to Vet's Memorial Park, Monterey (40.0 Miles)

Between New Brighton State Beach and Monterey, the bicycle route is composed principally of backroads and bike paths. The route passes through open farmlands where Brussels sprouts and artichokes are the major crops. The scenery is some of the least interesting on the coast, and no points of interest interrupt your ride. Terrain varies from gently rolling to level. The biggest hazard to cyclists, especially in the Monetery area, is dense fog.

As of 1989 the bridge over the Pajaro River was closed to all traffic. Rebuilding of the bridge should begin in 1990 and end sometime in 1991. Until the new bridge is completed, a detour must be followed which takes you several miles east, crossing Highway 1 twice before you return to the normal route. (Detour is detailed below.)

The day's ride ends at Vet's Memorial Park. This is a small city park with one small hiker-biker site that turns cyclists away only when it actually overflows. Arrive early to claim an area for your tent. Monterey attracts visitors from around the world, so expect an international crowd at the campsite.

The Monterey area more than makes up for the uneventful ride, and you can spend the remaining hours of the day enjoying this incredible town. Monterey has more places to see and explore than any other area of the coast. A special tour of Monterey includes stops at Fisherman's Wharf (to feed the sea lions and pick up something to eat for yourself), Cannery Row ("restored" to an elegance it never had when featured in Steinbeck's famous novel), Point Lobos Light Station (beautifully situated at the edge of the

Point Lobos Refuge), the wintering spot for monarch butterflies (these fragile insects fly all the way down from Alaska), and the beautiful 17-Mile Drive (possibly the most famous stretch of road on the entire California coast), which is included at the end of the route description. An afternoon is the absolute minimum amount of time you should devote to this area. To see it all, plan to spend an entire day.

The newest addition to this area, an aquarium located at the southern end of Cannery Row, is a masterpiece. Visitors are taken on a visual journey from the estuary at Elkhorn Slough to the tidelands, then down below the wharf through the kelp beds to the ocean floor. If you enjoy the ocean, a trip to the aquarium is a must. Plan to spend three or more hours there.

MILEAGE LOG

0.0 From New Brighton State Beach, return to the bike route by pedaling back up Park Ave.

0.6 Turn right at Soquel Dr., rejoining the Santa Cruz city bike route. Stay on Soquel Dr. for the next 4.8 miles.

2.5 *SIDE TRIP* to Sea Cliffs State Beach. Turn right (west) on State Park Dr. for 0.6 mile to the long, sandy beach, a favorite with sunbathers; picnic tables and restrooms. An old shipwreck has been converted into a pier for fishermen.

4.6 Confusing intersection. After passing Rio Del Mar Blvd., follow Soquel Dr. as it makes a sharp turn to the right.

5.4 Soquel Dr. ends. Turn right on Freedom Blvd.

5.7 After crossing Highway 1, turn left on Bonita Dr. This is the end of the Santa Cruz city bike route.

6.8 Bonita Dr. ends; go right on San Andreas Rd. and follow it 6.1 miles.

8.7 La Selva Beach; access to a sandy beach, popular with surfers. Beyond La Selva Beach, San Andreas Rd. heads inland through rich farmlands. Traffic varies from light to extremely busy during harvest season.

11.0 Sunset State Beach turnoff. Follow Sunset Beach Rd. 2.2 miles past fields of Brussels sprouts and artichokes to this isolated park. The campground offers hiker-biker sites, hot showers, and beach access. Cyclists spending the night at the park should buy food in Santa Cruz—no food available near the park.

12.9 San Andreas Rd. ends; go left (east) on Beach Rd., then take the first right (this is McGowan Rd., not signed here). Go straight on McGowen Rd., cross the Pajaro River bike path (to Watsonville), cycle over a narrow bridge, then cross the

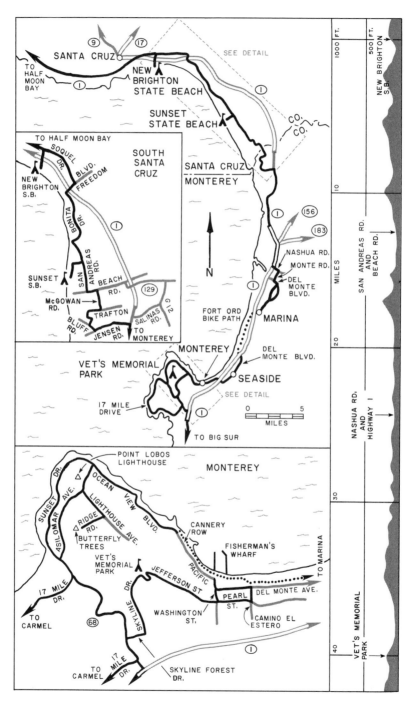

Santa Cruz–Monterey county line. ***DETOUR ROUTE.*** While the bridge across the Pajaro River is closed for construction, use the following route. When San Andreas Rd. ends, turn left (east) on Beach Rd. for 1.3 miles. Turn right on State Highway 129 (also called Riverside Dr.) for 1.9 miles. During this time you will cross Highway 1 (the bridge here is also closed to cyclists). Turn right on Elkhorn Dr. (also known as County Rd. G12) for another 1.9 miles to Salinas Rd., then go left for 1.6 miles to reach Highway 1. Go left across the highway and continue south, back on the main route. Note: Highway 1 is very busy in this area. Be patient; there will be a break in the traffic.

13.6 This is the halfway point between Oregon and Mexico.

14.1 At the end of McGowan Rd., take a right on Trafton Rd.

15.6 Trafton Rd. ends; turn left on Bluff Rd., cycling through a small residential community, and then past chicken and mushroom farms.

16.4 Bluff Rd. ends at Jensen Rd.; go left (east).

17.1 **(mp 100.00)** Return to Highway 1, opposite a fruit stand. The busy highway has good shoulders here.

17.9 **(mp 99.10)** Moss Landing; a long, narrow town.

18.9 **(mp 98.30)** Turnoff to Zmudowski State Beach. The beach lies 2 miles west; no facilities.

20.0 **(mp 97.00)** Moss Landing State Beach turnoff. The beach is located 0.5 mile to the southwest on Jetty Rd.; beach access, views of Moss Landing harbor, and restrooms, but no water.

20.5 **(mp 96.50)** Cross Elkhorn Slough.

20.7 **(mp 96.30)** Pass Moss Landing power plant, whose twin towers dominate the skyline. Highway 1 enters the business section of Moss Landing and passes the access to Elkhorn Slough Reserve.

23.5 **(mp 93.60)** Junction with Highway 156 (heading east) and Highway 183 (heading south). Stay on Highway 1, now a divided freeway.

25.2 **(mp 91.80)** Nashua Rd.; cyclists must exit Highway 1. At the end of the off ramp, turn left, crossing over the freeway.

25.5 Bicycle path from Castroville joins Nashua Rd. Continue straight.

25.9 Turn right on Monte Rd., paralleling Highway 1. No shoulders; traffic is light as you pass large artichoke fields.

27.1 Turn left on Del Monte Blvd. for 100 feet to a Y-intersection. Take either Del Monte Blvd. or Lapis Rd. They rejoin shortly.

28.6 Enter Marina on Del Monte Blvd.; several small grocery stores in this section.

29.5 Start two-way bike path paralleling Del Monte Blvd.

Pelicans drying their wings after plunging into the ocean for food

30.4 The bike path passes under Highway 1 then turns left, becoming the Fort Ord Bike Path as it parallels the freeway south through the Fort Ord area.

32.4 Seaside city limits. The bike path continues to parallel the freeway.

35.0 Bike path passes under Highway 1 and ends. The bike route returns to Del Monte Blvd. and it heads through a busy business district. Watch for cars parked on the shoulder.

36.6 Monterey; supermarkets, restaurants, hotels, and several bike shops.

36.7 Take the first right after entering Monterey, then go immediately left on a wide bike path.

38.4 Leave the bike path when it makes a sharp bend left to skirt Del Monte Ave. Cross Del Monte Ave. and cycle up Camino El Estero for two blocks.

38.6 Turn right on Pearl St.

38.8 Go straight, following Pearl St. through a confusing intersec-

Feeding the seals from Fishermen's Wharf in Monterey

tion with Abrego St. (even the street signs are confusing; Abrego St. changes names here, becoming Washington St.).

39.0 Pearl St. becomes Jefferson St. as it heads steeply up.

40.0 Vet's Memorial Park; picnic area and campground, hot showers, and hiker-biker camp. No beach access; however, the incessant barking of the sea lions can be heard day and night, keeping campers in tune with the ocean.

Monterey Tour

As mentioned in the introduction, a trip around Monterey is a must. Although you can ride from one attraction to the next on the tour, a lot of places cannot truly be explored from the seat of your bicycle, so carry a bike lock and chain. You can also enjoy the luxury of free bus service (summer only) from Fisherman's Wharf to Cannery Row and the aquarium.

From the intersection of Pearl St. and Washington St., ride down Washington St. to its end at the hotel–convention center. Walk your bike through the plaza to the waterfront and lock it up. Start your tour by exploring the wharf.

0.0 Fisherman's Wharf is divided into two parts, tourist and commercial. On the commercial wharf, join the pelicans in watching the fishermen unload their catch; on the tourist wharf, buy little baskets of fish to feed the barking sea lions, or purchase a seafood meal for yourself from outdoor vendors. Keep an eye open for sea otters, generally shy, floating on their backs beside the wharfs.

0.4 Leaving Fisherman's Wharf, ride along the waterfront on a wide bike path, watching for harbor seals and otters.

0.9 *SIDE TRIP* to the Coast Guard jetty. Descend off the bike path to the large parking area, then walk out to the end of the jetty where sea lions nap on the breakwater, watching an endless procession of skin divers.

1.1 The bicycle path crosses through the upper portion of Cannery Row, past shops and restaurants located in the old buildings made famous by John Steinbeck in his famous novel of the same name.

1.6 At the end of Cannery Row, descend one block to the aquarium built in an old cannery building. Plan to spend several hours here before continuing south. The bike path parallels the beautifully sculptured coastline. Watch for sea otters floating on their backs (and hundreds of skin divers floating on their stomachs) through the kelp beds.

2.7 Bike path ends. Go right on Ocean View Blvd. and continue to follow the coast.

3.9 Go straight through an intersection, entering Point Lobos Refuge.

4.6 Exit Point Lobos Refuge to meet Sunset Dr.; cycle along the waterfront past Asilomar State Beach (no facilities) to 17-Mile Drive. *SIDE TRIP* to lighthouse (open from 1:00 P.M. to 4:00 P.M. Saturdays and Sundays). On weekends, when Point Lobos Lighthouse is open to visitors, turn left on Sunset Dr. for 0.2 mile, then go left again on Asilomar Ave. to the lighthouse entrance. Deer often graze near the lighthouse. *SIDE TRIP* to butterfly trees. From September through March, you can take a side trip to the butterfly trees, wintering spots for the Monarch butterflies which migrate south from Alaska. Follow the directions to the lighthouse, except go right on Lighthouse Ave. immediately after turning onto Asilomar Ave. Cycle 0.5 mile to the Butterfly Grove Inn. Walk through the Inn's parking area to the trees.

6.2 Turn right on the 17-Mile Drive.

6.3 17-Mile Drive entrance station. You must stop here and sign a form waiving your rights to sue, should you be run over on this private road. You will receive an information guide and map of the scenic highlights along the drive. Bike route signs located along the drive make route-finding easy.

16.4 Pass Carmel gate and follow 17-Mile Drive as it climbs steeply up a tree-lined canyon.

17.0 Exit 17-Mile Drive at the Highway 1 gate. Follow Highway 68 back towards Monterey.

17.8 Turn right onto Skyline Forest Dr.

18.0 Turn left on Skyline Dr.

19.1 Vet's Memorial Park.

Vet's Memorial Park to Kirk Creek Campground (60.2 Miles)

South of Monterey, Highway 1 heads into a wild, undeveloped section of the coast. Rugged cliffs descend at near-vertical angles from the mountains to the pounding surf, leaving little room for man or his roads. As a consequence, Highway 1 is narrow and winding, as if etched along the coast with a shaky hand.

Riding the steeply rolling terrain south of Monterey is physically demanding. The road is narrow, with little to no shoulder when you need it. Traffic is moderate to heavy, consisting mainly of tourists and tour buses. If you can get yourself moving at dawn, you will have several relatively peaceful hours before the rush of vacationers hits the road around 9:00 A.M. to 10 A.M.

Stores, restaurants, and water stops are few and far between, so plan ahead to avoid shortages.

Between Monterey and Kirk Creek Campground, it's open riding country with three "must" stops. The first is Point Lobos State Reserve, an enchantingly beautiful headland which has received recognition as a Registered National Landmark. Small groves of the nearly extinct Monterey Cypress, sculptured by the wind into graceful shapes, thrive in the harsh environment of Point Lobos. Cycle the park's three miles of roads, then walk several of the short trails over the headlands and through the groves.

The second stop for the day is the Pfeiffer–Big Sur State Park. This park has two distinct sections, the ocean park with its walk-in campground and a back-to-nature atmosphere, and the redwoods park with every amenity to pamper the camper. Little of the area's mystique is visible to the passing cyclist. From the highway, it is the commercial aspects of the area rather than the natural ones that stand out. To get a better feel of the area, leave

On the coast, south of Carmel

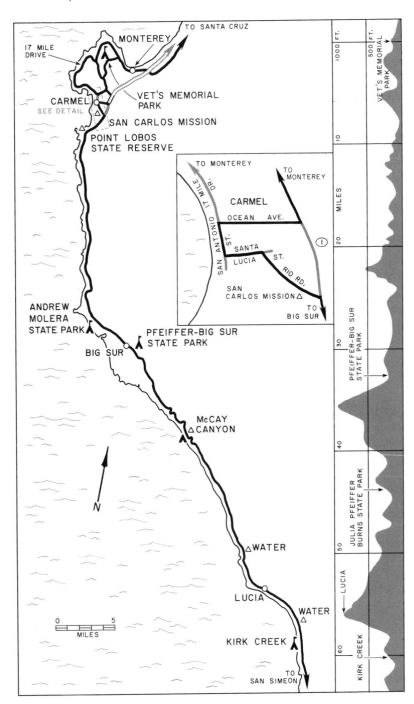

the bikes behind and hike up one of the park's trails to high viewpoints, narrow, stream-cut canyons, ocean beaches, and even a hot spring.

The third stop of special interest is Julia Pfeiffer Burns State Park, where a short trail leads to a beautiful vantage point over a waterfall and beach.

If a long and difficult ride and three "must" stops are more than you wish to tackle in one day, this section divides into two perfect halves. This allows a leisurely two days, leaving plenty of time to explore the area and relax on the beach.

MILEAGE LOG

0.0 Heading south from Vet's Memorial Park, follow Skyline Dr. steeply uphill.

1.1 Turn right on Skyline Forest Dr.

1.4 Take a left on Highway 68.

2.2 Passing a 17-Mile Drive entrance, descend the freeway ramp to southbound Highway 1. Freeway ends in 0.1 mile in a busy and shoulderless section of Carmel.

4.0 Exit right off hectic Highway 1 on Ocean Ave. and descend through Carmel, a tourist-oriented town with small shops, restaurants, and art galleries, including the Weston Gallery which features photographs by Edward Weston and Ansel Adams.

4.6 Turn left on San Antonio St. Straight ahead is a large parking area for Carmel Beach.

5.2 San Antonio St. ends; go left on Santa Lucia St.

5.8 Take a right on Rio Rd.

6.2 San Carlos Mission; the building has been restored to its original grandeur. Visitors are welcome from 9:30 A.M. to 5:00 P.M. for a small entrance fee.

6.8 (mp 72.65) Return to Highway 1 and head south. On the east side of the intersection are the last stores before Big Sur. Stock up on groceries as well as pastries from the bakery.

7.1 (mp 72.30) Cross the shoulderless Carmel River Bridge on Highway 1. The shoulder reappears on the opposite side and remains good, except at slide areas.

8.2 (mp 71.20) Carmel River State Beach; restrooms and beach access. The beach is a popular area for skin diving.

9.0 (mp 70.40) Point Lobos State Reserve; restrooms, running water, picnic tables, and trails. Plan to spend as much time here as possible.

9.5 (mp 69.9) Carmel Highlands, a residential area which lasts for several miles. No grocery stores. Highway 1 travels near

Point Lobos State Reserve

the coast, climbing over headlands, and passes through several slide areas where the shoulder disappears.

19.2 (mp 60.1) Rocky Creek Bridge.

19.8 (mp 59.5) Bixby Creek Bridge.

28.2 (mp 51.2) Andrew Molera State Park; camping, beach access, and hiking trails. The walk-in campground is located 0.3 mile from the road on a trail that is suitable for mountain bikes (bikes with narrow tires should be pushed). The camp area is located in an open field with pit toilets and water brought in by a tank trailer. No wood may be gathered or purchased for fires. The camp area is located 0.2 mile from a sandy beach.

30.1 (mp 49.3) Highway 1 heads inland, under the shade of the redwoods.

30.6 (mp 48.8) Enter Big Sur; several private campgrounds, grocery stores, motels, and restaurants.

32.1 (mp 47.3) Pfeiffer–Big Sur State Park; a large campground with hiker-biker site, hot showers, wading in the Big Sur River, hiking trails, a lodge, restaurant, and grocery store. (The next grocery store is 20 miles south in Lucia.) Beyond the campground, Highway 1 climbs a long hill and then drops back to the coast leaving the redwoods. Shoulders on the southbound side remain good; views are spectacular.

41.4 (mp 38.4) Julia Pfeiffer Burns State Park vista point. View and an information sign which discusses the park as well as the migration of monarch butterflies and whales.

43.9 (mp 35.9) McCay Canyon day-use area; restrooms, picnic tables, environmental camping (walk-in campsites located 0.2 mile from the road), and a short 0.25-mile hiking trail to a scenic vantage point overlooking the beach and a waterfall.

52.7 (mp 27.00) Water fountain on east side of the highway.

56.4 (mp 23.00) Lucia, a small town perched on the side of a hill, the last chance to purchase food before Kirk Creek Campground.

59.1 (mp 20.30) Drinking fountain.

60.2 (mp 19.20) Kirk Creek Campground, operated by the Los Padres National Forest; hiker-biker site, running water, beach access, but no electric lights, showers, or hot water. Closest grocery store is 3 miles south, in Pacific Grove.

Kirk Creek Campground to San Simeon State Beach (40.0 Miles)

From huge hills to almost flat coastal grasslands, the terrain is the key interest along these 40 miles. Leaving Kirk Creek Campground, the route continues to climb and dive its way for 22 miles along the rugged coast. Then, as if by magic, the hilly countryside is transformed into gentle, low rolling hills.

Once the terrain levels, the miles fly by. While speeding over the lowlands, keep an eye on the tumbling surf, where sea otters may be playing just a few yards offshore. If lucky enough to spot one of these wary animals, it is best to watch their antics from afar, as they are shy of humans.

Near San Simeon, a casual glance east is all that is needed to spot the Hearst Castle perched on Highway 1. The massive castle, built by William Randolph Hearst, houses one of the world's largest private collections of art treasures. These treasures may only be viewed by taking one or more of the four organized tours of the castle offered by the California State Parks. Each tour lasts approximately 1 hour and 45 minutes, and must be booked in advance by calling MISTIX, 1-800-444-7275 within California or 1-619-452-1950 out of state. For a brochure about the four tours, write MISTIX, P.O. Box 85705, San Diego, CA 92138-5705. Of course, you can always check at the visitor center for unreserved tickets when you arrive.

For the cyclist without extra time or money for a tour, stop at the Hearst Castle visitor center and visit the free museum for insights into the life and times of William Randolph Hearst, and information on how the castle was designed and built on this lonely stretch of coast.

MILEAGE LOG

0.0 (mp 19.20) Leave Kirk Creek Campground and head south along Highway 1 on a shoulder that comes and goes.

3.0 (mp 16.0) Pacific Valley; the small grocery store-restaurant-gas station on the left side of the highway also serves as a bus stop.

5.1 (mp 13.9) Sand Dollar picnic area; picnic tables, running water, and restrooms.

5.3 (mp 13.7) Plaskett Creek Campground on the east (left) side of Highway 1; hiker-biker site, running water, but no showers.

5.7 (mp 13.3) Jade Cove beach access; a stroll along this beach may turn up bits of jade. Bicycles may be left at Plaskett Creek Campground or at the trailhead.

7.1 (mp 11.90) Willow Creek picnic area; no facilities.

Hearst Castle

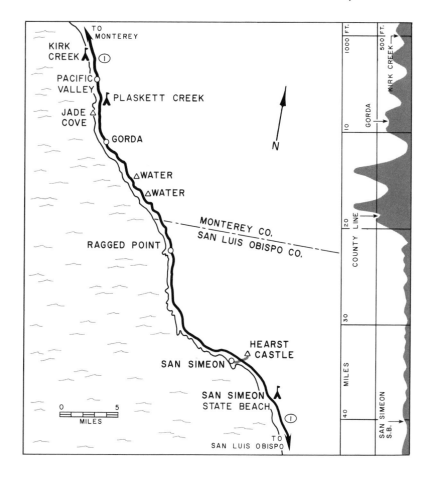

8.4 (mp 10.30) Gorda; a small store and restaurant mark the center of this community, which was put up for sale in 1988.

13.0 (mp 4.2) Drinking fountain on the left (east) side of the highway.

14.7 (mp 3.9) Drinking fountain on the left (east).

17.0 (mp 1.40) Leave Los Padres National Forest.

18.5 (mp 0.0 and 74.32) Leave Monterey County and enter San Luis Obispo County.

19.8 (mp 73.02) Ragged Point. If planning to stop for a bite to eat, start slowing down. When you are flying down the hill, it's easy to miss this small community of fast-food outlets and cliff-hanging houses.

22.6 (mp 70.19) Into the flatlands.

28.8 (mp 63.93) Piedras Blancas Lighthouse; no visitors allowed.

29.7 (mp 63.03) The road narrows as it skirts the edge of the coast. Keep an eye out for sea otters playing and bobbing for food.

31.2 (mp 62.1) Vista point; view of Hearst Castle, beach access, and tide pools. Beyond the vista point, the shoulder returns and remains good for the rest of the day.

34.8 (mp 58.5) San Simeon city limits.

35.4 (mp 57.9) Turn left (east) for 0.3 mile to the Hearst Castle visitor center; restrooms, water, tours, museum, gift shop, bike rack, lockers, and snack bar. To the right (west) is the town of San Simeon, which has a small grocery store, and William Randolph Hearst Memorial State Beach; picnic area, fishing pier, restrooms, running water, and beach access.

38.4 (mp 54.9) San Simeon's motel and restaurant row, which includes several small grocery stores.

40.0 (mp 53.2) San Simeon State Beach Campground. Turn left (east) off Highway 1 to reach the campground access. The campground has two parts. The first is San Simeon State Beach, small hiker-biker site at the edge of the freeway, and water, hot showers, and beach access. The second is the primitive Washburn Campground, located on a hill overlooking the beach area. This primitive area has neither hiker-biker site nor showers; however, it is clean, quiet, and scenic. For groups of three or more, this is less expensive than the hiker-biker site on the edge of Highway 1.

San Simeon State Beach to Pismo State Beach (52.6 Miles)

The ride from San Simeon State Beach to Pismo State Beach marks the beginning of the transition from middle to southern California. The quiet, lonely coast and spectacular scenery is replaced by freeways and large urban areas with a Spanish flavor. The distinctive smell of eucalyptus trees fills the air. Beaches are lined with palm trees, and hillsides are dotted with oaks. Ants are everywhere—so keep the tent door closed and don't leave food out. The ocean is warmer here and swimming is a refreshing, rather than heart-stopping, way to end the day's ride.

Between San Simeon and Pismo Beach, the country is open and excellent for riding. You can cover many miles and still have time to relax at the end of the day. With the exception of a brief scenic excursion along the coast at Cambria, the route follows Highway 1 (a 4-lane highway) south for 23.6 miles before exiting at Morro

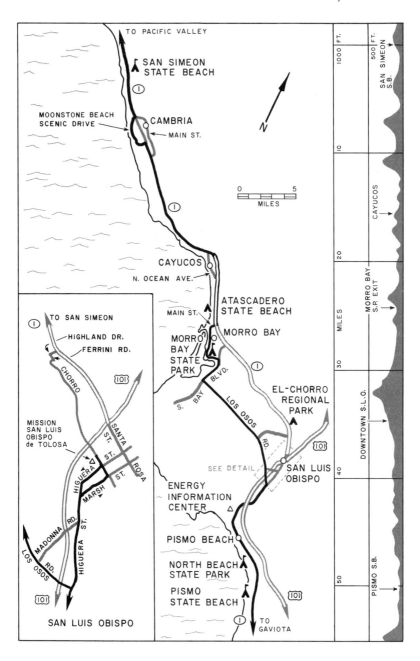

TO PACIFIC VALLEY

SAN SIMEON
STATE BEACH

MOONSTONE BEACH
SCENIC DRIVE

CAMBRIA
← MAIN ST.

N

0   5
MILES

CAYUCOS
N. OCEAN AVE.

ATASCADERO
STATE BEACH

MAIN ST.

MORRO
BAY   MORRO BAY
STATE
PARK

S. BAY BLVD.

LOS OSOS

EL-CHORRO
REGIONAL
PARK

RD.

SEE DETAIL

SAN LUIS
OBISPO

ENERGY
INFORMATION
CENTER

PISMO BEACH

NORTH BEACH
STATE PARK

PISMO
STATE BEACH

TO
GAVIOTA

TO SAN SIMEON

HIGHLAND DR.
FERRINI RD.

CHORRO

MISSION
SAN LUIS
OBISPO
de TOLOSA

SANTA ROSA ST.

HIGUERA ST.

MARSH ST.

MADONNA RD.

HIGUERA ST.

LOS OSOS RD.

SAN LUIS OBISPO

1000 FT.   500 FT.

SAN SIMEON S.B.

10

CAYUCOS

20

MORRO BAY
S.P. EXIT

MILES

30

DOWNTOWN S.L.O.

40

50

PISMO S.B.

Bay. The second half of the ride is entirely on back roads through well-developed farmlands. Temperatures in this section may be quite warm, especially in the San Luis Obispo area.

Chief attractions are Morro Bay, a popular tourist and fishing area, and the wind-sculptured sand dunes at Pismo Beach. An optional side trip takes you to visit Mission San Luis Obispo, founded in 1772.

The day ends at Oceano Campground, one of two camp areas in Pismo State Beach. The beach shore near the campground is a popular place to drive jeeps and cars. People come to surf-fish, or just watch the sunset. Inland from the beach is the sand dunes reserve, a natural area closed to motorized vehicles. It's a great place for exploring, sitting, sliding, or just looking.

MILEAGE LOG

0.0 (mp 53.20) Leave San Simeon State Beach on Highway 1. Shoulder width is ample, up to eight feet wide, except at bridges.

0.8 (mp 52.60) At Moonstone Beach Scenic Dr., turn left (west) off Highway 1 for a scenic ride along the coastline through Cambria.

1.1 Leffingwell Landing State Beach; picnic tables, water, and restrooms at the popular winter whale-watching site. Continue south, past long, sandy beaches.

2.3 (mp 50.80) Return to Highway 1. *ALTERNATE ROUTE.* Cross to the east side of Highway 1 and follow Main St. south through the center of Cambria past shops and grocery stores. Main St. loops back to Highway 1 in 2.4 miles.

4.7 (mp 48.20) Alternate route through Cambria returns to Highway 1. The route heads inland, traversing sun-baked pastureland for the next 10 miles.

15.4 (mp 36.90) Cayucos, a small tourist-oriented town; grocery stores.

15.6 (mp 36.70) *ALTERNATE ROUTE* through Cayucos. Cyclists wishing to shop in Cayucos exit Highway 1 on N. Ocean Ave. The road parallels the waterfront, passes through town, then returns to Highway 1 in 1.7 miles. Past the Cayucos exit, Highway 1 becomes freeway.

17.3 (mp 34.90) Cayucos Alternate Route returns to Highway 1.

19.5 (mp 32.70) Morro Bay city limits. Markets and shopping centers are visible from the freeway. The town has several state parks, long, sandy beaches, and a wildlife refuge.

20.5 (mp 32.00) Atascadero State Beach, a campground oriented to trailers; running water, restrooms, and cold outdoor showers; no hiker-biker site.

23.6 (mp 28.60) Exit Highway 1 at Main St. Go right on Main St., and follow the signs through town to Morro Bay State Park, cycling around Morro Bay and pass Morro Rock. The road parallels the bay, winding through a residential district before entering the park, where it turns into State Park Rd. Follow the park road past the golf course, museum, and marina. *SIDE TRIP* to Morro Rock. Go right off Main St. on Beach St.. and ride to its end. Turn right on Embarcadero for 1 mile to Morro Rock and the state park; restrooms, picnic tables, and water.

26.4 Morro Bay State Park campground entrance; hot showers. The hiker-biker site is located in the picnic area. Tents may not be set up until 5:00 P.M. during the summer and 4:00 P.M. during the winter. Tents must be down by 9:00 A.M. If camping at the park, no entrance fee is charged to visit the natural history museum or to enjoy its excellent view of Morro Rock. The rock is a national preserve and nesting ground for the rare and endangered peregrine falcon. Continue beyond the campground to S. Bay Blvd.

27.0 Turn right (south) on S. Bay Blvd. and cycle around Morro Bay. The road starts out narrow, then gradually widens to include a comfortable shoulder.

Morro Rock and Morro Bay

Sand dunes at Pismo Beach

31.0 Turn left on Los Osos Valley Rd., which heads east away from the ocean. Temperatures soar as the road rolls through open farmlands. (Expect to see numerous cyclists on this road; this is part of a popular training ride.)

31.8 Los Osos Oaks State Reserve; hiking trails.

37.9 Pass Foothills Blvd., access to Cal-Poly State University (California's famous agricultural college). The route continues straight on Los Osos Valley Blvd., entering the residential outskirts of San Luis Obispo.

40.1 Cross over a freeway (U.S. 101 and Highway 1 combined).

40.3 Los Osos Valley Rd. ends; go right on S. Higuera St. *SIDE TRIP* to Mission San Luis Obispo de Tolosa. Go right (north) on S. Higuera St. until the road divides in 2.4 miles. Continue north on Marsh St. (one-way) for 0.3 mile, then turn left on Chorro St. and continue 0.2 mile to the mission. Tour the mission, then stroll down to San Luis Obispo Creek. Restaurants, grocery stores, bakeries, and a bike shop are close by. The park has a restroom and water. To return to the route, take Higuera St. (one way south), back to S. Higuera St.

42.1 Cross under U.S. 101, staying on S. Higuera St.

42.2 Turn right on Ontario Rd. and parallel the freeway for the next 3 miles. Note the sirens located along the road. If trouble occurs with the nuclear power plant in Diablo Canyon, a warning signal will be heard, lasting from three to five minutes. Now, doesn't that make you feel good about riding through an area that has a nuclear power plant located on a fault?

44.3 Diablo Canyon Energy Information Center; picnic tables and running water. Before the nuclear reactor was built, there were elaborate and expensive displays on energy and conservation here.

45.2 Turn left on Avila Rd., passing a private campground and pool heated by a hot springs.

45.5 Turn right on Palisades Rd.

45.7 Pismo Beach. Stay on Palisades Rd. sandwiched between the freeway and beach. The road becomes Shell Beach Rd., then turns into Price St.

49.5 (mp 16.05) When the road divides, descend to the right on Dolliver St. (you are now back on Highway 1). Ride through the center of Pismo Beach on a wide bike lane.

50.7 (mp 14.70) North Beach State Park campground, the first of two. Pismo State Beach camp area; hiker-biker site, water, beach access, but no showers in this open-field park. Continue to the second campground.

52.1 (mp 13.24) Oceano city limits.

52.4 (mp 13.00) Turn right off Highway 1 at Pier Ave., passing the closest grocery store to the park.

52.6 Oceano Campground, the second Pismo State Beach camp area; hiker-biker site complete with bike rack, hot showers, and a trail to the beach. Keep valuables stored well out of reach of the flock of marauding ducks, and store food and touring bags out of reach of thieving raccoons. *SIDE TRIP* to Pismo Dune Preserve. The sand dunes are located 0.2 mile beyond the campground. Due to the large amount of loose sand, it is best to leave bikes at the campground and walk Pier Ave. or one of the campground trails to the beach. Head south on the beach for another 0.2 mile, cross a creek, then go inland through a low fence designed to keep motor vehicles out of the dunes. Walk beyond the reach of the dune grass to enjoy the sandy dunes. This is a great place to watch the sunset. The roads and houses near the Dunes Beach access have special problems. In winter, sand tries to engulf the surrounding area. The roads are marked with tall poles, the same as those used in snowbound mountain passes, to define the roads for snowplows.

Pismo State Beach to Gaviota State Beach (61.6 Miles)

For the next 61 miles, the route runs inland from the ocean, skirting the huge Vandenburg Air Force Base. Riding is the main activity for the day, and the majority of the ride is on back roads surrounded by eucalyptus groves or open farmland. Two major hills, each about 950 feet in elevation, offer elegant scenery on the long grind up, and thrilling descents.

Food and water stops are limited to three towns along the way: Guadalupe, Orcutt, and Lompoc. Temperatures along the route frequently reach 90 degrees during the summer, so start early and carry plenty of water. However, the greatest discomfort comes when the northern trade winds whip across the plowed fields, filling the air with dust.

A highly recommended alternative to the standard Pacific Coast Bike Route (and California Bicentennial Route) is the Santa Ynez Valley route, starting at Lompoc. The route heads inland to the Danish town of Solvang, through Santa Ynez Valley, then back to the coast at Santa Barbara. Solvang was founded and settled by Danes, who have kept its heritage alive through customs, architecture, and a friendly spirit. One facet of Danish life—cooking—is tastefully represented here. The slightest breeze is filled with tempting aromas from bakeries and fudge factories that line the city streets.

Santa Ynez Valley is scenic country and a superior cycling area, through rolling grass hills dotted with California oak trees. The bright blue sky here is a prime soaring area for hawks, ravens, and people in gleaming white glider planes. In the heart of the Santa Ynez Valley is Lake Cachuma County Park, a complete recreation area with everything from camping and swimming to miniature golf and horseback riding. The alternate route climbs over San Marcos Pass, then descends with outstanding views of the Southern California coast to Santa Barbara.

In short, the Santa Ynez Valley Alternate Route is a scenic, tasty, and downright enjoyable ride that bypasses a long stretch of riding on U.S. 101 (a busy freeway). The Alternate Route is not recommended in July or August, when temperatures soar into the hundreds.

MILEAGE LOG

0.0 From Oceano Campground, cycle back to Highway 1, then head south through peaceful countryside. Shoulders are narrow and traffic light.

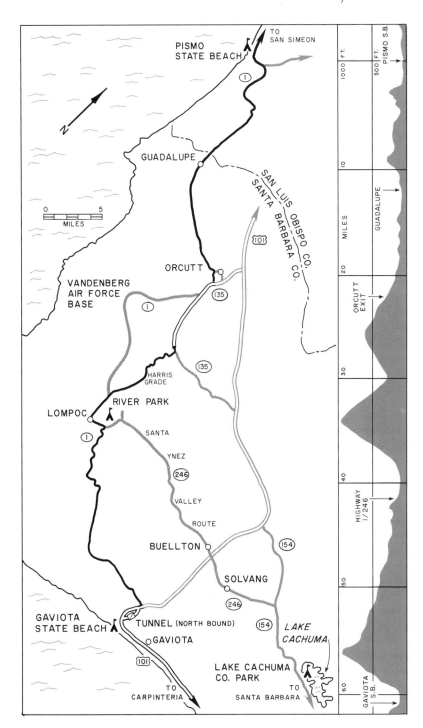

2.7 (mp 10.41) Intersection; turn right (south) following Highway 1 towards Guadalupe. After the turn, ascend a short, steep hill.

12.8 (mp 0.0 and 50.6) Leave San Luis Obispo County and enter Santa Barbara County at the city limits of Guadalupe. The first right inside town leads one block to Le Roy County Park; restrooms, picnic tables, and water. As you ride through town, you'll notice the Mexican grocery stores, restaurants, and bakeries, indicating a strong Mexican influence in Guadalupe. Signs are written both in Mexican and English.

15.1 (mp 48.3) Solomon Canyon Creek. Shoulder narrows.

24.1 (mp 35.0) Highway 1 merges with Highway 135 becoming a four-lane freeway with wide shoulders. Continue south towards Lompoc.

28.0 (mp 24.15) Highway 1 and Highway 135 divide. Go straight on Highway 135. Use caution crossing the Highway 1 exit; most traffic turns off here. *ALTERNATE ROUTE.* Highway 1 may be followed to Lompoc, bypassing a large hill. It's busy freeway all the way, with no scenery to speak of.

30.0 (mp 22.10) Freeway ends. The highway returns to two lanes and a narrow shoulder.

30.7 (mp 31.10) Turn right (south) on Harris Grade; Highway 135 continues straight. Over 600 feet of elevation are gained in the next 3 miles as the narrow, twisting road climbs over a small band of hills, reaching an elevation of 950 feet. Traffic is light.

34.0 (mp 27.80) Top of the hill. Enjoy the views across the open farmlands before starting the brisk trip down.

35.9 (mp 25.80) Historical marker noting the La Purisima Mission State Historical Park.

38.4 (mp 23.28) Bike route rejoins Highway 1; continue straight ahead. Truck traffic increases as the road widens to four lanes with no shoulder.

38.9 (mp 22.78) Lompoc. Just about everything needed can be found here—food, laundromats, bike shops, cafes, hotel, a campground, and the last grocery store before Gaviota State Park.

41.1 (mp 21.6) Turn left (south) on Ocean Ave., following Highway 1.

42.4 (mp 20.3) Turn right (south), still on Highway 1, towards Santa Barbara, starting a 13.5-mile uphill climb to an elevation of over 900 feet. The shoulder is good, except at bridges. Santa Ynez Valley Alternate Route to Santa Barbara starts

Left, *Solvang, on the Santa Ynez Valley Alternate Route*

from this intersection (see details below). *SIDE TRIP* to River Park Campground; hiker-biker site, picnic area, water, but no hot showers. When Highway 1 turns right, continue straight on Highway 246 for 0.5 mile to the campground.

56.0 (mp 2.1) Summit of hill and start of a fast, 2.5-mile descent to U.S. 101.

58.6 Intersection; Highway 1 joins U.S. 101. Enter on U.S. 101, a freeway with wide shoulders and lots of traffic. (If you're heading north, before turning off on Highway 1, you will encounter a short tunnel with a very narrow shoulder, and it frequently has a strong head wind. It's like trying to cycle out of a high-suction vacuum hose.) *SIDE TRIP* to Gaviota State Beach Hot Springs. At the junction of Highway 1 and U.S. 101, cross the freeway overpass, then go left on the frontage road to a parking area. A brisk 0.5-mile hike leads to springs and swimming area.

60.6 (mp 46.1) Rest area; tourist information, water, restrooms, and cool shade, for southbound travelers only.

61.1 (mp 45.6) Turnoff to Gaviota State Beach.

61.6 Gaviota State Beach; hiker-biker campsite, beach access, surfing, swimming, pier fishing, hiking trails, and a very limited grocery store. No hot showers. A small grocery store, restaurant, and gift shop is located 0.7 mile south of the campground on the east side of U.S. 101.

If time and energy are available, continue south on U.S. 101 for 9.1 miles to Refugio State Beach, which has a hiker-biker site located on the edge of a palm-lined beach, a small store, and hot showers.

Santa Ynez Valley Alternate Route

0.0 The junction of Highway 1 and 246 just south of Lompoc is the start of the alternate route through Santa Ynez Valley to Santa Barbara. Follow Highway 246 east over rolling terrain. Shoulders are one to eight feet wide, traffic occasionally heavy.

16.0 Enter Buellton, the home of Anderson's split pea soup (renowned throughout southern California for its flavor). Leaving Buellton, continue southeast on Highway 246, crossing U.S. 101 to Solvang.

19.5 Solvang; the main road through town is Mission St. (Highway 246); however, bakeries, fudge factories, wine-tasting rooms, and tourist traps are on Copenhagen St., one block west. Continue south from Solvang on Highway 246. Hills get steeper and traffic volume increases.

24.5 Turn right (south) on Highway 154. Shoulders remain good for a few miles, then deteriorate to nothing.

Highway 1 near Guadalupe

30.5 Lake Cachuma County Park, the recommended overnight stop for this alternate route. The campground has excellent facilities, including a hiker-biker site, hot showers, fishing, boat rentals, horseback riding, complete grocery store, swimming and wading pools, game room, miniature golf, and roller-skating.

36.5 Start of 4-mile climb to San Marcos Pass.

40.5 San Marcos Pass, elevation 2,225 feet. From the summit, it is a 7-mile rapid descent down a narrow, twisting road with heavy traffic.

47.5 Cyclists take the Foothill Rd. exit (State 192). At the base of the exit, turn left on Foothill Rd. and follow it for 2 miles through the outskirts of Santa Barbara.

50.0 At Alamar Ave., turn right and descend to State St.

50.2 Turn left on State St. and rejoin the coast bike route in 1.2 miles at the intersection of Mission St. and State St., 29.6 miles south of Gaviota State Beach.

Gaviota State Beach to Carpinteria State Beach (44.0 Miles)

Freeway, backroads, farmlands, and cities are mixed together throughout the ride from Gaviota State Beach to Carpinteria State Beach. Riding conditions are good, the freeway has a wide shoulder, city streets have wide bike lanes, and only one short, steep hill breaks the harmony of gently rolling terrain.

The chief point of interest in this section is Santa Barbara. The day's ride is short, leaving plenty of time to savor the city's strong Spanish flavor in an optional tour which includes the Santa Barbara Mission, founded in 1786; the county courthouse, modeled after a Spanish–Moorish palace with hand-painted ceilings, giant murals, and sweeping views over the city from the clock tower; the El Paseo, known as a "street in Spain," with sidewalk cafes and art galleries; and the Historical Society Museum depicting four eras of settlement: Indian, Spanish, Mexican, and American. The tour ends at Stearns Wharf in the beautiful harbor area, where the sight of sunbathers, roller-skaters, and wind surfers make for a strictly modern view of the area.

Cyclists passing through Santa Barbara in mid-August have a chance to catch the Fiesta Days celebration, which features a parade, street dancing, and every kind of Mexican food imaginable.

Carpinteria, the last stop for the day, claims the world's safest swimming beach, long and sandy with no undertow. Carpinteria State Park was build on an old Chumash Indian campsite; artifacts are still being uncovered. On the beach are several tar pits, where natural tar seeps out onto the sand.

MILEAGE LOG

0.0 Day's ride starts from Gaviota State Beach hiker-biker site.

0.5 (mp 46.3) Head south on U.S. 101. Shoulder is broad along the freeway, averaging four to eight feet except at bridges, where it completely disappears. Timing is very important when you cross a bridge; use caution.

1.2 (mp 45.6) Enter Gaviota. The city, composed of a gas station, telephone, and restaurant, is located on the east side of the freeway.

9.6 (mp 37.0) Turnoff to Refugio State Beach; scenic hiker-biker camp, hot showers, and small store. *ALTERNATE ROUTE.* A 2-mile bike path connects Refugio State Beach with El Capitan State Beach to the south, providing a scenic escape

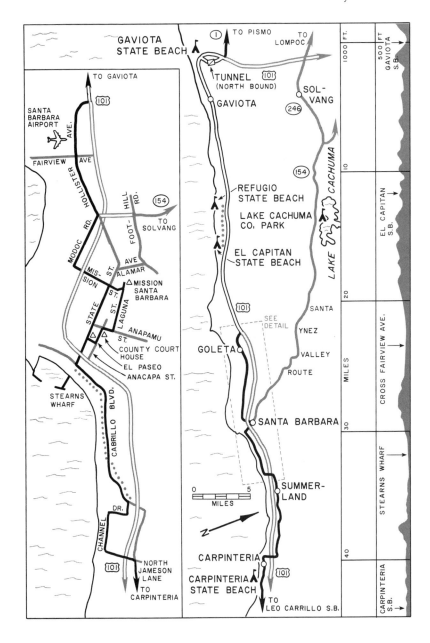

Mission Santa Barbara

from the noise and dirt of the freeway. The bike path skims along the edge of a bluff, overlooking the ocean and providing views up and down the coast.

11.3 (mp 34.3) El Capitan State Beach; large hiker-biker campsite located at the north end of the park in sight and sound of the freeway, hot showers, nature trail, small visitor center, camp store, sandy beach with lifeguards in the summer, and a 2-mile bike path to Refugio State Beach.

18.4 (mp 27.16) Hollister Ave. exit; bicycles must leave U.S. 101.

18.7 At top of freeway exit ramp, turn right on Hollister Ave. Numerous grocery stores, bike shops, restaurants, and motels, as well as heavy traffic for the next 20 miles. Most roads have a wide bike lane.

20.8 Cross Storke Rd., access to University of California at Santa Barbara.

23.1 Cross Fairview Ave., staying on Hollister Ave., at the center of the busy town of Goleta. Two large bicycle shops are located within four blocks (to the west).

26.6 Bear right on Modoc Rd. just before Hollister Ave. passes under a railroad bridge. Modoc Rd. changes to Catania Way after the first mile, which in turn becomes Parks Rd.

29.6 Turn left on Mission St. at the end of Parks Rd. Cycle under U.S. 101. Stay on Mission St. to State St.

30.1 Turn right on State St. and head down through the center of Santa Barbara. This intersection marks the rejoining of the Santa Ynez Valley Alternate Route to the coast bicycle route, and the beginning of the Santa Barbara tour. For details, see end of this mileage log.

32.1 After crossing U.S. 101, State St. ends at the waterfront. Turn left on Cabrillo Blvd. and cycle along the beach area. A city bike path is located between the road and beach for those who wish to brave the dense traffic of joggers, roller-skaters, and walkers.

33.5 Pass the entrance to Santa Barbara city zoo on the left.

34.3 Turn right on Channel Dr. opposite the Andree Clark Bird Refuge (just before passing under U.S. 101). Channel Dr. briefly returns to the beach, then heads inland, becoming Olive Mill Rd. as it crosses over U.S. 101.

35.6 Take the first right after the freeway on N. Jameson Lane. The road is shoulderless and moderately busy.

37.2 Go right, climbing Ortega Hill Rd. From the top of this short, steep hill, descend to the small community of Summerland; restaurants and a small grocery store. Paralleling the freeway, Ortega Hill Rd. becomes Lillie Ave., then Via Real.

Cycling along the palm-lined coast at Santa Barbara

42.5 Via Real ends. Turn right on Santa Ynez Ave. and cross to the west side of U.S. 101.

42.7 Take a sharp left on Carpinteria Ave. and follow the bike lane through town.

43.4 Turn right on Palm Ave. and follow it to the campground. (No signs point to the campground, so watch for the street sign.)

44.0 Carpinteria State Beach; hiker-biker site, hot showers, beach access, a small store, and a visitor center featuring the Indian history of the area. Several large grocery stores and numerous restaurants are located nearby. Excellent bus service to Santa Barbara. From Carpinteria south, hiker-biker sites attract a lot of transients. When you leave camp, carry all your valuables with you, and lock your bike.

Santa Barbara Tour

From the intersection of Mission and State streets, continue straight on Mission St. In 0.5 mile, Mission St. ends. Turn left for 0.2 mile up Laguna St. to the Santa Barbara Mission, known as the Queen of Missions because of its graceful architecture. Mission and museum may be toured for a small fee.

From the mission, ride down Laguna St. for 1.1 miles to Anapamu St., then go right 0.2 mile to Anacapa St. and turn left. The county courthouse on the left is the next stop. Walk through the halls, then climb to the top of the clock tower for a view of the whole city. Two and one-half blocks farther down Anacapa St., stop and lock your bikes up for a tour of the El Paseo, a shopping mall containing the Casa de la Guerra, the original adobe home of Jose de la Guerra, Commandante of the Presidio. Across the street, tour El Cuartel (the site of the original fortress founded by Spain in 1782) and the Presidio Gardens, located behind the post office. The Historical Society Museum is located one block south. After exploring the museum, take the first right and go west two blocks to State St., rejoining the main bike route. The tour may be continued from the end of State St. by heading out on Stearns Wharf or by cycling right, around the boat harbor and out on the breakwater, a scenic place to watch boats and eat lunch.

Carpinteria State Beach to Leo Carrillo State Beach (47.2 Miles)

Spanish architecture, palm trees, famous surfing beaches, and a mission all combine to produce that famous Southern California ambiance on the ride from Carpinteria State Beach to Leo Carrillo State Beach. Scenery varies from the Pacific Ocean, dotted with offshore oil rigs, to quiet farm country, to busy city streets.

Of course, the people play a large role in creating ambiance, and Southern Californians do more than their share. Many Californians spend a great deal of time outdoors swimming, sunbathing, sailing, walking, and, of course, bicycling. Take this opportunity to check out some of the extremes in cycling attire. (Some of these fashions will work their way to the conservative north in the next few years.)

Terrain is nearly level, except near Leo Carrillo State Beach, and miles go quickly. One short section of the ride is on the freeway, where broad shoulders give you some protection from the traffic. The most hazardous section is in the Oxnard–Port Hueneme area, where the bike route follows several shoulderless thoroughfares through town. Avoid traveling this section during rush-hour traffic.

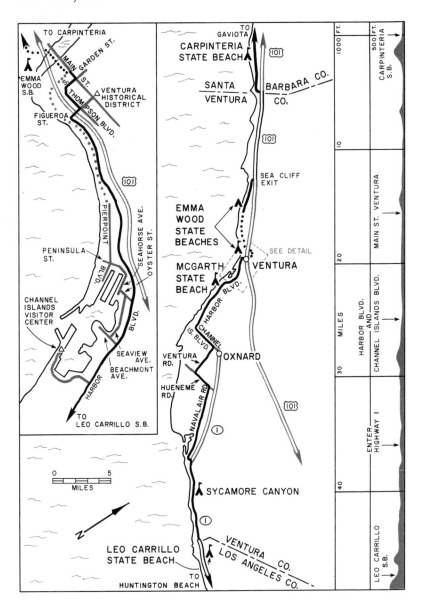

Sunrise over the Ventura Marina

Two side trips are recommended along the route. The first is to visit the restored San Buenaventura Mission and Ventura County Historical Museum in the Historical District of Ventura. The historical museum has indoor and outdoor exhibits depicting local history from the time of the Indians to oil exploration. The mission also has a museum with artifacts from the old mission (admission charged).

Farther south, at the Ventura Marina, the second side trip leads to the Channel Islands National Monument and Wildlife Refuge visitor center, which features displays of natural history on and around the islands. Charter boats take visitors out for half- or whole-day trips to observe the islands. Reservations for these trips should be made up to two weeks in advance. For the cyclists who do not have a day to devote to the islands, a 30-minute movie at the visitor center describes the area, its natural inhabitants, and geological history.

MILEAGE LOG

0.0 Leave Carpinteria State Beach and follow Palm Ave. back to Carpinteria Ave.

0.2 Turn right on Carpinteria Ave. and head south, paralleling U.S. 101.

2.2 At the end of Carpinteria Ave., turn left and go immediately right down the on ramp to U.S. 101 (mp 00.43) and follow it for the next 4.8 miles; U.S. 101 heads around a broad bay along the edge of the Pacific Ocean. At the north end of this bay is Rincon Point, an area which attracts surfers from around the world.

2.9 **(mp 00.00 and mp 43.80)** Leave Santa Barbara County, enter Ventura County.

7.0 **(mp 39.30)** Exit freeway at the small community of Sea Cliff; county parks, state beaches, homes, but no stores.

7.2 At the base of U.S. 101 exit ramp, turn right on Old Highway, passing the entrance to Hobson County Park; camping.

9.8 Faria County Park; camping, water, a small store, but no hiker-biker site.

13.3 Go up the freeway on ramp. To the right is the north entrance to Emma Wood State Beach and RV camping area.

13.7 At the top of the ramp, turn right on a narrow bike path.

14.6 Ventura city limits.

15.1 Bicycle path enters the south section of Emma Wood State Beach; picnic area, water, hiker-biker site, group campsites, cold outdoor showers, and beach access. Stay on the bicycle path as it passes under U.S. 101 and winds around a commercial campground.

15.6 Cross the Ventura River, then turn left (east) off the bike path to Main St. *ALTERNATE ROUTE.* The bike path turns west, offering a scenic route through Ventura, out to the beach, then around the Ventura County Fairgrounds. (In 1988, a portion of the bike path was closed due to storm damage, so part of the ride was through the fairgrounds parking lot.) The bike path passes through Surfers Point and Promenade Park, then through San Buenaventura State Beach, where it returns to the city streets and continues south on Pierpoint Blvd. for 1 mile. Go left on Peninsula St., then right on Seahorse Ave. Turn left on Oyster St., right on Seaview Ave., and left on Beachmont Ave. to return to the bike route at Harbor Blvd.

15.7 Pass Ortega Adobe Historical Site on the left (east) side of Main St.

15.8 Turn right on S. Garden St. *SIDE TRIP* to Ventura Historical District. Continue straight on Main St. 0.3 mile.

15.9 Follow S. Garden St. as it bends left (south) at the base of the freeway, becoming Thompson Blvd.

16.2 Turn right on Figueroa St. and cross under U.S. 101.

16.3 Take a left on Harbor Blvd. immediately after crossing the railroad tracks.

16.7 Beach Park, a small picnic area with tables but no water.

17.8 Cross San Pedro St. (the turnoff to Buenaventura State Beach;

a day-use area with restrooms, water, picnic tables, and beach access.)

18.2 Harbor Blvd. passes through a congested commercial ara with grocery stores. Continuing south, head through a residential district, then around the Ventura Harbor.

20.2 *SIDE TRIP* to Channel Islands National Monument and Wildlife Refuge visitor center. Turn right into the harbor area, then head left (west) for 1.3 miles down the spit to the visitor center; restrooms and running water.

20.7 McGarth State Beach; hiker-biker area, hot showers, beach access, and nature trail. Beyond the park entrance, Harbor Blvd. passes the Mandalay Steam Plant electric generating station, followed by an exclusive residential area.

25.0 Harbor Blvd. divides; stay left, heading east over Channel Islands Harbor into Oxnard, where Harbor Blvd. becomes Channel Islands Blvd. This is the start of a very congested area. Much of the road is narrow without a shoulder. Shops and grocery stores, located on the left (north) side of the road, are the last before Leo Carrillo State Beach.

27.1 At the eastern end of a large golf course, turn right on Ventura Rd. and ride the bike path for the next 1.2 miles.

28.8 Go left on Port Hueneme Rd. (pronounced "wye-nee-mee")

Evening view of the coast near Ventura

and enter the town of Port Hueneme. This is a navy area; gated roads and restricted sections abound. The road is very busy as it leaves the city, heading into farm country.

33.5 Turn right on Navalair Rd. just before Highway 1, passing naval installations and the airport.

34.7 Intersection. Continue straight past a display of rockets, or stop and inspect them, if you're so inclined.

36.3 Turn onto Highway 1, heading back towards the coast (mp 10.00). Use caution; the wide shoulder is used as a parking lot for those who do not wish to pay for parking at the state beaches, forcing cyclists onto the highway.

40.5 (mp 6.00) Enter Point Mugu State Park, which is comprised of several sections spread out along the coast. The first section, La Jolla, has a drive-in campground on the west side of the highway, and a walk-in campground on the east side. No hiker-biker facilities.

42.1 (mp 4.47) Sycamore Cove and Canyon; picnicking at the cove on the west side of the highway, camping in the canyon on the east side, hiker-biker site, running water, and several trails into the canyon. This campground is preferable to Leo Carrillo. If you can manage the longer ride through Los Angeles tomorrow, spend the night here.

46.5 (mp 00.00 and mp 62.87) Leave Ventura County and enter Los Angeles County.

47.2 (mp 62.10) Leo Carrillo State Beach, the last campground north of Los Angeles; hiker-biker site, hot showers, beach access, and a very small camp store (open in summer only). No stores or restaurants nearby. This campground is at the end of the bus line from Los Angeles, providing easy access to and from the city.

Leo Carrillo State Beach to Newport Dunes Aquatic Park (77.3 Miles)

Heading south from Leo Carrillo State Beach, Highway 1 has a moderate shoulder and low traffic volume for the first 7 miles. Near Malibu, the amount of traffic rapidly increases and the shoulder virtually disappears, setting the scene for the next 53 miles. While cycling through Malibu, keep in mind that this is one of the few places in the country where hilltop property annually becomes beach-front property. The effects of sliding are visible everywhere.

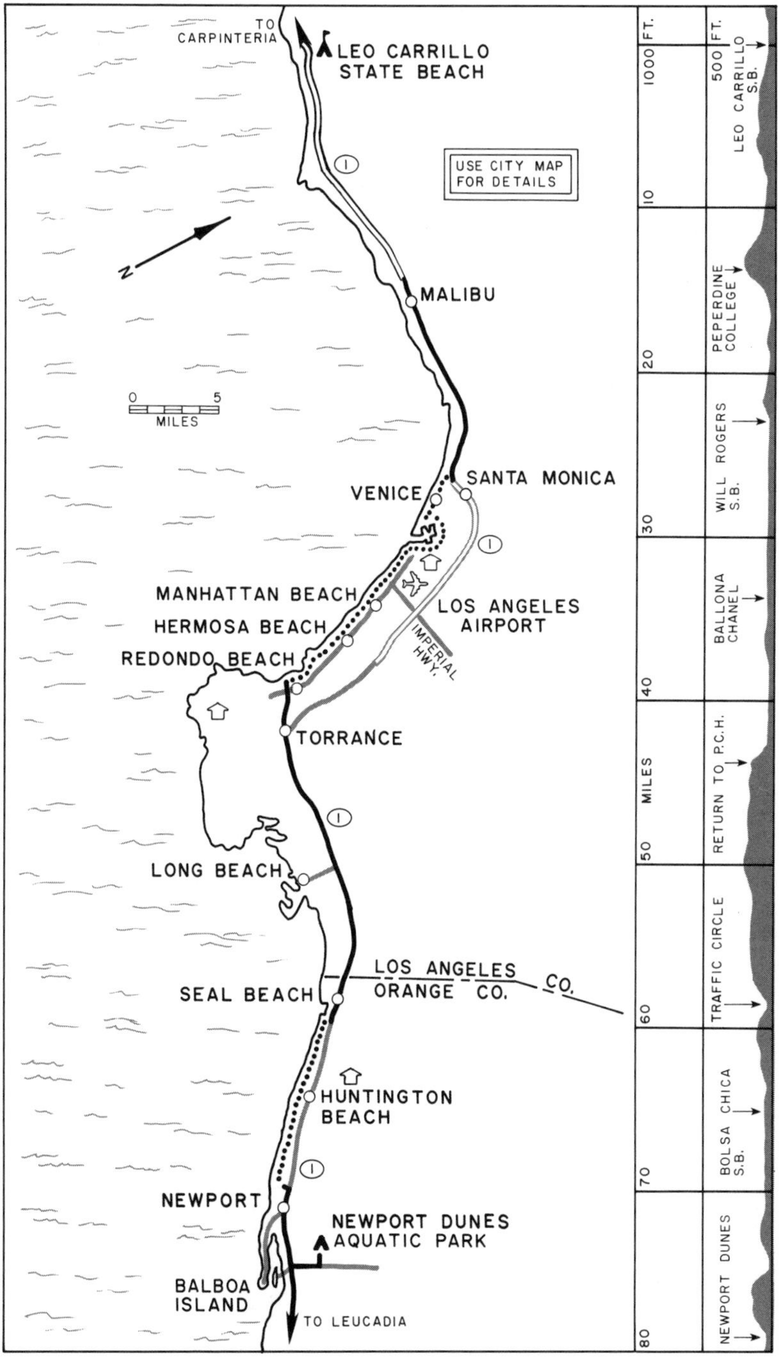

TO
CARPINTERIA

LEO CARRILLO
STATE BEACH

1

USE CITY MAP
FOR DETAILS

N

MALIBU

0   5
MILES

VENICE   SANTA MONICA

1

MANHATTAN BEACH

HERMOSA BEACH

REDONDO BEACH

LOS ANGELES
AIRPORT

IMPERIAL HWY.

TORRANCE

1

LONG BEACH

LOS ANGELES
ORANGE CO.

CO.

SEAL BEACH

HUNTINGTON
BEACH

1

NEWPORT

NEWPORT DUNES
AQUATIC PARK

BALBOA
ISLAND

TO LEUCADIA

1000 FT.   500 FT.   LEO CARRILLO S.B.

10

PEPERDINE COLLEGE

20

WILL ROGERS S.B.

30

BALLONA CHANEL

40

RETURN TO P.C.H.

MILES

50

TRAFFIC CIRCLE

60

BOLSA CHICA S.B.

70

NEWPORT DUNES

80

South of Malibu, Highway 1 (now called the Pacific Coast Highway) enters the gigantic sprawl of Los Angeles. Cyclists must leave the main highway and make their way along a series of bike paths and city streets.

Travel through any large city is hectic. Travel through the nine cities that make up the Los Angeles coast area gives the word "hectic" a whole new meaning. Do not expect to make good time. City streets are shoulderless, busy, and constantly interrupted by stoplights. Wildcat growth combined with rolling hills causes streets to change direction or dead end. The easy-to-follow bike path that weaves along the beaches for part of the way is usually jammed with people, causing travel to be slow and frustrating. It is advisable to have a city map with you at all times to aid in navigation through the twisting jungle of streets, bike paths, and people.

On a rare smog-free day, Los Angeles is a beautiful city. From the bike path, views extend up and down the coast, and east to

A day at the beach

the San Bernardino Mountains. Start the day at first light to reach the bike path before the midday haze sets in, and before the rush of morning commuter traffic. Take your time, enjoy the beaches, and be ready to head back to the city streets before 1:00 P.M. to avoid the afternoon rush hour.

South of Redondo Beach, the route follows the Pacific Coast Highway inland for a 20-mile stretch. The smell of car exhaust and stench of oil refineries dominate until the route returns to the refreshing ocean air at Huntington Beach.

If you have any extra time near the end of the day's ride, take a ride to Balboa Island. The island specialty is frozen bananas dipped in chocolate, with a topping of your choice—a real taste treat. The island can be reached by a short side trip at the campground turnoff, or by following an alternate route which takes you to the Wedge (a famous body-surfing area), before crossing to the island on a ferry.

As there are no public campgrounds between Leo Carrillo State Beach and Dana Point, 94.4 miles south near Capistrano, the suggested ride is long, and ends at Newport Dunes Aquatic Park. The facility is privately owned, and tent sites are expensive. The campground is on the bus line and less expensive than a hostel for groups of two or more.

If 77.3 miles seems a bit far to ride in a day, you may shorten your ride by stopping at one of three hostels along the route. The Westchester YMCA hostel is located near the Los Angeles International Airport at 8015 S. Sepulveda Blvd. Call ahead for reservations and directions, 213-642-8277. The Los Angeles International Hostel is scenically located in Angels Gate Park near Long Beach. The address is 3601 S. Gaffey St., Bldg. 613, San Pedro. Call ahead for reservations and cycling directions, 213-831-8109. Colonial Inn Hostel in Huntington Beach is the easiest of the three hostels to reach from the bike route. This hostel is near the beaches, within riding distance of Disneyland, and on bus routes to Hollywood. It is essential to call ahead for reservations, 714-536-9184.

MILEAGE LOG

0.0 (62.10) Head south from Leo Carrillo State Beach on Pacific Coast Highway.
2.5 (59.70) El Pescador State Beach; the first of three beach accesses.
6.9 (mp 55.1) Zuma Beach County Park; one of many excellent swimming beaches in Los Angeles County.
7.8 (mp 54.2) Malibu; shoulder decreases while the number of cars, people, and general urban clutter increases.
13.4 (mp 48.1) Pepperdine College.

15.4 (mp 46.1) Pass Malibu Pier to the right (south). This is a favorite hangout for sunbathers and surfers, who flock to the rocky point just west of the pier nearly every day of the year.

21.8 (mp 40.0) J. Paul Getty Museum, located on the left side of the highway up on the hill (barely). This museum contains a world-renowned collection of sculpture and paintings. (The museum may be descending to sea level in the near future.)

22.5 (mp 29.3) Will Rogers State Beach. The beach extends for several miles and has more than one entrance. This is the last milepost on the route south.

24.7 The first beach bike path begins. It continues for 0.3 mile, then returns to the highway.

25.7 Start of Los Angeles Bike Path. The turnoff to the bike path is not marked. Look for a small driveway 0.3 mile after the second pedestrian overpass. The driveway is marked with a sign reading KEEP THIS DRIVEWAY CLEAR FOR EMERGENCY VEHICLES. Once on the path, route-finding is easy.

29.1 Venice Beach, where the people of Los Angeles come to look and be looked at. The beach is easily recognizable by a large pavilion for roller-skaters, dancers, weightlifters, and masses of people. Modern roller-skating got its big start here, and is still a popular activity. Check out Muscle Beach, an open gym where body builders grunt and strain, trying to achieve the perfect body.

29.8 At the end of Venice Beach, turn left (northeast) off the bike path onto Washington St. and follow the green bike-route signs.

30.5 Turn right (southeast) off Washington St. to the Marina Del Rey Bike Path. This turn is somewhat obscure; look for four apartment buildings shaped like half circles to the right. You'll see them just before you reach the turn.

31.0 Cross Bali Way and enter the narrow alleyways of Marina Del Rey boat basin.

31.9 Bike path returns to the street. Turn right on Fiji Way and follow it to its end.

32.5 End of Fiji Way; the bike path starts again. Go straight for 200 feet, then turn right (west) between Ballona Channel and the entrance to the boat basin.

33.2 Cross the Ballona Channel and go right, following the bike path back to the beach. To reach the Los Angeles International Airport (LAX), continue straight from the end of the bridge onto Pacific Ave., follow it to Vista Del Mar, turn right, and ride 1.6 miles past the end of the runway. Go left on Imperial.

41.0 Beach path enters the city of Redondo Beach and temporarily ends. Go left, then take the first right on Harbor Dr., staying on the bike route.

Volley ball tournament

41.5 Leave the bike route by turning left on Beryl St. for one block.

41.6 Turn right on Catalina Ave. passing Redondo Beach municipal pier. (The pier was badly burnt in 1987; however, many shops and restaurants still operate in the section that remains.)

42.4 Turn right at Pearl St., which becomes Esplanade as it follows the coast south.

43.5 Turn left on I. St., heading up to rejoin the Pacific Coast Highway.

44.0 Turn right on Pacific Coast Highway and enter the city of Torrance. Following the highway for the next 27 miles is not easy on the nerves. Traffic is heavy, shoulders irregular, and the air foul. But cheer up, and think of resting on the beach at the day's end.

48.9 Enter Los Angeles.

54.6 Pass an entrance to the Long Beach Freeway. This can be a dangerous interchange, with drivers vying for position to get on and off the freeway. Cyclists continue on the Pacific Coast Highway.

Venice Beach

55.7 Continue straight, past the Long Beach Blvd. intersection. Two retired giants, the Queen Mary and the Spruce Goose, are both located in Long Beach but due to freeway restrictions, neither can be reached by bicycle.

58.4 Drop down a short hill and go halfway around a traffic circle. Veer right on the Pacific Coast Highway, following signs to Newport. Most of the big-city clutter is left behind here; however, traffic remains heavy.

61.8 Leave Los Angeles County, enter Orange County and the city of Seal Beach.

65.6 Start of the Bolsa Chica State Beach bike path to Huntington Beach. Like most Southern California bike paths, it's crowded and difficult to ride but safer than the highway.

70.2 Turnoff to Colonial Inn Hostel. To reach the hostel, turn left on 8th St. for four blocks (0.3 mile) to Pecan St. The hostel is located on the corner at 421 8th St. It has 28 beds, showers, a full kitchen, and bicycle storage. Check-in is from 4:30 P.M. to 10:30 P.M.

70.4 Huntington Beach Pier, the best vantage point along the coast to watch surfers. Surfing was first introduced in California at Huntington Beach, and the tradition is still going strong. Continue south on the shoulder or the beach bike path. (The path is recommended for all out-of-staters.)

71.4 Huntington State Beach entrance; restrooms, water, and beach access.

73.8 Newport Beach city limits. Huntington Beach bike path ends; return to the Pacific Coast Highway, which has a wide shoulder here.

74.8 Balboa Island Alternate Route to Corona Del Mar State Beach. (For details, see end of this mileage log.) The main route continues south around the east side of Newport Bay on the Pacific Coast Highway. The highway descends, crosses a wide bridge, then climbs steeply, paralleling the Newport Dunes Aquatic Park.

77.3 Intersection of Jamboree Rd. and Pacific Coast Highway. Go left (east) down a short hill to Newport Dunes Aquatic Park, the first campground south of Leo Carrillo State Beach. It's an expensive private area that's never full. Facilities include

Surfer at Huntington Beach

hot showers, laundry, information center, and a swimming beach. Public transport provides access to the attractions of the south Los Angeles area (Disneyland, Knotts Berry Farm, Long Beach, and surfing beaches). *SIDE TRIP* to Balboa Island. Go right (west) off Pacific Coast Highway on Jamboree Rd. and descend 0.3 mile to the island and frozen bananas. The Balboa Island Alternate Route ends here.

Balboa Island Alternate Route

Turn right (southwest) on Balboa Blvd. for a shoulderless 3.5 miles down the long sandspit that protects Newport Bay and Balboa Island. The main section of the spit is covered with shops, businesses, and private homes. The west side has a pier, fish market, and state park, which ends at The Wedge, a famous and very dangerous body-surfing area. On the east side are Newport Bay Harbor and Balboa Island. To return to the main route, ride 2.7 miles down the spit and catch the ferry to Balboa Island. Ride back to the Highway via a bridge on the east side of the island.

Newport Dunes Aquatic Park to San Elijo State Beach (58.4 Miles)

South of Newport Beach, the coast is a popular vacation area for Californians attempting to escape the heat and smog of the interior. Throughout the summer, the four major state park campgrounds and numerous state beaches along this 58.4 mile section are full to overflowing. The towns along the coast attempt to accommodate the vast influx of tourists by lining the streets with restaurants, motels, fast-foods, and surf shops.

Roads traveled along the coast vary from busy thoroughfares to quiet residential streets. Shoulders are nonexistent in towns and better in the open country. Terrain is gently rolling—excellent for riding.

The bicycle route follows the busy Pacific Coast Highway until it merges with Interstate 5 near San Clemente. San Clemente is traversed by a series of confusing city streets, followed by a relaxing ride on the nearly deserted roads of Camp Pendleton—quiet riding when the army is not on maneuvers. Past the camp, negotiate busy city streets and highways to complete the day. Grocery stores and bike shops are numerous along the route.

Take time for one important side trip to the San Juan Capistrano

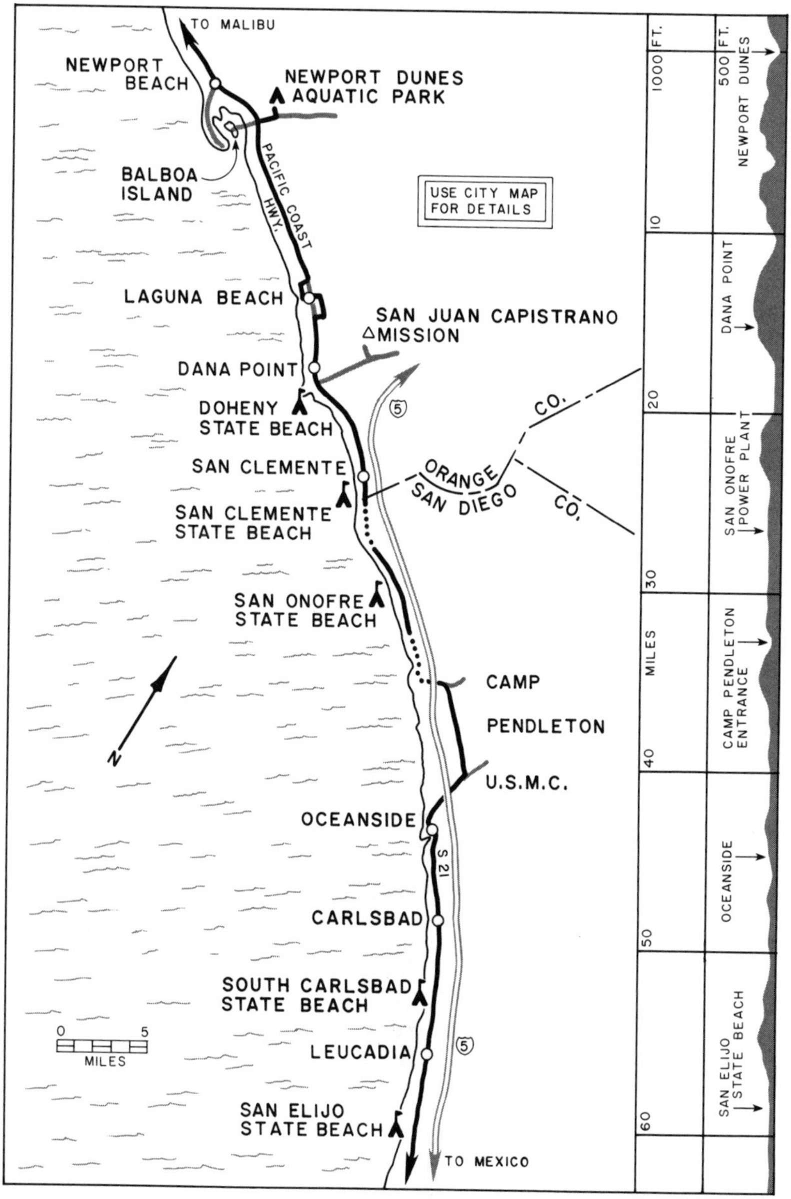
TO MALIBU
NEWPORT BEACH
NEWPORT DUNES AQUATIC PARK
BALBOA ISLAND
PACIFIC COAST HWY.
USE CITY MAP FOR DETAILS
LAGUNA BEACH
SAN JUAN CAPISTRANO MISSION
DANA POINT
DOHENY STATE BEACH
5
SAN CLEMENTE
ORANGE CO.
SAN DIEGO CO.
SAN CLEMENTE STATE BEACH
SAN ONOFRE STATE BEACH
CAMP PENDLETON U.S.M.C.
N
OCEANSIDE
S 21
CARLSBAD
SOUTH CARLSBAD STATE BEACH
0 5 MILES
LEUCADIA
5
SAN ELIJO STATE BEACH
TO MEXICO
1000 FT.
500 FT.
10
20
30
MILES
40
50
60
NEWPORT DUNES
DANA POINT
SAN ONOFRE POWER PLANT
CAMP PENDLETON ENTRANCE
OCEANSIDE
SAN ELIJO STATE BEACH

Mission, a short 3 miles off the Pacific Coast Highway. Every year, on March 19, the swallows return to Capistrano, heralding the beginning of spring. The swallows stay at the mission and a nearby shopping center through the second week of October. Even if you are not on hand to witness the return of the swallows to Capistrano, the mission is worth a visit. Founded in 1776, it was destroyed by an earthquake in 1812. A new mission was built behind the ruins of the old church, creating an elegant setting for the gardens.

The day's ride ends at San Elijo State Beach, the last public campground north of the Mexican border.

MILEAGE LOG

0.0 Leave Newport Dunes Aquatic Park and go right on Jamboree Rd. to the Pacific Coast Highway.

0.2 Turn left on Pacific Coast Highway and head south.

1.7 Turnoff to South Corona Del Mar Beach Park; restrooms, water, and views north to Newport Harbor, The Wedge, and

Newport Beach

Balboa Island. The park is located 0.3 mile off the Pacific Coast Highway on Marguerite Ave.

2.5 The Pacific Coast Highway enters open country.

3.9 Turnoff to Crystal Cove State Beach; no facilities.

5.7 Laguna Beach; grocery stores. Pacific Coast Highway is narrow and congested. In 1.2 miles, at the base of the hill, the bike route turns off the highway.

6.9 Turn off the Pacific Coast Highway on Cliff Dr., leaving the congested main highway. Stay on Cliff Dr. as it bends left, then twists and turns through a complicated residential area.

7.3 Heisler Park; restrooms, water, benches, picnic tables, and views, as well as access to a beach, which is an ecological reserve.

7.9 Return briefly to Pacific Coast Highway. *SIDE TRIP* to the Art-A-Fair and Sawdust Festival, held throughout July and August. To visit the fair, turn right (south) on Pacific Coast Highway at the end of Cliff Dr., then take an immediate left (east) on Broadway. When Broadway merges into Laguna Canyon Rd., the displays and arts and crafts shows are on the right (south) side of the road.

8.3 Turn left (east) off Pacific Coast Highway on Legion St.

8.5 Go right (south) on Catalina St.

8.8 Catalina St. ends temporarily; turn right on Thalia St., then take the first left back on Catalina St.

9.3 Catalina St. becomes Calliope St. Take the first left on Glenneyre St.

9.6 At Diamond St., turn right and return to Pacific Coast Highway. The highway soon widens to include a good shoulder.

10.9 Aliso Beach County Park entrance; restrooms, water, and a pier.

13.4 Pacific Coast Highway leaves the city for another short stint through open country, past a large supermarket on the east side of the road.

13.8 Salt Creek Beach County Park; a picturesque day-use area with restrooms, water, pavilion, fountain, and beach access.

15.5 Dana Point, a long, narrow town spread along the highway; small grocery store and restaurants.

16.1 At the base of the hill below Dana Point, turn right on Dana Point Harbor Dr. and follow the city bike-route signs. (Less than 0.5 mile south, Pacific Coast Highway merges with Interstate 5 and ends.) *SIDE TRIP* to Mission San Juan Capistrano. Head inland (east) here for 3.4 miles to the mission. Admission charged.

16.2 Go left on Park Lantern Rd., cycling into Doheny State Beach; hiker-biker site, showers, and beach access. Pass the park entrance booth, then follow the park road paralleling the Pacific Coast Highway. When the park road forks, stay left on the Old Coast Highway. Cross a short bridge, then go through the day-use parking area.

18.5 At the end of the parking area, continue south along the edge of a sandy beach on a bicycle path.

18.6 Bicycle path ends at the entrance to Capistrano State Beach. Go left to the Old Coast Highway and continue south on a wide bicycle lane. (Northbound bicycle lane varies from wide to nonexistent, depending on recent slides.)

20.1 San Clemente, a city with narrow, busy streets. The bike route turns off onto side roads 0.2 mile ahead.

20.3 Turn right (west) on Pico St. and follow it through the twists and turns of a residential area. Follow street signs carefully.

20.4 Go left on Boca de la Playa and take an immediate left on Calle las Bolas. Follow signs carefully.

20.5 Turn right on Ave. Florencia.

20.6 Take a sharp left on Ave. de la Grulla.

20.7 Turn right at Calle Puente and follow it for 0.5 mile.

21.3 Bear right on Ave. Palizada.

21.4 At N. Calle Seville, steer left.

21.5 Go straight on Ave. Santa Barbara.

21.6 Swing right on S. Ola Vista.

22.2 At Ave. Valencia, turn left.

22.3 Take a right on Ave. del Presidente and relax a bit on the wide bike lane. Parallel Interstate 5 for the next 1.5 miles.

22.7 San Clemente State Beach; picnicking, camping, hiker-biker site, solar-powered showers, and impressive views of the ocean at the base of weathered sandstone cliffs. A small grocery store is located across the Interstate 5 overpass.

23.6 Leave Orange County, enter San Diego County.

23.8 Ave. del Presidente ends. Continue straight on a bike path which starts just before the freeway entrance. The path parallels Interstate 5 on a section of the Old Coast Highway, past the access to Trestles Beach, one of the most crowded surfing areas on the southern coast.

25.3 Bike path ends. Go left around the gate and head up the wide bike lane on the San Onofre State Beach access road.

26.8 Pass the San Onofre nuclear plant. Expect considerable traffic when the work shifts change.

28.0 Entrance booth for San Onofre State Beach campground. The bike path heads straight through the 3-mile-long campground, which is sandwiched between the freeway and the ocean. Hiker-biker camp, cold outdoor showers, a small store (rarely open), beach access, and no electricity. For camping, San Clemente is recommended over San Onofre.

Mission San Juan Capistrano

San Elijo State Beach Campground

31.1 At the southern end of San Onofre State Park is the entrance to Camp Pendleton restricted area. Allow enough time to cycle completely through the 12 miles of Camp Pendleton before the camp closes at dusk. Entrance into the camp requires negotiating the narrowly spaced bars on the left-hand side of a gate. Beyond the barrier, the road belongs to the cyclists and army tanks.

32.8 The bike road turns inland, passing under Interstate 5.

33.0 After passing under the freeway, the road branches. Stay to the right.

34.4 Bike road ends; go left (east) on an unnamed road, passing under the Santa Fe Railroad.

34.6 Official camp entrance checkpoint. Sign in, and receive an official map. Continuing, bear right as the road splits.

35.1 Intersection and first stop sign; go right. (Route-finding through the camp is easy; at every major intersection, go right.)

41.9 Cycle around a small pond to arrive at a major intersection. Turn right on Vandenberg Blvd.

43.3 Exit Camp Pendleton and follow Harbor Dr. south.

43.7 Pass under Interstate 5 and take the first left on Hill St., entering Oceanside.

44.6 Turn right (west) on 6th St. (If you're looking for restaurants or groceries, stay on Hill St., busy but rideable, if you are hungry enough.)

44.8 Cross railroad tracks and turn left on Pacific St. Use caution on this street; it's the main access to Oceanside's palm-lined, sandy beaches, and receives heavy auto and pedestrian use.

46.7 Turn left at Cassidy St. Pass under a bridge and head east, inland.

47.0 Take a right at Hill St. (also known as State 21). The road is narrow and congested for the first few blocks, until the bike lane begins.

47.5 State 21 dips across Buena Vista Lagoon (a bird sanctuary) and enters the town of Carlsbad.

48.5 Carlsbad State Beach; no facilities.

49.9 Pass the massive San Diego Gas and Power Company.

52.6 South Carlsbad State Beach campground; small store, laundromat, solar-heated showers, and beach access. In 1988 no hiker-biker site was offered due to a problem with transients. No bikers will be turned away; however, you may be asked to pay full price for your site.

54.2 Leucadia, a congested town with small shops and grocery stores.

55.7 Encinitas.

56.4 Moonlight State Beach; beach access and water.

57.4 Cardiff by the Sea; a roadside park with restrooms and water.

58.4 San Elijo State Beach; campsites, small store, hot showers, and beach access. In 1988 the hiker-biker site was closed to discourage transients from moving in every night. A space will be found for anyone arriving on a bicycle; however, you may have to pay full price. A large grocery store and bike shop are located directly across the road from the campground. This is the last public campground before San Diego. It's noisy and unpleasant, so if you have some extra cash, this may be the time to treat yourself to a motel

San Elijo State Beach to the Mexican Border (45.3 Miles)

The final leg of California, and of the entire Pacific Coast Bike Route, consists of 45.3 challenging miles. The challenge is not the terrain—there are only two hills of notable size. The challenge comes from riding an entire day through cities.

The first 6 miles to Torrey Pines State Reserve are the easiest; the towns are small and somewhat spread apart. Beyond the state reserve, it's uphill to La Jolla Mesa and the start of the San Diego urban sprawl. The remainder of the ride is spent weaving through a maze of residential and industrial streets of downtown La Jolla, San Diego, National City, Chula Vista, and finally San Ysidro.

San Diego is a friendly city with many fascinating places to visit. Make your first stop at the Torrey Pines State Reserve, the only place in the world where these trees grow. A little farther south, hours may be spent at Scripps Institute Aquarium watching a marvelous variety of colorful shoreline inhabitants in a man-made tide pool, or at the glass-fronted fish tanks that contain creatures of the deep and not-so-deep. The best time to visit the aquarium is around 1:00 P.M., when the fish are fed.

A little farther south, performing sea animals tickle the fancies of the young and old alike at Sea World, located near San Diego Mission Bay. Open daily.

The San Diego area beaches are excellent; surfing is good, body-surfing very popular, sunbathing outstanding, and people-watching unequaled on the entire coast. Try Mission Beach if you are staying in the central San Diego area, and Imperial Beach if you are in the south. If you need a surfboard, boogie board, or skate board, you may rent them at the beach.

If spending a few days in San Diego, visit Balboa Park, home to a fascinating collection of museums, a velodrome, and the famous San Diego Zoo. San Diego Wildlife Park, located 30 miles north of downtown, is an extension of the zoo; it is worth a long visit. The wildlife park may be reached by bicycle if you don't mind the heat, or by bus if you do.

If you are staying several days in the San Diego area, the Coronado Peninsula makes an excellent and easy day ride. To get to the peninsula, take a passenger ferry from downtown San Diego, or take bike routes from Imperial Beach.

Reaching the California–Mexican border is a great thrill, and a good place to turn around and head back north. If planning to visit Mexico for the day, it is best to leave the bike in a secure place and

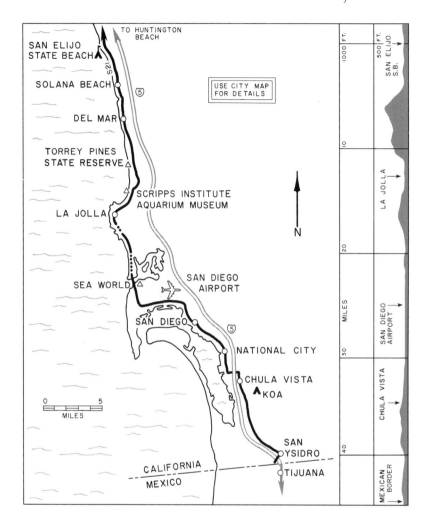

take the bus or train to the border. The streets and traffic south of the border are no place for cyclists.

The closest campground to the border is the San Diego Metro KOA in Chula Vista, about 7 miles south of the train and bus stations, and 9 miles south of the airport. San Diego has three hostels and numerous motels.

San Diego city has a hot line for lost or confused cyclists. During regular business hours, dial 231-BIKE, and a cheerful, helpful voice will guide you to your destination.

MILEAGE LOG

0.0 From San Elijo State Beach, head south on County Highway S21, which has an excellent bike lane.

0.5 Cardiff by the Sea; a sunning and swimming beach with chemical toilets and no running water.

2.1 Solana Beach. Turnoff to Solana Beach County Park to the right (west); picnic tables, restrooms, running water, and ocean views.

3.5 Del Mar. The buildings here have a Danish flavor, and so do the pastries. Beyond Del Mar, the highway rambles along the coast; shoulders moderate.

5.9 San Diego city limits. Pass Torrey Pines State Beach on the right (west) side of County Highway S21.

6.6 *SIDE TRIP* to Torrey Pines State Reserve. Go left off the highway up a steep, mile-long hill to scenic views and the rarest pine trees native to the United States. Trails, restrooms, water, and a visitor center.

8.8 County Highway S21 becomes Torrey Pines Blvd. Shoulders narrow and traffic gets heavier as the road passes around the western edge of the University of California at San Diego.

9.6 Turn right (west) on N. Torrey Pines Rd.

10.7 Turn right on La Jolla Shores Dr. Start a steep descent, keeping a steady finger on the brakes and an eye out for pedestrians. The Scripps Institute Aquarium Museum is located at the bottom of the hill.

12.0 Scripps Institute Aquarium Museum. Just as the hill starts to bottom out, keep an eye on the right for signs to the aquarium. A small donation is requested at the entrance.

12.9 Bear right, following Torrey Pines Rd., and enter La Jolla. The route through residential streets is marked by green city bike-route signs.

13.7 Turn left on Prospect Pl. for one block.

13.8 Turn right on Virginia.

14.2 Turn left on High St.

14.3 Turn right on Pearl St.

14.4 Turn left on Grand.

14.6 Turn right on Genter St.

14.7 Turn left on Fay Ave.

15.0 Cross Nautilus St. to the sidewalk on the south side. Turn right (west) and coast down the sidewalk a half block to a bicycle path. The path is 0.6 mile long and easy to follow. (Northbound folks will have one junction at 0.4 mile; keep right.)

15.6 Bike path ends, head left for one-half block, then go right on Beaumont Ave.

16.0 Turn right on Camino de la Costa for one block.

16.1 Turn left on La Jolla Hermosa Ave.

16.7 Following the city bike-route signs, pass the Bird Rock Elementary School and take the first left up a narrow alley.

16.9 Cycle past the school playfield and take a right on another unnamed alley.

17.0 Take a left on the first normal-looking city street, Agate St.

17.1 Turn right on La Jolla Mesa Rd. and follow it as it merges with La Jolla Blvd., which eventually becomes Mission Blvd.

17.6 *ALTERNATE ROUTE* along the beach. The main route stays on Mission Blvd.; however, if you want a view of San Diego beach life and don't mind cycling through crowds, turn right on Law St. for 0.1 mile, then go left (south) on a bicycle path overlooking the coast. Follow the bike path south for 2.2 miles, then leave it just before passing a large pavilion. Turn left (east) on Ventura Plaza, which becomes Mission Bay Dr. after crossing Mission Blvd.

19.9 Turn left onto Mission Bay Dr., just before passing an abandoned amusement park. Mission Bay Dr. crosses Mission Bay Channel on a wide bridge.

20.4 After the bridge, exit right on Quivira Rd., then go left (south), paralleling Mission Bay Dr. *SIDE TRIP* to San Diego Sea World. Turn left after crossing Mission Bay Channel Bridge on Dana Landing Rd. (opposite the Quivira Rd. exit), and follow it to the right for 0.5 mile. Cross a major four-lane road, then follow Perez Cove Way to the entrance of Sea World in 0.2 mile. Plan to spend at least three hours here; large admission charged.

20.8 Turn left off Quivira Rd., opposite the entrance to a shopping center, then make a quick right on Sunset Cliffs Blvd. and ride over the San Diego River.

21.3 At the south end of the bridge, merge left in preparation for a left turn on Nimitz Blvd. This is a tricky intersection in heavy traffic. From here on, traffic is heavy at all times. Nearing the heart of San Diego's downtown and business district, expect slow progress, lots of stoplights, and a few bumpy railroad tracks.

23.7 Nimitz Blvd. ends in the heart of a naval training center. Turn left on Harbor Dr. and ride over a large bridge, either on the road or on the wide sidewalk that doubles as a bicycle path. The road now parallels the West Basin of the San Diego Bay.

24.3 Spanish Marine Bayside Park. A nice place to relax; restrooms, water, picnic tables. You may leave the road here and ride a winding bike path through the park for the next 6 miles.

25.8 San Diego International Airport exit.

26.6 *SIDE TRIP* to Balboa Park and the San Diego Zoo. Turn left on Laurel St. for a very steep climb 1.7 miles east to the entrance of Balboa Park. Continue straight into the park on El Prado to reach the information center, museums, and zoo.

27.8 Intersection of Harbor Dr. and Broadway. The Amtrack station is located two blocks left up Broadway. The Greyhound bus station is a couple blocks beyond, at the corner of Broadway and First Ave. The passenger ferry to the Coronado Peninsula departs near this intersection. The bike route continues to follow Harbor Dr. south.

28.2 Harbor Dr. ends temporarily. Turn right on Pacific for one block to its end, then follow the roadway left back on to Harbor Dr.

31.9 Enter National City.

32.7 Turn right (west) on 13th St., just before Harbor Dr., which passes under Interstate 5 for one short block, then turn left (south) on Cleveland Ave.

33.4 Turn left (east) on W. 24th St.

33.7 Turn right (south) on Hoover Ave.

34.2 At the end of Hoover Ave., turn left (east) on W. 33rd St.

34.4 Go right (south) on National Ave. and cross two bridges over the Sweetwater River.

34.8 Leave National City and enter Chula Vista. Turn left (east) on C St. immediately after crossing the second bridge.

35.1 Turn right (south) on 5th Ave., entering a residential area. Intersections in this section have shallow culverts across them; ride carefully.

35.3 If planning to spend the night at the San Diego Metropolitan KOA campground, go left on D St. for 0.7 mile. Turn left (north) on 2nd Ave. for 0.8 mile to the campground located at 111 N. 2nd Ave., 619-427-3601 for reservations.

36.7 A shopping center is located in the middle of 5th Ave., so go left on H. St. for one block.

36.8 Turn right on Fig Ave. to I Ave.

36.9 Take a right on I Ave., then go left back onto 5th Ave.

38.3 Turn right (west) on Palomar St. and descend to the second intersection.

38.5 Turn left (south) on Broadway, which becomes Beyer Blvd. The terrain opens up a little, and the last few miles to the border slip by.

41.2 Pass under Highway 75, then turn right (south) on Dairy Mart Rd.

41.6 Turn left (east) on San Ysidro Blvd., just before Interstate 5.

44.0 Pass under Highway 805, entering the very Mexican town of San Ysidro. Streets are jammed, lined with places to change your money. Everyone speaks Spanish; very few know any English.

44.7 Turn right on Camino de la Plaza. Cross over Interstate 5 and turn left, following the signs to bus and taxi parking.

45.3 YAH HOO! THE MEXICAN BORDER, 1987.3 miles south of Powell River, British Columbia.

The California–Mexico border, the southern end of the Pacific Coast Bicycle Route

RECOMMENDED READING

Bicycle Touring

Armstrong, Diana. *Bicycle-Camping*. New York: Dial Press, 1981.

Bridge, Raymond. *Bike Touring: The Sierra Club Guide to Outings on Wheels*. San Francisco: Sierra Club, 1979.

Coello, Dennis L. *Living on Two Wheels: The Complete Guide to Buying, Commuting, and Touring*. Berkeley, CA: Ross Books, 1982.

Wilhelm, Tim, and Glenda Wilhelm. *The Bicycle Touring Book: The Complete Guide to Bicycle Recreation*. Emmaus, PA: Rodale Press, 1980.

Bicycle Maintenance

Cuthbertson, Tom, and Rick Morrall. *The Bag Book*. Berkeley, CA: Ten Speed Press, 1981.

de la Rosa, Denise M., and Michael J. Kolin. *Understanding, Maintaining, and Riding the Ten-speed Bicycle*. Emmaus, PA: Rodale Press, 1979.

Editors of *Bicycling Magazine* and Richard Jow. *Reconditioning the Bicycle*. Emmaus, PA: Rodale Press, 1979.

Marr, Dick. *Bicycling Gearing: A Practical Guide*. Seattle: The Mountaineers, 1989.

Sloanes, Eugene A. *Bicycle Maintenance Manual*. New York: Simon and Schuster, 1981.

Area Bicycle Tour Guides

British Columbia

Perrin, Tim, and Janet Wilson. *Exploring by Bicycle: Southwest British Columbia and the San Juan Islands*. Vancouver, B.C.: Douglas and McIntyre, 1979.

California

Jackson, Joan. *50 Biking Holidays: From Old Monterey to the Golden Gate*. Santa Cruz, CA: Valley Publishers, 1981.

Washington

Woods, Erin and Bill. *Bicycling the Backroads around Puget Sound*, 3d ed. Seattle: The Mountaineers, 1989.

———— *Bicycling the Backroads of Northwest Washington*, 2d ed. Seattle: The Mountaineers, 1984.

———— *Bicycling the Backroads of Southwest Washington*, 2d ed. Seattle: The Mountaineers, 1988.

INDEX

About the authors:

Tom Kirkendall and Vicky Spring, residents of Edmonds, Washington, are both experienced, enthusiastic outdoor people. The couple spend their summers as hikers, backpackers and cyclists; when the snow falls, they pin on cross-country skis. Both Vicky and Tom studied at the Brooks Institute of Photography in Santa Barbara, California, and are now building their careers together as outdoor photographers and guidebook authors. Vicky had something of a head start in the field, beginning in the days when she carried a backpack of camera gear for her well-known outdoor photographer father, Ira Spring.

Vicky and Tom are the authors of *Cross-Country Ski Trails of Washington's Cascades and Olympics;* she is co-author and photographer of *94 Hikes* and *95 Hikes in the Canadian Rockies;* and he is author/photographer of *Mountain Bike Adventures in Washington's North Cascades & Puget Sound Basin* and *in Washington's South Cascades & Olympics,* all published by The Mountaineers.